TWAYNE'S WORLD AUTHORS SERIES

A Survey of the World's Literature

Sylvia E. Bowman, Indiana University

GENERAL EDITOR

AUSTRALIA

Joseph Jones, University of Texas

EDITOR

Marjorie Barnard
and
M. Barnard Eldershaw

(TWAS 257)

TWAYNE'S WORLD AUTHORS SERIES (TWAS)

The purpose of TWAS is to survey the major writers —novelists, dramatists, historians, poets, philosophers, and critics—of the nations of the world. Among the national literatures covered are those of Australia, Canada, China, Eastern Europe, France, Germany, Greece, India, Italy, Japan, Latin America, the Netherlands, New Zealand, Poland, Russia, Scandinavia, Spain, and the African nations, as well as Hebrew, Yiddish, and Latin Classical literatures. This survey is complemented by Twayne's United States Authors Series and English Authors Series.

The intent of each volume in these series is to present a critical-analytical study of the works of the writer; to include biographical and historical material that may be necessary for understanding, appreciation, and critical appraisal of the writer; and to present all material in clear, concise English—but not to vitiate the scholarly content of the work by doing so.

Marjorie Barnard
and
M. Barnard Eldershaw

By LOUISE E. RORABACHER

Twayne Publishers, Inc.   ::   New York

To

Carol H. Lawrence

who shares my regard for the Australia they depicted

Preface

Writing of M. Barnard Eldershaw and her works is like trying to pin down Proteus. First, she was a very versatile writer, doing significant work in each of several important and diverse literary fields. Second, she was a considerably prolific writer, as the appended bibliographies will attest. Third, and most disconcerting, she was two writers as well as one—two extremely able but very different people who not only subordinated themselves to a remarkably successful collaboration under a combined name but who each emerged, now and again, to publish works of her own.

In these circumstances it has seemed best to make this a single study covering not only the collaborative works of M. Barnard Eldershaw but also those of her component authors, Marjorie Barnard and Flora Eldershaw, when they wrote separately. Actually the writer who supplies the joint surname, Miss Eldershaw, did very little literary work alone. Miss Barnard, however, has produced a great many things in her own right, not only during the period of the partnership but in the quarter of a century since its dissolution. This study, then, looks into the many and varied works of two writers known jointly as M. Barnard Eldershaw, and into those of Marjorie Barnard.

In the preface to her study of her friend and fellow countrywoman Miles Franklin, Miss Barnard remarks that "Miles writing is indivisible from Miles living."[1] But Miles was almost wholly a writer of novels, heavily autobiographical novels at that. The subjects of this study were far more objective in both choice of material and approach to it. Their lives, being thus of less concern to their readers, have been touched on relatively lightly here.

I never met Miss Eldershaw. She died in middle life before I first went to Australia, and my knowledge of her as a person is limited to memories generously shared with me by her family and friends. I did meet Miss Barnard and came to know her well. Yet her life too is treated briefly here in deference to her own expressed wish. Her sense of privacy is so strong that despite being a historian she has never (most unfortunately) saved letters. She has been a great writer of them, however, and has been good enough to let me use my judgment in quoting from her own to two of her friends and literary contemporaries, Vance and Nettie Palmer, which since their deaths have been turned over to the Australian National Library in Canberra. Theirs was a large and largely literary correspondence ("like belonging to a club," Miss Barnard recalls) from 1930 to 1959—three decades that cover almost the entire period of the Barnard-Eldershaw collaboration and that of the greatest Barnard creativity as well. These letters are invaluable as revelations not only of the personality of their writer but of the genesis of the books, the problems of execution, the reception—all recorded with a freshness and validity that no maturer recollections of those earlier years could possibly supply. I have drawn upon them heavily.

For the use of these and other materials and facilities I owe thanks to the National Library in Canberra, of whose collection of Australiana I have been a grateful reader from the days of its quonset huts and warehouses to its present magnificent building on the verge of beautiful Lake Burley Griffin—a period during which I have known many kindnesses, personal and professional, at the hands of its Chief Librarian, Australian Studies, Mrs. Pauline Fanning. I owe only slightly less to the Mitchell Library in Sydney and to its staff. My gratitude must also include another institution far removed—Purdue University of Lafayette, Indiana, which helped with time and money in the early stages of this study.

My special thanks go to two individuals for their willing cooperation in providing information and insights: P. H. Eldershaw, one of Flora's younger brothers, and Tom Inglis Moore, author, scholar, and lifetime friend of Flora and her family. My debt to Miss Barnard herself is incalculable.

Contents

Acknowledgments

For permission to use material in this book, grateful acknowledgment is hereby made to the following:

Angus and Robertson (Publishers) Pty. Ltd., Sydney, for selections from Marjorie Barnard's *A History of Australia*, published by them;

The Australian National Library, Canberra, for the use of Marjorie Barnard's letters to Vance and Nettie Palmer, now in its keeping;

Marjorie Barnard, Sydney, for selections from M. Barnard Eldershaw's "The Plover" and from her own *The Persimmon Tree*, published by the Clarendon Press, Sydney, and from M. Barnard Eldershaw's *Essays in Australian Fiction*, published by the Melbourne University Press, Melbourne;

John Farquharson Ltd., Business Managers for Authors, London, for selections from M. Barnard Eldershaw's *A House Is Built, Green Memory, The Glasshouse, Plaque with Laurel*, and *Phillip of Australia*, all published by George G. Harrap & Company Ltd., London; and for selections from their *My Australia*, published by Jarrolds, London;

Georgian House Pty. Ltd., Melbourne, for selections from M. Barnard Eldershaw's *Tomorrow and Tomorrow*, published by them;

Meanjin Quarterly, Melbourne, for selections from various articles and reviews by Marjorie Barnard and by Flora Eldershaw, published in the *Meanjin Quarterly*; and for selections from Nettie Palmer's *Fourteen Years*: Extracts from a Private Journal 1925-1939, published by the Meanjin Press, Melbourne;

Southerly, Sydney, for selections from various reviews by Marjorie Barnard;

Twayne Publishers, Inc., New York, for selections from Marjorie Barnard's *Miles Franklin*, published by them.

Chronology

1897   FE born March 16, Darlinghurst (Sydney); reared on station in Riverina; early education in Wagga Wagga. MB born August 16 in Ashfield (Sydney); reared in a succession of other western Sydney suburbs.

1904   MB begins education under governesses. Later attends Cambridge School, Hunters Hill, then spends four years in Sydney Girls High School.

1916   MB enters University of Sydney and meets FE, already a second-year student.

1918   FE takes her B.A. degree but continues as secretary of the University's Women's Union (1917-1921).

1920   MB graduates with numerous honors. Takes library training at Sydney Teachers College, works in Public Library, then library of Sydney Technical College, 12 years. MB's first publication, *The Ivory Gate* (for children).

1921   FE teaches in Cremorne Grammar School (Sydney), 2 years.

1922   MB's father builds at Longueville; still her home.

1923   FE teaches at Presbyterian Ladies College, Croydon.

1928   MBE win half of *Bulletin* prize with first novel.

1929   *A House Is Built* is published and acclaimed in London.

1930   MB begins correspondence with Vance and Nettie Palmer.

1931   MBE's second novel, *Green Memory*, published in London. FE addresses Australian English Association on "Contemporary Australian Women Writers"; in 1935, on "Australian Literature Society Medallists."

1933   MB makes first trip to England with her mother. FE addresses Royal Australian Historical Society on "History as the Raw Material of Literature"; in 1940, on "Captain John Piper."

1934   FE, on leave, spends year in England and Europe.

1935   MB resigns library position for full-time writing. FE president of Fellowship of Australian Writers.

1936   MBE publish third novel, *The Glasshouse*, in London. FE edits *Australian Writers Annual*, an anthology.

1937   MBE's fourth novel, *Plaque with Laurel*, published in London. MB begins several years of short stories in *Home*.

1938   MB publishes numerous historical articles in *Home*. FE edits Women's Sesquicentennial *The Peaceful Army*. MBE turn to history with *Phillip of Australia*, London; their *Essays in Australian Fiction* out in Melbourne.

1939 MBE's *The Life and Times of Captain John Piper* is published in Sydney for the Australian Limited Editions Society; their *My Australia* appears in London. FE becomes member of Advisory Board of Commonwealth Literary Fund.

1940 MB's father dies; she remains at home with mother.

1941 FE leaves Presbyterian Ladies College for work with the Department of Reconstruction in Canberra. MB's *Macquarie's World* is published in Sydney for the Australian Limited Editions Society.

1942 MB goes back to work at the Public Library; soon shifts to technical library of CSIRO. FE back to Sydney for a time, then to Melbourne with the Welfare Division, Department of Labor and National Service.

1943 MB publishes in Sydney her *Australian Outline,* first of several minor histories over next twenty years; also *The Persimmon Tree,* a collection of her short stories. FE again president of Fellowship of Australian Writers.

1946 MBE edit annual anthology *Coast to Coast.*

1947 MBE's fifth and last novel, *Tomorrow and Tomorrow,* published in Melbourne, ends the collaboration.

1948 FE enters private practice as industrial consultant.

1949 MB's mother dies. Much book reviewing during 1950's.

1950 FE made Fellow of Australian Institute of Management. MB resigns from CSIRO, last regular employment.

1951 MB goes abroad with friends; again in 1964, 1967, 1971.

1952 "The Landscape Writers" appears in *Meanjin* under FE's name.

1953 FE in poor health; resigns Advisory Board of CLF.

1956 FE dies September 20 after long overwork and illness.

1962 MB's longest work, *A History of Australia,* published in Sydney after five years of research and writing.

1967 MB's critical study *Miles Franklin* is published in U.S.

1970 MB's article "How 'Tomorrow and Tomorrow' Came to be Written" appears in *Meanjin.*

CHAPTER 1

The Collaboration

I The Setting

THE year 1929 was remarkable in Australian letters. Like the dawn, it glowed the brighter for the relative darkness out of which it emerged. The great upsurge of nationalistic spirit that had swept in the truly Australian short story in the 1890's had worn out its impetus if not its welcome. The new century which, through the birth of the Commonwealth in 1901, had produced an Australian nation, had failed as yet to produce a truly Australian literature. Miles Franklin's *My Brilliant Career* (1901), hailed by the *Bulletin's* famous early critic A. G. Stephens as "the very first Australian novel to be published,"[1] had been a hopeful beginning—for a youthful writer, a youthful nation, and a youthful century alike—but decades were to elapse before its author published anything else. Two years later Joseph Furphy, after much excision and revision, published under the pseudonym "Tom Collins" that fascinating book of fiction *Such Is Life* (1903), which has since come to wear for many the accolade that Stephens had bestowed on Miss Franklin's first-born; but more than forty years passed before it received in fair measure the attention it deserved.

Now, in 1929, there came both fulfillment and further promise in plenty. Henry Handel Richardson, with *Ultima Thule*, completed her slowly and carefully wrought trilogy *The Fortunes of Richard Mahony*, which was to draw serious international attention for the first time to an essentially Australian novel. Katharine Susannah Prichard published *Coonardoo*, a very Australian novel indeed, being a serious study of an aboriginal-white relationship. And, more important for our purpose here, there appeared for the first time on the Australian literary scene the figure of M. Barnard Eldershaw, springing full-panoplied from the youthful but extremely well-equipped heads of two friends

13

and writing partners, Marjorie Faith Barnard and Flora Sydney Patricia Eldershaw.

Both of these young women, having been born in 1897, had been growing to maturity (like the new nation, only four years their junior) in the new century. They had no pioneering to do as women writers; in Australia, as in her mother England, literature, especially fiction, had long been the creative woman artist's most accepted endeavor. Within a half century of the arrival of the First Fleet in 1788, Mary Vidal had produced her didactic *Tales for the Bush* (1845)—*for* rather than *of* the bush, unfortunately, but memorable for having been published in Australia as well as written there. Another decade saw the emergence of "the first Australian woman novelist," Scottish-born Catherine Helen Spence, the best-known of whose several novels is the realistic, largely domestic *Clara Morison* (1854); and of Caroline Woolmer Leakey, whose melodramatic *The Broad Arrow* (1859) is still a source of information about early convict life.

The year in which Marjorie Barnard and Flora Eldershaw were born witnessed the publication of the last novel by Jessie Couvreur ("Tasma") and her death. In this same year Ada Cambridge and Rosa Praed (the latter the first genuine "born in Australia" author on the list) each published a volume of fiction, each only midway in a prolific writing career. And now Australian-born women authors begin to multiply. One of them, Barbara Baynton, was this year in only her mid-thirties, soaking up the morbid impressions of her native land that were shortly to emerge in the brief but arresting collection of short stories called *Bush Studies* (1902). Another in her mid-thirties, Mary Jean Cameron, was in far-off Paraguay hopefully but futilely helping William Lane's efforts to found a workers' paradise; in this year she was married by him to William Gilmore, and as Mary Gilmore, poet and editor, she was to span almost a century of Australian life and literature (1865-1962). In this year Ethel Richardson, recently married to J. G. Robertson and living with him at the University of Strasbourg, began as Henry Handel Richardson to write her first novel, *Maurice Guest* (1908), and thus to develop the talent which she was later to turn to such excellent use in fiction drawn from her Australian girlhood (*The Getting of Wisdom*, 1910; *The Fortunes of Richard Mahony*, 1930; *The End of a Childhood*, 1934). In this year Miles Franklin

(p. 167) was only a slip of an eighteen-year-old but, restive under the restrictions to which her sex was heir, had already completed her first novel of protest (*My Brilliant Career*, not published for six years). And in this year Katharine Susannah Prichard, only thirteen and making a belated start on a formal education in the State schools of Victoria, was showing distinct signs of the literary talent that was to put her into the front ranks of Australian novelists.

This is the literary tradition to which Marjorie Barnard and Flora Eldershaw were heir, these the generation of women writers into which they were born. Geoffrey Dutton is not alone in astutely noting "the extraordinary prevalence of women writers in Australian literature."[2]

II   *The Actors*

"I think collaboration (in creative work) is impossible," Miss Barnard once wrote; "but now and then it happens."[3] That it succeeded for M. Barnard Eldershaw is owing to the happy combination of likenesses and differences that the partners brought to it. Both were born, as we have seen, in the same year (Flora exactly five months the elder) in Australia of Australian parents; both became omnivorous readers; both attended the University of Sydney where they fell alike under the spell of historian George Arnold Wood, whose influence in shaping their interests and their values was immeasurable. Both had to spend most of their lives working to support their pens, but both managed some travel, at home and abroad. Both loved, belatedly; neither married.

Some similarities are necessary to the common bond of understanding basic to a successful collaboration; but if two writers are to succeed together creatively, they must be different enough to strike sparks from each other. Here again the Barnard-Eldershaw team was blessed. Flora was reared in the Riverina, a rich wool and wheat area in southern New South Wales west of Canberra, on a large sheep station of which her father was manager; Marjorie in Sydney, where her father was a chartered accountant with a business firm. Flora grew up in the rough-and-tumble of a country family, middle child among four brothers and two sisters; Marjorie was an only surviving child who spent her life in her parents' succession of suburban homes. Flora's upbringing was Roman Catholic, Marjorie's Presbyterian (although both turned away in youth from their orthodox beginnings). Both were brilliant young women but very different in personality: Flora was charming, vivacious, outgoing, aggressive, interested in people, organizations, causes; Marjorie was philosophic and artistic, shy and retiring, generous, happy to play an apparrent second fiddle. The feministic bent common to their generation of women might be called dominant in Flora, recessive in Marjorie.

They met at the University of Sydney when Marjorie was a first-year, Flora a second-year student. Each had a long trip abroad during the years of their partnership (that pilgrimage "home"—to England—essential to every educated Australian of British blood). Apart from that and rare but rewarding vacation trips in Australia, Marjorie was largely homebound in her youth, and home meant Sydney: birth in the western suburb of Ashfield, then of Croydon, then of Eastwood (where home included two acres and a half and gave her, from the age of three to eleven, her earliest taste of "country" life). But Longueville was to be the center of her existence. When she was eleven, her father built a home up the river; when she was twenty-five, another, nearer to Sydney Harbor, in which she still lives almost a half century later. The house is a substantial brick on a rocky hillside across from a park on the Lane Cove River, its twenty-one front steps up from street level rewarding the climber with a magnificent view from its wide verandah of the river, a great sweep of the harbor, and Sydney's bridge and skyline—a suitable setting for the chronicler of the area that she was to become. From Longueville she commuted to the city by ferry as the beginning of her daily trips—to the University as a student and to her work as librarian and user of libraries later. In autumn 1948 she wrote to Nettie Palmer, "It's dark when I come home now but the river in the morning was never so beautiful.... For 45 years (woman and girl) I've made this little voyage and it has never ceased to be a source of joy."[4] Of the almost two hundred letters of hers in the Palmer collection, scarcely a dozen bear any heading but the familiar "2 Stuart Street." There she lived with and for her parents until their deaths, her father's in 1940, her mother's in 1949. By the time she was alone, she was in her fifties, with most of her writing, especially her more creative writing, done.

Flora's life was shorter and far less settled. Her birthplace too is recorded as Sydney, but only by the circumstances of her mother's having come for the event to the flat that the family maintained in Darlinghurst. Flora was native to the Riverina, growing up under the spell that Marjorie too was to find there later during visits to that lovely countryside. The station that her father managed during Flora's childhood was near Wagga Wagga; there she was reared and began her education, and there she was to return in 1956 (to the home of her elder sister Molly) to die. But in the meantime her addresses had been many. College for her was no daily ferry ride but the break of leaving home for Sydney. Later employment took her to the suburbs of Cremorne and Croydon, still later to Canberra and Melbourne. Far from a stable address like her friend Marjorie's, Flora's was a list of schools and city flats and, when her health began to fail in the 1950's, the homes of various friends and relatives.

Flora emerges personally and professionally from the words of her family, her friends, her colleagues, several of whom published tributes to her both before and after her death. Our earliest glimpse cames from poet and critic Tom Inglis Moore, a boyhood friend of Flora's younger brother Pat, who remembers her as an active girl "playing 'kick the tin' in the moonlight of a paddock." For him she was then only "one of an exceptionally interesting and attractive family,"[5] and a serious, even solemn girl—an odd impression in terms of later judgments, but he was seeing her against the high good humor of the eldest sister, Molly, the family storyteller. He also remembers Flora at that time as devout. With a Protestant father and a Roman Catholic mother, the children were brought up in their mother's faith. After her early years of school at Wagga Wagga, Flora was sent to a convent to live while she attended the University of Sydney. There, in wartime, the issue of conscription carried her head-on into a conflict between conscience and authority. Following conscience she left not only the convent (for an apartment with her brother Pat) but the Church, to become what Moore calls a genial agnostic.

At the University she excelled in history and Latin in spite of indulging many extracurricular interests: music, theater, debat-

ing, sport. Here her future collaborator first met her, and later
reported:

Our first contact was not entirely happy. I was the greenest of green
"freshers." Flora was established in her second year. Chance had
given me the locker immediately above hers. Its untidy contents
frequently spilled out into her more ordered domain. My then meagre
person was continually underfoot, and Flora's brown eyes flashed
with indignation more often than they smiled. But within the year
we were close friends. She widened my horizons and quickened
my mind.

Marjorie further remembers Flora from their college days as "a
vivid girl, eager for life," "a dark-haired, vivacious girl, a fountain
of energy, ideas and laughter," and especially recalls "how full
of fire and wit she was when she led the women students against
the men in the Union Hall or in Manning House. She sat on
many committees but was never a 'committee woman.' "[6]

Tom Moore, also at the University, found Flora above all
capable—sensible and constructive, with a clear logical mind,
practical ability, feet always on the ground. Flora was very
active in organizing the Sydney University Women's Union, and
served as its secretary for several years. Her first teaching position
after leaving the University (equipped with a B.A. degree)
was at the Cremorne Grammar School (1921-1923); her longest
commitment (1923-1940) was with Presbyterian Ladies' College
in Croydon, where she became Senior Mistress teaching English,
history, classics. There she put to good use her university experience in the theater and the shaping influence of Professor
Wood's history classes by writing two remarkable pageants
(one on world history, one on Australian) for student production. This is our first record of her as a creative writer.

It was during this Croydon period that she obtained leave for
a full year (1934) abroad. It is indicative of the differences
between the Barnard and the Eldershaw temperaments that
Marjorie had spent her own six-months' leave the previous year
on a quiet pilgrimage to England with her mother, and had
found London overwhelming; Flora traveled widely through
Europe, attending conferences on both sides of the Channel and
bearding London publishers. Her collegiate—or merely Australian?—interest in sports led her to attend the first Test there,

whereas Marjorie not only confessed that this was an interest they didn't share, but that she herself (a very untypical Australian in this respect) could understand neither the games nor their attraction.

Both women joined Sydney's Fellowship of Australian Writers soon after their first novel had established their eligibility, and Flora inevitably became very active in its work. For two years (1935 and 1943) she served as its president, an unusual position for a woman to attain to in those days. This led to a still higher honor. Flora was one of the Fellowship's deputation to Canberra to urge upon the Prime Minister a widening of the scope of the Commonwealth Literary Fund (since 1908 a source of small pensions for needy writers) to include its present functions of aid to working writers, book publishers, and literary periodicals. As a result she became a member of the Fund's new Advisory Board—its first and only woman member, serving from 1939 to 1953, when ill health forced her to resign. Tom Moore, also on the Board, has commented on her remarkable capacity for organization and administration, but Vance Palmer is our best authority on her impact in that very important position. He found her

exuberant, gay, inexhaustible! There seemed no limits to her vitality. She could emerge from a dreary night's journey under war-conditions and take her place, fresh and expectant, at the conference table, ready for a long day's discussions and decisions. Her powers of concentration were remarkable. How often have I seen her settle down in a 'plane, take a couple of ill-typed manuscripts from her case and bury herself deep in them, shutting out all diversions! By the time we alighted she would have her opinion of them formulated and could be depended upon to express it in a clear and concise way.[7]

Her experience, her extraordinary memory for detail, her unerring literary judgment, and her passionate devotion to the work of the Literary Fund made her, in Palmer's judgment, the Advisory Board's most valuable member. And this in spite of what, in that time and place, might have been the handicap of her sex. Palmer, writing from the vantage of the mid-50's, is worth quoting again on this subject.

Not the least of Flora's gifts was her ability to work with men in a jolly, unself-conscious way. Our tradition does not make public life easy for a woman. Frontier prejudices still linger in offices and other places: women are uncertain, hysterical creatures, liable to go off at an emotional tangent, not comfortable to have anything to do with except in a romantic or domestic way! Flora, when she came up against such notions, was not in the least disconcerted. She met them with her robust good-humour which made such a piquant contrast with her feminine sensibility. I knew men (Chifley was one of them) who were at first inclined to resent her presence at a male gathering, but later they could not help letting a radiant look light up their faces as soon as she came into the room. She had a largeness, a racy humour, a sense of abundance that was inspiriting.[8]

During Flora's fifteen years of important service to this Board, her professional life had undergone several changes. Increasingly restive at Presbyterian Ladies' College (where the religion she had abjured nonetheless kept her from the advancement she deserved), she broke away, with the advent of the war, to wider service with the Department of Reconstruction in the then small young capital city of Canberra. Later she was transferred to the Welfare Division of the Department of Labor and National Service in Melbourne, where she had the privilege of getting to know personally the Palmers, who had long befriended M. Barnard Eldershaw and their work; for a time she shared an apartment with their daughter Aileen. Nettie describes her at this time as having "shrewd, lively brown eyes, good hands and neat feet,"[9] and as having retained her country instincts, being an excellent cook and gardener, still at ease with sheep and horses, capable of coping with flood or bush-fire. But she had also become a person with a prompt grasp of problems, balanced, progressive, helpful—a brilliant public speaker and committee member. It is of this period that Vance writes: "All her latent energies were called upon and with her reputation as a writer and her achievements as a woman of action she became one of the most striking figures in the national life."[10] But she hadn't lost her perspective. Nettie, interviewing her in a broadcast, asked her to explain what terms like "induction procedures" used in her new work meant; Flora was happy to "translate," but with her very real respect for language, was amused into a "You've jerked me out of the jargon of my job."[11]

When she finally left Government service in 1948, she had the experience necessary to going into private practice as an industrial consultant, but in the 50's the enormous demands she had put upon her energies for a quarter of a century began to take their toll. Again it is Nettie Palmer who makes this drain vivid to us in speaking of the "three lives" of Flora's prime, when she taught all day, worked evenings on committees, then wrote into the wee hours. When on September 20, 1956, she died at the age of 59, it is Vance who summed up the circumstances: "In a sense, most of her friends could feel no shock at the news of Flora Eldershaw's death. She had been a sick woman for so long life had become little more than a burden to her. She did not want to live unless she could regain her full powers; and as the days went on, the prospect of this grew more hopeless."[12]

Back in 1932 Marjorie wrote, of the circumstances that prevented her and Flora from going abroad together, "It is a pity. We would have enjoyed it more together. We like the same things."[13] This compatibility, as we have already noted, grew out of personalities and circumstances that were complementary rather than similar. Raised as an only child (a brother died in infancy), Marjorie knew nothing of the give-and-take that life on a Riverina station held for the Eldershaw children. She was seven before her father let her learn the alphabet, but from that time on, with the assistance of two successive governesses, she knew such intimacy with the printed—and written—word as never to be utterly lonely. Two matters relating to her parents bespeak her extraordinary precocity: from seven to eleven, writing poetry and stories as gifts for her mother, she cunningly made them deliberately childish so that they would be acceptable; from eight on, she felt estranged from her father over the issue of religion, about which he was and remained more than a little fanatical. At eleven she attended Cambridge School at Hunters Hill; at fourteen she began her four years at the Sydney Girls' High School, state-supported, "big" (as she remembers its five hundred students), efficient, good. Then, during the war years, the University of Sydney. Marjorie's father, who had little sympathy with the lives of his wife and daughter at best, had none for the idea of Marjorie's going to the University; but he fed and housed her and gave her a weekly allowance—£1 a week to cover all other expenses including commuting, so that she remembers she "didn't get into the habit of clothes."

Marjorie's nature and her circumstances both precluded the kind of active participation in extracurricular activities that her friend Flora knew; she was totally absorbed in the academic. With her B.A. degree she won first class honors in history, a University medal, and an opportunity to go on to Oxford for graduate work. Her father predictably refused both permission and funds, and Marjorie came to feel later that it was all for the best: with no respect for the sterility of much scholarship, she thinks that graduate training might have stifled her creativity.

Now at loose ends, she drifted into library work through a kind of apprenticeship, and for more than a dozen years (1923-1935) she worked regularly as a librarian—first in the Public Library of New South Wales, then at Sydney Technical College, where she shortly became head librarian. There was no question but that she was good for the job, much doubt as to how good the job was for an aspiring creative writer. In 1932 she admits to Nettie Palmer that "After ten years on a holiday ration of three weeks a year one is liable to attacks of claustrophobia!"[14] To Vance a couple of years later she reports, "Am exceedingly busy doing researches on electric clocks, honey, calculating machines, ethyl acetate, and welded bridges simultaneously in a horrid jumble. Feel rather battered and after hauling heavy books can hardly hold my pen."[15]

We shall look with more attention at her decision to leave this work for full-time writing in 1935, and at her decision to go back to work in 1942. This second stretch began in the Public Library again but she soon left, this time for a more challenging position with CSIRO (the Commonwealth Scientific and Industrial Research Organization). Here she was head of the most complex scientific library in Australia, located at the University of Sydney—a physics library behind such projects as the development of the radar system that helped save Darwin during World War II. In 1950, her mother's death the previous year having left her modestly independent, Marjorie forswore scheduled employment for the last time, free for the rest of her life to go back to her writing and to take long trips abroad.

Since the personality of Marjorie Barnard will emerge largely through her letters to the Palmers, we should pause here to note more particularly who this couple was and how she felt about them. Marjorie's own words will best serve our purpose. In an appreciation written in 1959, she describes them both as "poets in youth and lecturers in maturity. . . . Nettie Palmer with her scholarship and her gift for languages looks outward, seeing Australia in a world context; Vance looks inward, at home or in exile, preoccupied with the intimate textures of Australian life." Since 1915 they had, between them, covered

the whole field of literary endeavour. Vance Palmer as novelist, short story writer, dramatist, essayist, editor, reviewer of books most constant. Nettie Palmer, who claims that she is not creative, is biographer, essayist, diarist, critic, letter writer. Above all perhaps she is a writer of letters, weaving a network of sympathetic communication between the great and the small, the arrived and the hopeful of the Australian literary world. . . . there can scarcely be a writer of any promise in Australia who does not owe something to the Palmers. They have read almost everything on publication and they have welcomed almost every young writer who showed the gleam. . . . Nettie, by her correspondence with the known and the unknown, created the finest and most enduring literary club in Australia. Vance Palmer, as in all else, has been a partner in this generosity.

As a writer, once young and hesitant, I want to record my gratitude to Vance and Nettie Palmer for their reassurance, help and friendship over many a long year.[16]

It is significant that the first letter in the National Library's Barnard-Palmer collection is Marjorie's answer to an inquiry from Nettie as to how the second M. Barnard Eldershaw novel was coming on. The two had never met, didn't meet for several years. The inquiry was prompted solely by Nettie's interest in *A House Is Built* and her concern for the literary future of its young Australian authors.

This section has been but a preliminary sketch of the lives and personalities of the two women who wrote together as M. Barnard Eldershaw. More details will inevitably be revealed in the ensuing discussions of their works. But before we examine these in detail, let us look as closely as possible at the workings of that curious phenomenon, the collaboration.

III *The Action*

Authors have used pseudonyms for various reasons: to conceal identity, to denote a phase of personality, to mislead as to sex.

The name "M. Barnard Eldershaw" appears to have originated for none of these. The two young and entirely unknown authors had no desire—made no attempt—to remain unknown. From the first it was common knowledge that this pen name signified two women named Marjorie Barnard and Flora Eldershaw, and it was used thereafter for every type of writing that they jointly produced.[17] One might wonder, then, why a pseudonym at all (one of the team was a trained librarian, surely conscious of the bibliographical difficulties that would ensue!). Later pairs of Australian women writers were simply to use their two complete names: Miles Franklin and Dymphna Cusack did, in publishing their wickedly satirical *Pioneers on Parade* (1939), a novel so certain to raise a furor that one could have understood their taking at least temporary refuge in an adopted name. So did Miss Cusack and Florence James in publishing their less controversial novel *Come In, Spinner* (1951). Why not, then, "Marjorie Barnard and Flora Eldershaw?"

The choice of a combined name, it appears, was not to conceal, not to confuse, not to typify, but to indicate a kind of collaboration so close, so carefully welded, that a single joint name made up of pieces of both seemed a truer reflection of it than their two complete names would have been. But why not just "Barnard Eldershaw," the simpler form to which some reviewers and bibliographers have reduced it? On this subject history and the surviving member of the pair utter nothing of significance. There is a certain staginess about "M. Barnard Eldershaw" that may perhaps be forgiven their youth. If the use of both given initial and surname for Marjorie recognized her greater share in the collaboration, it was an emphasis increasingly well-deserved during the score of years that the partnership nominally existed. That the use of Flora's surname as the final one consequently gets her the major attention in literary indexes, bibliographies, and library card catalogs is less fortunate.

Even the authors fell into the trap of grammatical number set by their pseudonym. The first person singular was usually used—purposely, Marjorie told me, to represent the two minds as a single writing entity. Thus when we find their study of Captain Piper concluding with "I searched the newspaper files of the day," it is an "I" which means not Marjorie Barnard, who probably did the searching, but M. Barnard Eldershaw, who were responsible jointly for the finished book. But inconsistencies inevitably crept in. In an article "The Period Novel" (p. 138), "we" is used for the authors of *A House Is Built*, "I" for the M. Barnard Eldershaw writing the essay. Throughout their *Essays in Australian Fiction*, all opinions are expressed with "I," but the acknowledgments with "we." This problem arose for the authors only in their non-fiction, of course, but is ever present for readers and reviewers and literary historians.

Looking at the joint authorship of *Pioneers on Parade* in her study of Miles Franklin (1967), Marjorie decides that since it is impossible to say what contributions each author made, she will treat it as Miles's book, just as, writing on Dymphna Cusack, she would treat it as hers. A prolonged collaboration like that of Barnard and Eldershaw cannot be dismissed so easily; it is mandatory (not to mention irresistible) to ferret out as accurately as possible the contribution of each writer to each book. But here Marjorie, the only sure source of information left, has been of little help, remaining generally true to her further contention in *Miles Franklin* that "Collaborators should not publicly claim their contributions to a shared book; it is not fair to the book."[18]

From the time their first published work, the novel *A House Is Built*, appeared, the success of the collaboration as such has been a matter of comment. As discerning a literary critic as Nettie Palmer recorded in her journal in 1933, "It isn't easy to understand how a literary partnership is carried on, but in this case it seems to work well. At any rate it has so far, for there are no visible gaps or joins in *A House Is Built*."[19] The methods by which the collaborators achieved such smoothness varied over the years from a completely shared effort to one in which the work of conception was shared but Marjorie did most, even all, of the actual writing. This first novel was the result of thoroughgoing teamwork. Like all their books, it was written under two grave difficulties: little time to write and still less to work together. Marjorie was tied to her library work, her commuting, her home and family; Flora was penned up in residence at Presbyterian Ladies' College. But they nonetheless conceived the story jointly, blocked it out in chapters, assigned each to one or the other, then worked together on the resulting manuscript to eliminate any discrepancies, to smooth over any "joins."

The astonishing thing about this system is that stylistic differences from chapter to chapter did not betray them, for there are reasons to believe that their styles varied indeed. Marjorie, all artist, thinks in metaphor, the common denominator of her writing whether it be fiction, history, criticism, or letters, and of much of her conversation as well. Nettie Palmer recorded of their first meeting early in 1933 the impression of "a spontaneous brilliance of expression that made you catch your breath."[20] Flora, when she met her a year later, Nettie found "sometimes using inexpressive words."[21] In such work as is known to be Flora's alone—a few letters and written speeches—I have not found a memorable phrase. Yet this stylistic disparity does not show in their published work.

To say that Marjorie is the greater stylist is not by any means to minimize Flora's value to the partnership. She contributed her own set of indispensable strengths. Tom Inglis Moore, familiar with Flora's drive and energy, her firms opinions, and her constructiveness, believes that these qualities operated in the organization of their works, which then flowered under Marjorie's sensitivity and imagination. Certainly they complemented each other, and they knew it. Working together was not merely a doubling of their strength but a great multiplication of their spirits. In all their difficult years of writing together, there was no flagging of their mutual respect and admiration, affection and dependence. As Nettie Palmer observed, "Any difference in the characters of the two women doesn't make for a difference in their point-of-view or values."[22]

Marjorie still speaks of Flora's fine critical sense; she drew strength from it. Writing of a lecture on Vance Palmer that she had completed just as she was getting ready to make her first trip abroad, Marjorie expressed concern that in her exhaustion she had been unable to give it her best, but took comfort in the fact that "Teenie [Flora's family nickname] will tune it up."[23] When she first visited the Palmers in Melbourne, en route, Nettie apparently made suggestions for Marjorie's marketing a Barnard-Eldershaw play while she was in London. Marjorie wrote back her thanks, but added, "I doubt however if I have the courage to do anything with it. Much better to leave it for Teenie to handle next year. She is our shop window."[24] She was also a shield and defender. Concerning a critical literary friend, Marjorie comforts herself that the woman "wouldn't last half an hour with Teenie."[25] Of English editors who had lost one of the team's manuscripts, Flora writes from London, "Don't worry, I'll be nasty to them." And Marjorie adds, in reporting this to the Palmers, "She can be very competently nasty too, bless her heart."[26] Confessing to the difficulty she always found in going back over anything she had written in order to revise it, Marjorie exclaimed, "How magnificent to have a partner—to throw the thing in her lap and say 'See if you can make something of it' and then think of something else."[27]

In the workings of the collaboration there developed a curious kind of partnership to which each contributed according to her special ability (or time, or energy, or inclination), from which each drew according to her need. This is the "larder" to which Marjorie frequently refers. When Flora, early in their career, gave a speech on "Contemporary Australian Women Writers," Marjorie confessed confidentially to Mrs. Palmer (whom she had not yet met), "It is our joint work though in the circumstances I do not claim my share. Flora speaks very well—brilliantly—and I very badly, so I have given up the practice entirely and if any one wants to hear our views refer them to her. The least I can do in return for getting out of all the bother is to help anonymously with the speeches, isn't it?"[28] This became a pattern, with Flora the "shop window" for the pair. There are frequent references in the Barnard-Palmer correspondence to the long hours that Marjorie put into the writing of lectures for Flora—sometimes public lectures, sometimes lectures for her teaching needs.

Flora made an occasional contribution to the larder. In January 1935 Marjorie wrote to Vance Palmer, presumably to forestall any misunderstanding: "Teenie has written a review of *The Swayne Family* [Vance's new novel, about which Marjorie had written him a long and glowing personal report a couple of months earlier] and sent it to *Desiderata*, over our common name. We don't see exactly eye to eye here but I refrained from shoving my oar into the pie this time."[29] If, as it appears, Marjorie was shy about expressing her opinion of what Flora had written, that was part of her characteristic modesty, even self-doubt. Writing late in 1933 to prepare Nettie Palmer for her first meeting with Flora, who was on her way to Europe, Marjorie said, "She is worth ten of me in every way. I set that down in black and white in case you should think I didn't realize it."[30]

The meeting took place, resulting in two vignettes in Nettie's journal that are our best portraits of the young collaborators at this early point in their career.

Until I met her [Flora], I'd thought of Marjorie Barnard as the directive part of that composite, the Barnard-Eldershaws. Chiefly, I suppose, because I'd come into contact with Marjorie first and found she had so definite a personality, in letters and then in talk. There was that day last March, after years of correspondence, when she rang up to say she was in Melbourne on her way to Europe, and would I meet her in town. How musical her voice sounded on the phone, and how it lifted at the end of every phrase: "You'll easily know me—I'm middle-aged—I wear brown—I wear glasses—I'll be watching for you." (Middle-aged meant precisely thirty-five, or half-way.)

Next evening, when she came to dinner, I remember being still conscious of that musical lilt in her voice. With it was a sort of demureness that, at every fifth moment, was swept away by a most unusual frankness. . . . I knew from her letters that she had all the significant virtues—loyalty, selflessness, industry and, of course, sincerity.

Flora Eldershaw was a vaguer figure in my mind. Yet as soon as she got down from the bus yesterday it was plain that she couldn't be disposed of as part of a composite. A fine head, a broad, generous brow, she's physically powerful, though much too fatigued for her years. She must have called up her reserves and resources continually. Yet it's the extent of these that impresses you. A thinker, a personality in her own right, a robust woman of action, she seems to include the goodness of all her experiences.[31]

Nettie, having taken this look into the "shop window," was moved, when next she wrote, to ask what was, to one of Marjorie's temperament, an ill-advised question. Marjorie replied:

You ask me if I am going to be "powerful enough" to keep up with her when she returns. I stared sombrely at that question for a long time. There must always be something like that to fear. There has always been disparity; perhaps a little more won't matter. The

natural end of our collaboration (nothing external will ever destroy
it I think) will be bitter enough for me. It comforts me to empty
my little vial into her fountain and see it lifted. I don't know why
I should need comfort, but I do.[32]

In the face of such apparent self-abasement, however, one
broods over a later remark of Marjorie's: "May it not be my
vanity to put away vanity?"[33]

Fortunately Marjorie was able to act with less diffidence,
more courage, than she dared express to her friends. In 1935
she took a major leap: after having spent all of her post-graduate
life in various demanding library positions, she resigned, free-
ing herself at age 38 to devote her whole time to writing. She
was financially secure, for not only was she still living at home
but her mother had persuaded her father to give his daughter
an allowance to this end. But that didn't end the soul-searching.
Nor did the pressing need that she felt for time to write overcome her diffidence about her ability. A letter to Nettie Palmer
while her resignation was still tentative indicates that she is
now thinking of a writing career beyond the limits of the collaboration, and also expresses her doubts and indicates something of what fed them.

If I give this up am I going to be worth my salt? I know you have
a certain faith in my literary ability—but it's faith, not knowledge,
isn't it? For after all you've seen nothing I've written alone and
there's no particular reason to think that any of the virtues of our
joint work are my contribution. (People have not scrupled to suggest
on public platforms that I was being carried by my brilliant collaborator or to ask her privately why she did it.) It has been honest,
however. The partnership will continue. That gives me some courage.[34]

It will continue, she adds a couple of weeks later, for the novel
in progress (*The Glasshouse*, their third) and for the critical
work that she hopes to do. "Anything else I'll probably have to
do alone—over a pseudonym so as not in any way to prejudice
Teenie's reputation. We'll settle that definitely between us."[35]

If it was easy at that time for people to underestimate Marjorie's share in the collaboration, it may be equally tempting
now to overestimate it. There is no doubt that with her new
freedom, Marjorie put the greater number of hours into their
joint ventures, hours of research as well as writing. But to dis-

count Flora's continued importance to the partnership is to fail to understand the nature of her contribution which, if proportionately smaller, remained just as vital to her partner. When the possibility arose in 1936 that Flora might leave Croydon for Western Australia, Marjorie was deeply concerned: "If she went there I don't know what would happen about our writing. But it hasn't happened yet."[36] Even when separation did occur, some years later, the collaboration survived it for a time in something more than name.

But at this time years of work together still lay ahead of them. While Marjorie's new leisure did permit her to write more and more (reviews, history, short stories) on her own and in her own name, M. Barnard Eldershaw, in the following decade, did most of their joint work too, adding more novels, notable criticism, and excellent histories to their score. Marjorie's account of their relationship after she left her work and was able to throw herself wholly into their unfinished third novel is illuminating: "Teenie is being very noble about this book. You can imagine how easily she might envy me my greater leisure to wrestle with it or be jealous of the time I spend alone with our common property. But she isn't. The atmosphere between us is so clear that any speck would show up monstrously."[37]

The method of collaboration used in the first novel appears to have been followed in the second, *Green Memory,* which, though it represents a stylistic falling off, reads with equal consistency. But if the problem of method was solved, the problem of finding time to work together remained. Early in their career Marjorie reported, "We are going away for this weekend and hope to do some work. When we do get a little time we're so anxious to lay it out to the best advantage that we become paralyzed. It's silly."[38] Not that the pressure didn't have its saving grace: with an appealing candor she once admitted of this problem of time that "if we didn't have to snatch it we'd probably never write at all."[39]

Occasionally they were able to take trips together—for a weekend, a fortnight, even a rare month—to the mountains, to Tasmania, to Flora's family home in the Riverina, that place of never-ending delight to Sydney-bred Marjorie. But it was always difficult for either to get away (especially for Marjorie, with her family responsibilities), and still more difficult for them both to

go at the same time. As for staying at home, the privacy for concentrated work, alone or together, must have been equally lacking with Marjorie's parents or Flora's students and colleagues.
It was not until 1936 that they attained in some measure to a
"room of their own." Marjorie reported late that year to the
Palmers: "Teenie and I have set up housekeeping in an abridged
and intermittent sort of way. We have a room in Orwell Street,
Potts Point. It is small with a barred and viewless window but
quite habitable when we had put away the Stags at Bay and the
malevolent china dog. We are able to give minute parties there
and it is our own."[40] This move must have greatly increased
their opportunities for thrashing out their mutual writing problems, although they were still bound to spend most of their
time with home and family on the one hand, school and students
on the other. At least they could more easily mingle with their
own literary kind.[41] And high time—both were approaching
forty.

CHAPTER 2

The Early Novels

I A House Is Built

IN 1928 Sydney's weekly *Bulletin,* long the successful promoter of the Australian short story, offered a prize of £1000 for the best Australian novel to be submitted that year. Among the inevitable flotsam that drifted into the net were two such superior catches that the prize was divided between them: *Coonardoo,* a study of an aboriginal woman by Katharine Susannah Prichard, an already well-established West Australian novelist, and *A House Is Built,* a story of nineteenth-century Sydney by M. Barnard Eldershaw, who came into literary existence with this book. Time has not questioned the wisdom of either choice.[1]

A House had been written by two unknown young women who approached their task with nothing but keen intelligence, a love of their country's history, and the enthusiasm of inexperience, but these did well suffice. In spite of living apart and being regularly employed, they had dashed off the manuscript in a few months.

To have won the *Bulletin* prize with this first book must have been heady indeed; any pain from sharing would have been mitigated by the already solid reputation of their co-winner. Prompt serialization in the *Bulletin* itself (under the title *The Quartermaster*) must have been gratifying too. But if these two newcomers needed their bubble pricked, a flat rejection from the prominent Australian publisher to whom the book rights were first offered must have done the job. Perhaps his refusal is understandable at that time in a country that even yet tends to undervalue its own. Happily he lived to regret it.

Happily too the manuscript was shortly accepted by a London publisher, Harrap, and consequently, like so many Australian books, *A House* first appeared in England. Happily indeed for its obscure young authors, since it thus drew the attention of influential English critics who would never have heard of it had

32

it been published in Sydney. No less a figure than novelist Arnold
Bennett reviewed the book in the London *Evening Standard* in
such phrases as "this extraordinary book," "a phenomenon of
modern fiction," "epical," "emotional power," concluding with
the prediction that "If more is not heard of the Misses Eldershaw and Barnard I shall be surprised."[2]

Although this first novel was not to be published in Australia
for sixteen years, an American edition appeared almost immediately. In England the book went into three reprintings in as
many months. Within its first decade nearly thirty thousand
copies had appeared, a figure which looms larger when one
remembers that the authors were previously unknown, the subject
Australian, and the decade the depressed 30's. It has never been
out of print since. If nearly a half century of continual accessi-
bility in bookstores and a firm place on school reading lists make
a classic, this is one of Australia's few.[3] No history of Australian
literature had appeared prior to the publication of *A House Is
Built*; none since has presumed to ignore it.

This firm place of the book in the hearts of its countrymen,
and women, and children, is unquestionably owing in part to its
subject matter. Yet earlier novels had been written of Australia's
past, and weightier ones since, with none as steadily popular.
Not that this was a cheap bid for success through romance or
melodrama. M. Barnard Eldershaw took a new approach to the
early days, managing to create fiction without an aborigine and
with scarcely a convict or a squatter, with no rebellions and no
outback hardships. There is the Gold Rush, to be sure, but even
it is seen largely at a remove, from the comforts of Sydney, and
is introduced mainly for its long-range economic results.

The history here is sound rather than spectacular, yet these
two young female disciples of Professor Wood are novelists first,
historians second, and there is no smell of the lamp. There is
much evidence of judicious choice and limitation, however. *A
House* is a story not of discovery but of growth. Of the century
and a half between the settling of Australia and the writing of
the book, the story occupies almost the middle half century
(the 1830's to the 1880's); of the continent whose vastness was
already recognized through settlement as well as exploration,
the scene is almost entirely the tiny area occupied by the rapidly
expanding commercial center, Sydney.

Within these limits of time and place there is room for a number of typical early Australian themes. There is the close relationship of the new settlement to England, a cultural dependence more inescapable than the political and economic ties. Opposing it are the early efforts of these colonists to resist the dictates of twelve-thousand-miles-distant Britain and to shape their own tastes and destiny. There is the painful and painfully slow process by which Englishmen in Australia became Australians. There are even (through reminiscent "stories within the story") brief glimpses of convict beginnings, outback loneliness, whaling perils, and pioneering hardships. But the major theme of the book is economic—the ups and downs (mainly ups) of Sydney as the business heart of developing Australia in the middle half of the nineteenth century. This being a novel, economic facts are given a living habitation and a name through character and action. Thus Steinbeck made the Depression live for Americans through the vicissitudes of the unforgettable Joads. But *A House* is built on the opposite end of the economic scale; in its theme of the "merchant prince" struggling to establish and maintain a commercial dynasty, it is closer kin to England's Forsytes and Germany's Buddenbrooks.

An English novel of public life opening in 1837 could hardly have forgone at least a reference to Victoria's accession. James Hyde, protagonist of *A House,* is English to the bone—by birth and by long service as quartermaster on His Majesty's ships. But as the novel opens, he is 110 days from home, in Sydney, thinking not of England's present but of Australia's future. Being fifty but with the energy and ambition of a young man, he decides to go back and resign from the "blind alley" of the Navy, and he shortly returns to Sydney to "build a house" for the motherless son and two daughters who soon join him from England. Experienced in buying and selling,[4] he sets up a store on the Sydney waterfront for the supplying of ships; by natural ability, hard work, and courage, he soon branches out into other areas that enable him to survive the depressions and bank failures of the times. During the Gold Rush of the 1850's his imaginative recognition that more money is to be made by supplying the diggers than by digging establishes him firmly among Sydney's wealthy.

English James Hyde is and English he remains, as does his son and heir William, who sent back to England not only for a bride but later for all the hideously Victorian furnishings of the family's third and final Sydney home. But his grandsons are native-born, and the "house" James builds for them is Australian. He would have been unperturbed could he have heard his bitterest business rival say of him, with typically English snobbery, "He is the only ancestor the Hydes have."[5] For he found great satisfaction in the fact that his son "William had been born in a London lodging-house to nothing in particular, William's son in a commodious and elegant house to an ever-increasing inheritance."[6] Australia was as short on ancestors as it still is on ruined castles, but it was long on commercial opportunities, and it was England's James Hydes whose diligence and daring helped set the bourgeois and egalitarian tone that one still finds conspicuous in Australian society.

This is no place to enter into the curious schizophrenia that has permitted Australians as a people to feel, as someone has said of Sydney's taxi drivers, "as good as anybody else if not a little better," yet still maintain a strong sense of the superiority of all things English to anything they know "down under." This state of mind has been a subject of satire in some hands; in *A House* the tone is gentler but clearly ironic. Both of its authors were Australian-born, and neither had yet been "home," but they knew England and the English inevitably and intimately. When Fanny Hyde, the elder daughter and hostess, sets the table for guests, she includes "cornucopias of imitation marble gushing asters on the damask. The cornucopias had come from England, packed carefully in her underlinen. Her aunt Sophia had presented them to her to be a leaven of refinement in the barbaric new world."[7] James Hyde had left England with no regrets. Out of all his seafaring he had chosen Australia as the proper place to make a fortune, and he had no thought of going "home" even to spend it. But when the family moved to a house with a garden, he "still obstinately grew cucumbers because he would not let a little thing like climate deflect him from his good English habits."[8]

It is his son William, however, who, while helping to build an Australian fortune, remains a thorough English snob. Only a Naval quartermaster's son in England, "sitting on a high stool"[9] in his uncle's counting-house, he nonetheless resents in Sydney having to "hobnob with swaggering captains and greasy traders."[10] Without aristocratic origins, he has the upperclass Englishman's scorn of trade even while fattening on it. Only he, of all the Hydes, finds their first home, in rooms over the wharfside store, ignominious. It is he who insists on the family's remove to a more suitable house before he imports his made-in-England bride, Adela. And when she finds life disappointingly the same as she had known it in England, it is he who utters "with pride and complacency" the point of view that the nineteenth-century Englishman made famous the world over:

"I have striven to reproduce our English life as far as possible.... What finer thing can we do for Australia than make it like another England? Australia of itself is nothing.... It has no personality of its own, only a resistance. It is for us with British perseverance to break down that resistance, to plant English life here in its entirety...."

Adela had sat through this oration with twitching lips and modestly downcast eyes. She saw an Empire built up on antimacassars and top-hats, Australia a brand snatched from the burning to the glory of gentility.[11]

Being limited for the most part to a single strand of plot, the story is on the whole well-knit. There is no departure from chronological sequence (an advantage in a historical novel) from that moment on 16 June 1837 when James Hyde, still a Navy man, looks down on Sydney from Flagstaff Hill and decides to return as a settler, to the April evening forty-five years and two generations later, when his surviving grandson, "the mouse that the mountain had brought forth,"[12] draws the curtains at Firenze, the tastefully refurnished family mansion, the night before his marriage. The building of the house of Hyde through expanding commercial interests is neatly measured for us by the three books of which the novel is composed, each named after the location of one of the three homes that the Hydes successively occupy on their way up: "Windmill Street" (the rooms over the store), "The City Road" (the house near Paramatta Road), and "The Hill" (the elegant Italianate residence in Hunters Hill). Only a couple of times do we leave the Sydney in which the Hyde firm is abuilding, and then for two purposes, story and history: to Camden to allow Fanny to recuperate from thwarted love while we get a needed glimpse into Australian country life with its plenty and its drought; and to the gold fields to allow James to enlarge his empire while we get an insight into the greatest economic event to occur in Australia during the entire nineteenth century.

Less clearly purposeful are some of the incidental "stories within the story." The dinner conversations of Captain Hildebrand and his mate Meikle give us a valuable insight into the dangerous seafaring upon which the Hyde fortune is indirectly founded. The story of Mr. Murther, from whom the first Hyde home is bought, pays tribute to the convict strain, and Gran Godling's reminiscences, to pioneering life in Australia—both useful insights into history. But the story of the self-punishment of drunken Dave, whom James runs across near the gold fields, reads rather like an anecdote that its authors could not resist including solely for its horror—or worse, for its moral. Surely the weakest bit of plotting appears in the report of Captain Hildebrand, Fanny's first love, happening to rob Mr. Moore, her second. The population of Australia was small, true, but this is an overuse of coincidence hardly to be justified by either a need to introduce the thread of bushranging into the historical skein or a desire for a neat Dickensian tying up of all threads.

But there is room for no carping in the handling of the main plot, which is an inexorable intertwining of action and character that many more experienced novelists might envy. The house has been built in every sense: James Hyde's daring and his son William's stability have achieved for the family one of the finest residences and one of the most widespread and flourishing businesses in the largest and most thriving city on the new continent, and the third generation in the person of young James has not only been taken into the business but has already taken to it. A cheaper story might have ended here with total success, Horatio Alger style, and a sacrifice of realism. A less discerning one might have closed with financial failure, stressing the material side of the "house" to the neglect of the family itself. A less well-managed one might have allowed tragedy to strike through a gratuitous accident. But in the able young hands of Barnard and Eldershaw, old James is brought down not by such a stroke as would have been medically possible to one of his type at any time but by one induced through the shock of learning of his grandson's disloyalty to the house of Hyde. And young James is disloyal not from selfishness but from the strongest of human motivations, love. Further, his beloved betrays him not from coquetry but from a family loyalty of her own which a Hyde would be the first to understand if not to forgive. And young James's inability to confide in his mother (and thus gain an emotional release that might have spared him from dashing out into the storm to search for it in danger) has the deepest of roots in the relationship of his mother to his father, to his younger brother Lionel, and to himself. At no time does the threefold meaning of the "house"—as business, as home, and as family—emerge so significantly.

The reputation of *A House Is Built* as a historical novel has tended to obscure its other virtues. Australian students today may find the book on reading lists of background material for a study of nineteenth-century Australia, but in it they will discover a group of very credible characters, quite capable of remaining upright if their historical background were removed. Readers who still like to feel that they can determine the sex of a novelist by the works (despite all evidence to the contrary) may be gratified by the attention paid here to food and clothes, by the remarkably acute insights into the psychology of children, by the true-to-life women characters. They may note further that Fanny's Captain Hildebrand, like Jane Eyre's Rochester, reads like a young lady's idea of a romantic figure. But no one can question the authenticity, the virility of James Hyde, the major character in the book and a timeless one surely. Son William is as sharp a contrast to his father as daughter Fanny is to her sister Maud, but all ring true; such strong family differences do exist—and we know nothing of the mother. Special tribute should be paid to the drawing of some of the minor characters as well: Benjamin Shirley, with a loyalty to man, and woman, that belies—or perhaps tries to make up for— his convict heritage; and best of all, surely the most Dickensian, Adela's cousin Esther, who manages to satisfy so perfectly our expectations of a "poor relation," and who remains so thoroughly the spinster despite her eventual wife-and-motherhood.

There is little broad humor in the book; these were neither humorous times nor people. Lusty old James gives us one delightful moment when, hearing predatory Mrs. Giles's silly daughter

Euphemia exclaim "Ravishing!" he reflects, "That's just what that girl does want."[13] Most of the humor, like this, is verbal, and of a rather wry, dry, caustic variety that is often credited with being typically Australian. When young William's early dissatisfactions in Sydney led James Hyde to a frank fatherly talk with him, the son's "sense of injustice was shaken. It is hard to do without a sense of injustice when you have got used to one."[14] In the Rocks area of Sydney through which daughters Fanny and Maud move with a delightful sense of danger, "Many of the houses were owned by Chinese. They may have been opium-dens or not, for a Chinese who does not run an opium-den looks just as sinister as one who does."[15] When the Franklins came to live on Hunters Hill, their ornate tastes led them to stud their garden with a stucco pavilion, white statues, immense urns, massive white seats: "In fact, everything that the art of the plasterer could do was done for the garden."[16]

There is one incident of high good humor told with a Dickensian robustness that deserves looking at though it is unfortunately too long to quote here. It involves William, characteristically ashamed of having to ride with the driver of one of the Hyde's freight wagons. One morning, to avoid being seen by any of his stylish friends, he insisted on starting off before George, the driver, had properly secured the load. Over William's head was suspended, "like sinister mistletoe,"[17] a washstand with a large circle cut out of the upper shelf to hold a basin. When he sees young Mr. Humphrey Gillam and his four elegant and eligible sisters approaching by carriage, William makes George whip up the horses and turn into a side street. The two vehicles are almost abreast when the pitching wagon swerves around the corner, precipitating the washstand upside down over William's head and shoulders. The wagon stops, the carriage stops, and a delighted crowd gathers to supply sprightly comments while Mr. Humphrey helps George to set the victim onto the road and free him—from all but his mortification.

This incident is of course particularly amusing because it happened to stiff-necked William. (His genial father laughed uproariously when he heard about it; had it happened to *him*, we are reminded, he would have happily told it on himself.) This spirited episode has not only a folksy humor but a further quality that is to be pervasive in the Barnard-Eldershaw canon—

irony. William suffers this humiliation not gratuitously but precisely because he is trying so hard to avoid it.

Such irony of incident is frequent in this book, as witness Cousin Esther's good intentions always coming to embarrassingly bad ends. Adela serves five long years of waiting, defies her father, and crosses unknown seas to an unknown land for William's love, only to find it a far remove from her anticipation. Fanny interprets Captain Hildebrand's "silence and remoteness" as a feeling of unworthiness and so arranges a supreme "gesture of faith that would leave him in no doubt,"[18] only to find him preoccupied with his work and annoyed by her proposed sacrifice. Young James endangers the family god, its business, to win Laurel's love, little dreaming that she was motivated only by a desire for family revenge.

But the overruling irony of the book is of course the fate of the house of Hyde. The high hopes of lusty old James and the more reserved but equally dedicated William do not end with a bang but subside with something of a whimper. Firenze, the *ne plus ultra* of homes, remains, and so does the firm of Hyde, for even unbusinesslike Lionel is sufficiently loyal to it to withstand his mother's urging that he sell. But the family has collapsed; the loss of young James deeply affects them all. Old James has been mortally stricken by the revelation of the boy's perfidy and death. William, mercifully spared a knowledge of the perfidy, nonetheless dies prematurely "of a broken heart" over the loss of his son. The loss for Lionel, never close to his elder brother, is incalculable; it reroutes the whole course of his pleasant gentleman's existence into the unfamiliar, uncongenial channel of the business. "He lacked the business sense, the necessary sense of its importance in the scheme of life.... It seemed to him incredible and comic that it should matter vitally whether he should offer tenpence or tenpence halfpenny for an article, even though the multiplication table convinced him that the difference sometimes involved thousands of pounds."[19] Two conceivable avenues of help are closed to him: capable Aunt Fanny because she is a woman, and the sons of Aunt Maud because they aren't titular Hydes.

James Hyde, your house is in poor hands in the third generation. And the fourth? Time and the authors utter nothing, but what can the prophetic reader hope from the progeny (if they have the vigor to produce any) of sensitive music-and-mama-loving Lionel and his about-to-be-wedded wife, daughter of the ridiculous Esther and the perpetually insolvent Bardon? Ironically, the family of Hyde, by whom Adela was repelled as a bride because it was so "invincible," has been brought low. But through its efforts, and those of other families like it, Sydney, the background against which the Hyde drama has been played, and partly played out, has prospered mightily.

II   Green Memory

One of the strengths as well as potential weaknesses of the team of Barnard and Eldershaw as novelists is their persistent unwillingness to repeat themselves. Thoroughly versed in their nation's past and established by *A House Is Built* as purveyors of it in fiction, they were surely capable of playing upon that initial success by repeating themselves endlessly on the theme of Australia's development—of going into factory production with it as their fellow countrywoman and contemporary Maisie Grieg was doing on the theme of love. Fortunately, as they approached a second novel, they changed their subject matter and their approach; unfortunately, they produced two years later a very inferior book.

Again Harrap published it in London, but this time there were no reprintings, no American or Australian editions. *Green Memory* (1931) is justifiably forgotten, important only in an examination of its authors' entire works.

Seldom does an opportunity arise to weigh the accomplishment of a book so exactly against an author's intention, especially an intention clearly stated before publication rather than after the reviews. Again we have the Palmers to thank. When Nettie Palmer, alerted by *A House*, wrote graciously to these young authors she had never met to ask them for particulars about their next book, the manuscript of *Green Memory* was already in England awaiting publication. Marjorie's reply would at first sight indicate a second historical novel not unlike their first, for it is set, she explains, in Sydney in the early 1860's, the action taking place at Darling Point and in a terrace house on the hill above Wooloomooloo. But the prospectus that follows, and the book itself, belie the expectation.

Green Memory is the story of a family that keeps green their father's memory to their own undoing. The protagonists are Lucy Haven and her younger sister Charlotte. Lucy was her father's favorite and the envy that Charlotte felt for her sister during his lifetime develops after his tragic and shadowed death into a silent struggle for the guardianship of his memory. For this Lucy sacrifices her own happiness and the liberty of the younger children in a fruitless effort to carry out, in poverty, the plans her father had made for his sons in affluence. For this Charlotte robs her husband of happiness and dedicates his child. Yet it is in his younger children, Gerald and Mina, that Alfred Haven finds his true memorial for they inherit the weakness he hid under his charm and, like him, they cannot face adversity.

Lucy has beauty, intelligence and courage but Charlotte stands for the easy way and in the end it is Charlotte who brings Lucy's plans to nothing. Lucy goes at last to her lover but it is in defeat, and the ineradicable years lie between them, though Richard refuses to see them. In the dream that ends the book the man beside her changes from Richard to her father and Lucy knows that she cannot cast out his memory even now when she has lost her last illusions about him.[20]

The book itself suffers from two contradictory circumstances that together doom it: the failure of the authors to develop the story as planned, and the nature of the plan itself. There is a rigor verging on the artificial about this synopsis. Remembering the rich humanity of character, motivation, and action in *A House*, one fears that writers who develop this plot will be touched with some of its stiffness. This fear is realized. We find ourselves in a morality play with Lucy standing for Pride, Richard for Faithfulness, Charles for Dependability, Gerald for Weakness. But worse for one's hopes than any fault of intent is the failure of the intention to emerge in the writing. The struggle that was meant to be the center of the action—between the two sisters over the preservation of their father's memory—too often eludes us. True, Lucy had been closest to him before the knowledge of his culpability as a Government official reached the family, and only she fully understood the circumstances. But the effect on her? While the rest of the family are, on the evening of the revelation, atwitter with unquestioning love and loyalty and turning their anger on Mr. Haven's "traducers," Lucy utters "a bitter, mocking little laugh," and proceeds to enlighten them (in an outburst that her father happens to overhear): " 'He has given away secret information and abused a trust, but because he did not do it for money he is innocent. He didn't ruin us for money, it was for his vanity. Do you think that is any nobler? To please a stranger, a man he hardly knew, he has brought us into this impossible position.' "[21]

There is every reason why Lucy, of all the family, should have made this speech. She not only knows about the past but has enough thought for the future to grasp at once what it all means to the family, as her sheltered mother and younger brothers and sisters cannot yet do. Then why should she, of all the family, wish to keep the father's memory green? Albert Haven was charming but weak and unstable, hardly a man to admire or emulate in either his living or his dying. As time passes, one feels that Lucy's tight rein on the family is less an effort to mold their futures along the lines that Father would have followed than it is plain strong-minded bossiness. She worships at the altar of her own selfish pride, surely, rather than at one dedicated to her father's memory. And she is so fully occupied with her almost impossible self-set task that she has no time, even if inclination, to brood over him.

That Lucy never regained her girlhood illusions about her father is clear when she reveals to her brother-in-law "the unbearable truth" about her sister Charlotte, his wife, some years after Mr. Haven's suicide. " 'Poor Michael!' she said very low. 'She has loved a dead man best.' And then, 'He wasn't worth it, Michael. He wasn't worth all we have suffered for him, the cruelties we have committed, Charlotte and I.' "[22] Yet her father's hold on Lucy is still there, however inexplicably, at the end. She and her once-betrothed and always-faithful Richard are reunited, after four years of pride and prejudice. But the closing passage of the book indicates that Father's memory is still all too green. In a dream that night, despite her new-found happiness, Lucy finds herself afraid, as well she may be:

"Richard," she cried, "take me away," but Richard was no longer there. Her father stood beside her, and her heart leaped as it never had for Richard. The last of the light fell on him, so that she saw him very distinctly—his clear brow and fine shining eyes, his long, eloquent hands, the cornelian ring. But he was looking beyond her toward the trees, his face haggard and desperate. She caught his arm in terror.

"What is it, Papa?"

Lucy's terror woke her. The first pale light of morning was flowing into the room, grey and meaningless. The tomorrow that she had longed for had come, but she was not free. "Richard!" she whispered. "Richard!" but the other was beside her still, and she knew now that he would never leave her.[23]

This is unexpected, contrived, overwrought.

Charlotte, the second daughter, feels only "apprehension, distress, and pity" over her father's predicament, and no more than a normal sorrow, apparently, over his subsequent escape by suicide. She might even have found a secret satisfaction in it all, since it opens the way for her to marry Michael, the socially inferior but wealthy young man she loves. What more could she do for her family than to achieve a sharable financial security? Her desire to give a home to her youngest sister, Mina, and the shelter she later offers to others in the family when Lucy's over-rigorous regime collapses, read like generous understanding rather than sisterly jealousy. The only blot on her pleasant and prosperous marriage was a little normal difficulty with her in-laws, and that slowly ironed itself out. It is therefore a jolt to the reader to learn toward the close of the book how heavily the dead man's hand has been resting on her. Lucy explains it all to Charlotte's loyal but confused husband. Yes, his wife had married him for love. "But afterwards she was afraid she had cut herself off from Papa altogether. She couldn't give him up— to me. When Alfred [her son] was born I think her purpose solidified. . . . She has taken Papa's responsibilities from me, and now she means our father to live again in Alfred."[24]

We would like to think that all of this is in Lucy's head, imaginings produced by bitterness about her own loss of control over the family. But the authors present with perfect seriousness Charlotte's rather sinister plans for keeping Papa's memory green by shaping her infant son in his image, and her consequent mild alienation from her genial husband. The reader, however, finds the whole idea gratuitous and unrealistic.

Probably the greatest disappointment that *Green Memory* inflicted upon some of the expectant readers of *A House Is Built* was its failure to be more than nominally an historical novel.

Sydney, which loomed so large in the first book, is no more important to *Green Memory* than St. Petersburg to *Crime and Punishment* (which has been dramatized very successfully against a twentieth-century San Francisco setting). The 1860's, which in the *House* gave us the great burst of population and prosperity following Australia's Gold Rush, could in this second book have been any other decade in which government servants are culpable, families meet with misfortune, and overbearing young ladies get their comeuppance.

Not that *Green Memory* isn't a Victorian novel, all right, in dress, transportation, mores; but it reads more as though it were written *in* the period than *of* it. Perhaps the authors, staunch middle-class Australians themselves, were ill at ease in the upper-class life they attempted to portray here. Gone are the youth and vigor of *A House*, most of what humor it had, and even the delightfully ironic touches in which it abounded. *A House* is a remarkable first novel in that it reads like the work of assured and experienced writers. *Green Memory*, equally remarkably, reads like a first novel. It is a stiff book. The style is stiff, even the characters often seem stiff, seldom three-dimensional.

But if the authors did not succeed this time in writing a good book, it is gratifying to find them incapable of writing a wholly bad one. The major characters may too often read like figures in a morality play, but a few of the minor ones are memorably real: Mama, charming but helpless; Uncle Aubrey, kindly but overprecise; Michael, honest tradesman, alternately awed and annoyed by the relative aristocracy into which he had married. Too, the keen insights into childhood conspicuous in the sensitive presentation of William's two sons in *A House* reappear in this book, notably in the portrayal of the youngest Haven child, Mina, through whose authentically eight-year-old eyes we are introduced to the family in Chapter 1. The next youngest, Gerald, fills substantially enough the role of inherited weakness to which both were assigned; Mina fortunately transcends it. Even a lay psychologist recognizes that she, from the moment she finds her father's body after his failure to stand up to his failure, is the child whose life is most deeply marred by the suicide and the quality of family life that follows. But unlike Gerald, she is also a developing and thoroughly credible charac-

ter, more sinned against than sinning. Less convincing is our
tour through the mind of baby Albert—possibly because he is
too young for us to remember ourselves in him, possibly because
this exploration seems to serve no useful purpose.

The plot of *Green Memory*, like that of *A House Is Built*, follows a straight chronological line, interrupted by only one of
the stories-within-the-story that mark the earlier novel. That
is the girlhood of Miss Clarke, so minor a character that it is
hard to justify the time spent in detailing her background.
Like that of Dave in *A House*, it creates a suspicion that its
authors found it too romantically interesting to omit—or even
needed it to fill up space in a novel that runs to less than three
hundred pages of large print.

What one yearns for in all of the Barnard-Eldershaw novels are
those intimate glimpses and loving interpretations of the Australian countryside that are so conspicuous in much of their
nonfiction. Only a few appear in *A House*, which hardly leaves
Sydney; none in *Green Memory*, which never does. The gum
trees, the most conspicuous and loved feature of the Australian
landscape, appear briefly but for a symbolic purpose. Lucy, the
only English-born Haven child, hated the frieze of lemon
gums that faced her window with "their air of ancient magic,"
the only natives left in an Australian garden full of English trees
and flowers. They symbolized for her "the strange, submerged
foreignness of Australia."[25] The most noteworthy use of setting
here is an urban one—a description of the Sydney waterfront in
the area of The Rocks, where Gerald barely survives when, like
his father before him, he tries to escape his wrongdoing by running away.

There is no need to spend more time on the details of this
generally unsatisfactory book. The important question that it
raised for the authors' future was what went wrong. Marjorie,
who has always believed in writing rapidly, warmed by the first
fires of inspiration, provided one answer. The Palmers had apparently grown concerned, when the first highly successful book,
published in mid-1929, was not promptly followed by a second.
Marjorie's reply in late 1930 is worth quoting because it details
the difficulties under which the collaboration had worked from
the beginning.

You speak of our slow rate of production. It is unfortunately too slow. *Green Memory* took nearly two years to write and suffered for it. Only an exceptional mind—like Henry Handel Richardson's—can concentrate on a book for years without the idea becoming either stale or exaggerated. Everyone, I suppose, has a best speed and it is nearly as disastrous to drag as to rush a book. I wish that we could work steadily *and constantly* at ours. As it is the work is done in gushes when we can lay our hands on a little spare time and then often has to wait months with the knowledge that the spirit we have been trying to grasp is melting back into air. To work eight hours a day, travel for another two and after that perform the duties (and pleasures) of a daughter and amateur housemaid, leaves me little time and less mental energy to write. Miss Eldershaw is in rather worse case as teaching is a more exacting profession than library work.[26]

And yet, under these same demanding circumstances, the well-conceived, solidly built *House* had been completed in about six months. Some other explanation must be found for the fact that they moved directly from what is in many ways their best novel (as well as the most popular) to what is unquestionably their weakest.

A long time after I had begun puzzling over this falling off, I came across an illuminating passage in a Barnard essay on Seaforth Mackenzie. The excellence of his first and third novels she feels "arose out of the impact of experience, real or imaginative, on a creative mind"; the weakness of his second and fourth, from his trying "to recapture spontaneity by artificial means." She continues, in words that one cannot help applying to M. Barnard Eldershaw's first two:

Thus a "real" novel is shortly followed by a "forged" novel. Let me make myself plain: this is a very natural and not infrequent state of affairs and no turpitude attaches to the word "forged." A writer, whose gift is sensitive rather than robust and prolific, achieves either subjective or objective success with a novel and has a very natural desire to repeat it without waiting for the genuine and often infrequent stirring of the creative impulse. He tries to make good the deficiency by substituting the tricks of the writer's trade, or imitating tried recipes for successful novels. Shakespeare could make good a phony tale, but for a writer whose real strength is in his delicacy, the handling of dross is fatal.[27]

Wherever the trouble lay, the young novelists were uncomfortably aware of their failure. Commenting to Nettie Palmer on an unfavorable review of *Green Memory* by a Miss Foster, Marjorie mused:

It is impossible to evaluate one's own work by exterior canons. We can only measure it against what we aimed at. It fell far short of that—but we never intended the things Miss Foster thinks we should have intended. Katharses and mortal agonies are as far from our intention as from our ability to execute. Miss Foster's criticism really points to a far deeper fault than she attacks. It shows that we cannot make ourselves understood at all, that our philosophy and artistic outlook have remained alike undecipherable. It is a melancholy thought. But we are not as cast down as we ought to be, because we still hope to clarify our style and our objects in the future. I understand how a dog must feel, head down, following a scent. It's the scent that matters, not the criticisms, good or bad. Failure to attain is just as bitter if no one notices that you have failed—and uncomprehending praise only rubs it in.[28]

In other words, down, but not out.

CHAPTER 3

The Later Novels

I   The Glasshouse

IN 1933 Marjorie Barnard returned from her first trip abroad
on a Norwegian cargo ship, the *Talleyrand*. Her report to
Nettie Palmer on that voyage indicates how profoundly it had
stirred her spirit and her imagination.

We had a magnificent voyage. Life at sea, at once constricted and
immense, fills me with excitement and happiness. It is like living
in a sonnet. It is better than an island for it moves. Thoughts
flourish in the moist salt air, the empty stretch of sky and sea are
like a dare to the human mind, the sunsets and the darkness are
heroic, the lonely, meaningless patterns of bird flight like the key
to a secret beauty . . . and then your life is espaliered upon a rhythm,
the rhythm of the boat, its bells, its routine, its whole rigid and
ordered life . . . and last you have a whole row of human specimens
held in a vise for your inspection. It is the best laboratory in the
world for studying human nature.[1]

The result, for a young novelist casting about for a third
book, was almost inevitable, though considerably delayed. On
her return Marjorie was immediately caught up in the pattern
of her life and work as daughter and librarian. As a writer she
was engrossed in the collaboration's struggle with the short story
(p. 78) and with the preparation of literary lectures for Flora
to deliver. A still greater impediment to the third novel they had
been casting about for since before the second was off the press
was Flora's absence during her own year abroad. But in January
1935, within a month after Flora returned to the team, Marjorie
was able to report to Vance Palmer:

We've begun a book—the story of a voyage, twelve passengers on
a cargo ship. It's to be a conglomerate, stories inset, not "true"
stories but the stories that one passenger makes up about the others,

with all the consequent cross commentaries, art upon life, fact upon invention; pinned down upon the routine of the ship, held between the sky and the sea. It's going to be difficult and whether we succeed at all will depend on whether we can carry the ghost in our mind through the long drawn out business of writing, and whether we can strike the right balance between the parts and the whole. It's really too young to be talked about at all yet. For us it is in its happiest stage—all hopes and nothing yet disproved. I'm terribly happy—dangerously.[2]

Thus began what was to be published in 1936 as *The Glasshouse* (the crew's term for the superstructure that housed the Captain and the passengers). The book had been conceived in a healthy mood of continuing experimentation, leaving the historical Sydney of the first two novels for the present on the high seas. For the first time the writers had an opportunity to draw directly on personal experience. After publication Marjorie admitted freely, "Yes, I travelled Norwegian, coming home in the Talleyrand, sailing out of Antwerp in a thunderstorm [the scene with which the book opens]. The ship is drawn from the life."[3]

But it is in no sense mere reportage. The characters and the situations of the framework are the products of the collaborators' imaginations, just as the inset stories are conceived by the chief character, novelist Stirling Armstrong. It is these minor stories that constitute the major experiment in *The Glasshouse*. The setting of the novel itself is necessarily limited to the cargo ship *Therikion* (plus a couple of brief shore excursions); the characters, to its twelve passengers and a small handful of its crew. Its main though slight action is the developing but hopeless love between the novelist and the captain. But into this conventional fiction fabric is set a scattering of minor stories. These are no Canterbury Tales told *by* the wayfarers but *about* a selected few; no flashbacks into their own pasts but stories which Stirling Armstrong makes up around them—for amusement, for malice, for literary exercise—and keeps to herself.

It is easy to say of the first two novels that *Green Memory* is a lesser book than *A House Is Built*. This third is so different from either that overall comparisons would be fruitless. The most casual reader, however, will notice a great change—for the better —in style. Gone is the stiffness, the artificiality. There is a spontaneity, a sophistication about *The Glasshouse* that suggests maturity and growing confidence. About the same length as the other two, this book seems slighter, partly from the material itself, partly from the division of attention among the interspersed stories. It is nonetheless a meaty and refreshing book, full of a variety of well-developed characters, chewable observations and reflections, and vivid figures of speech. The reader won't soon forget Mr. Cartwright's "gooseberry eyes," the partly-drawn-up gangway "dangling impotently," or young Lois Weatherell, unaffected by the storm that has kept others away from the first shipboard supper, "cruising adventurously among the archipelago of tinned delicacies."[4]

On the *Therikion* (departing Antwerp for Australian ports via the Cape) the characters are few enough to be drawn with some depth and considerable adeptness. This small laboratory gives the authors a chance to demonstrate what will be a conspicuous strength in their next novel—their keen perception of the gradations by which individuals become a group. Stirling Armstrong, on that first evening out, was reluctant "to take her plunge, a cold-blooded standing plunge too, into the social relationships that would inevitably enmesh her during the voyage."[5] The first group meal produced only "angular fragmentary conversation. They had been as wary with one another as people in a railway carriage."[6] The next day posed the problem of "constantly meeting one another in the morning promenade. This was a nuisance. Must one smile and speak every time? Having begun, could you stop?"[7] But shortly they became a microcosm. By the time they got to Cape Town they had developed such a sense of identity that they resented the addition of a new passenger. The consumptive French boy's serious hemorrhage later drew them as nothing before into a whole, "united in anxiety," while with his recovery "The tension of anxiety relaxed, and in its place irritations grew up like toadstools."[8]

Though *The Glasshouse*, like its predecessors, was published by Harrap in England, it is authentically Australian—from diction (the mobs, paddocks, and cowees of the outback) to viewpoint. For the Australian in Australia, going "home" might designate a trip to England, but for exile Stirling Armstrong, long in London pent, it meant a return to her native Australia, for which she was authentically homesick. In Cape Town she experienced "the faint aromatic taste of the air that is like Australian air."[9] Earlier, docked at Lisbon, she had found unexpected comfort in the land's brown hills: "I didn't know how tired I was of green."[10] She was equally weary of the "ten thousand young Englishmen" of whom passenger George Devlin reminds her: "His stereotyped good looks, the polished and impervious surface of his negligent manners, the conventional unconventionality of his clothes, were protective sheathings which encased him well. The trouble was that all the energy went into the armour. When you got it off, if ever you were so unfortunate, there was nothing underneath."[11] Stirling muses on such a young Englishman's view of the social differentiations in the "vast nutrient mass" of the Empire: from *pukka* India, Americanized Canada, dark Africa, to "the shabby fringes, the Antipodes, Australia in fact, where one just didn't go. The inhabitants were deplorable, and not with the interesting decorative deplorableness of a subject people which serves to floodlight the qualities of the ruling race, but with the uncomfortable deplorableness of common relations."[12]

If Australian Stirling seems anti-English, the reason appears when, asked if this is her first trip to Australia, she replies: " 'I am an Australian.' Always when she said that it was as if she had bared her heart to a blow. Years in England had done that to her, a spiritual gesture she had never weeded out."[13] A long conversation between the two returning exiles, Stirling and Dr. Gregory, reveals the hold, both realistic and sentimental, that their often derided home land has upon them. The special problem of the Australian author appears when he suggests that she try setting her next novel in Australia, even though the two of her six so set had gone unnoticed. She replies, "If I try to be honest, no one would understand; if I showed the country and the life as an imitation of somewhere else, it isn't worth doing. *There isn't an idiom yet.*"[14] (Italics mine.)

If one of the values of *The Glasshouse* is these glimpses into the Australian point of view, another is its detailed study of the mind of a writer at work. No one would be justified in calling this an autobiographical novel, but Stirling Armstrong has more than a casual resemblance to her presumably major creator, Marjorie Barnard. Both are Australian, both are novelists, both are "middle-aged spinsters with small but steady incomes, inconspicuous exteriors and reflective minds,"[15] both are chronic insomniacs, both have experienced England and a cargo ship home, neither has as yet been seriously in love. In personality they are as akin as in fact. Both are diffident in their human relationships and very sensitive to them, both swing from self-confidence as persons and writers to a humble conviction of "insignificance, convention, nonentity." Marjorie was in agreement with many of Stirling's reflections on the philosophy and practice of the creative writer. If she wasn't guilty of the deliberate malice with which Stirling approached some of her shipboard subjects, she shared with her a keen nose for the ironic, in literature and in life.

All of which raises the question of how the Barnard-Eldershaw collaboration worked on this third book. Marjorie once confessed to Nettie Palmer, "We might have had better results if we had divided the work logically, one writing the stories, the other the main story—but it did not fall out like that."[16] Exactly how it did fall out we don't know but can make some shrewd guesses. This ship that had been "petrified in the channel"[17] for weeks when both skippers were fully employed was the first thing that Marjorie turned to after resigning from the library in March 1935. With full time for it, and Flora still tied to her teaching, Marjorie undoubtedly did the lion's share of the writing. Not that Flora was just a silent partner. They spent Easter together at Kurrajong Heights and "between long walks and large meals, did quite a lot of writing and planning."[18] But when, early in July, the manuscript was completed and Marjorie reported, "It has been written in 3½ months, a practically unbroken concentration,"[19] we can deduce that the concentrating must have been largely her own, for in Australia these were winter months when Flora would have been bound to her classroom.

What Flora presumably contributed, then, was a full share in the planning, a smaller one in the writing. If the figure of novelist Stirling Armstrong owes more to Marjorie than to Flora, Flora surely supplied Stirling's rural girlhood. And Flora's robustness and knowledge of her profession both appear unmistakably in the most fully developed character among the other passengers—Stirling's cabinmate and abomination, teacher Gloria Williamson.

Brilliant flashes appear throughout the book, but the parts are greater than the whole, which strikes one as thin. This is owing partly to the inevitable superficiality of shipboard life even when it endures for several weeks, partly to the interruption of the inset stories, partly to the main theme. Middle-aged Stirling's brief passion for the Norwegian captain lacks conviction for the reader as much as it lacked opportunity for the lovers. Just how far it went is left a matter of conjecture, so delicately is it related. They walked, they talked (within the limits of his halting English), they even embraced—but always confined to the *Therikion*'s small exposed decks. Once Stirling went with him to his sitting-room for coffee, but what with his family's photographs about, they found the atmosphere so oppressive that they escaped to the deck again. Later she stood a watch with him, bundled in a huge waterproof cape in order to survive the exposure of the open bridge. They talked a little, but "She was aware that he was only giving her a part of his attention."[20] She got even less of it when they docked at Fremantle. By this time, conscious of the hopelessness of whatever attachment this had become, she had decided to make a sudden break by debarking there rather than spending another fortnight on board en route to Sydney, as she had originally planned. Going to his office to say farewell, she found the captain drinking with the agent's representative and the customs officer. He could only take her hand at the door and say, " 'So it is good-bye. I am sorry our voyage is over.' "[21]

The relationship was not only brief but unlikely. True, Stirling had apparently never loved before, but she was no ignorant, impressionable girl like Lois Weatherell, no psychotic like sex-deprived Corinne Cartwright. True too, she was lonely, and so was the captain, but both were accustomed to that state, and this was no cheap shipboard romance like those of the doctor with a couple of other women passengers. There is sometimes a kind of naïveté about its presentation. In one of their walks on a windy deck the captain had to support Stirling with his arm. "To her his strength, to him her weakness, was a subtle and significant discovery."[22] Maybe, but one that would seem more natural to a Juliet and her Romeo than to a middle-aged woman and a long-married man.

The greatest problem in this book is the inset stories. In both the earlier novels we have noted the use of unrelated stories about minor characters—stories that sometimes seemed more space-fillers than artistic necessities. We get them again here— if not in the captain's past, at least in his mate's. But here we have as well a different use of stories—these eight that Stirling imagines for her own satisfaction about a selection of her fellow-passengers. They appear at the times she wrote them, running from three to fifteen pages in length (altogether they occupy close to a third of the book), and in mood from tenderness (Raymond Becque's story) to humor (George Devlin's), to tragedy (Corinne Cartwright's), to irony (Gloria Williamson's and David Priestley's), even to melodrama (Doctor Gregory's).

Each of these is well written and interesting enough in itself, but the link between them and the main narrative is too often so obscure that they constitute a distraction rather than an embellishment. Doubts that the Palmers expressed about their use give us a welcome chance to learn in more detail what the authors had intended. To Vance (whose praise of the ship's company pleased her, since "One is so horribly afraid of showing the hoof of the lady novelist in a man's world"), Marjorie explained that properly handled, the inset stories

should not have watered down the theme but supplied side lights on it and relief from it, substituting symbols and so elucidating it indirectly. . . . The stories were an unsuccessful effort to reproduce the main theme in other terms and so get roundness into a flat story. We weren't subtle enough to get that effect without stating it. If it had come off it would have created a feeling of completion in the mind of the reader which would have been its justification.[23]

To Nettie, who liked the book otherwise, finding it an advance over the first two, she admitted "We didn't really pull it off,"[24] but stuck to the worth of the idea, admitting failure only in the performance.

The Glasshouse failed not only to live up to its authors' intentions but also to attract much of a reading public, particularly in Australia, where it was seldom in stock even in its early months. It is therefore ironic that eight years later it should have appeared in an Australian edition of 25,000 copies. This betokened not popularity but exigency, however. As a wartime move, a couple of dozen books on all kinds of native subjects were republished in those numbers in cheap paperback form known

as the Australian Pocket Library. M. Barnard Eldershaw clearly
merited inclusion, but reprint rights to the natural choice, *A
House Is Built,* could not be obtained (it was still selling too
well in hard covers). Hence *The Glasshouse* came home at last.
Despite its flaws it was better written than most of its running
mates in the APL, and doubtless provided some pleasant reading hours for the Australian and American service men for whom
the library was originally conceived.

II   Plaque with Laurel

The Glasshouse had taken M. Barnard Eldershaw not only out
of Australian history but out of Australia. Their next was to
be set in the Australia of their own times but concerned a very
specialized group in a very limited setting—the result of two
experienced and maturing authors casting a couple of pairs of
perceptive, even jaundiced eyes about the literary world of
which they were now a recognized part. In October 1935, with
The Glasshouse still in the publisher's hands, they went to
look at Canberra, the capital city, as a background for their new
project. Marjorie reported to Nettie Palmer:

> We are shuddering on the horrid brink of another novel. So far
> it's not much more than a design—a three-day literary conference
> in Canberra at which a plaque is unveiled in the National Library
> to the memory of a writer, dead five years or so. His story is to
> piece itself together behind the comedy, inconsequence and vanity
> of such a gathering. Behind it all the beautiful and naturally
> decorative background of the Canberra scene. It is going to be
> technically difficult. We'll probably write it in forced marches as
> before. It suits us best. We lose weigh every time we let our theme
> get cold.[25]

Actually this writing took discouragingly long, by her standards—around eight months. There was the usual dearth of
collaborative time, a problem unsolved by Marjorie's own greater
leisure. With only the first chapter written, Christmas took Flora
away for the holidays, and Marjorie found it "tough luck we
can't be together now, especially while it is in its precarious
early stages."[26] At Easter she herself was ill for a time—"nothing
important, just one more idiot obstruction to work. It took some
time to get the novel going again but a couple of weeks ago I

developed a fine turn of speed and got the thing practically finished."[27] This, in June, indicates that she was doing most of the writing; but Flora was as necessary as ever to the critical shaping, and in July they managed to be together for a week during the "last agonies" of the work. Composition complete, Marjorie as usual undertook the final typing ("slowly, painstakingly and persistently on my wayward little twenty-year-old portable").[28] In August *Plaque with Laurel* left for London (Harrap, as usual), to return between covers early in March 1937.

The framing narrative is simple, straightforward, and brief. On a Friday morning in October two busses and a variety of private cars leave Sydney for the two-hundred-mile drive to Canberra, carrying numerous members of the Australian Writers' Guild to its annual three-day Conference. A few guests are included, for there was to be a special event in this year's program, the unveiling of a plaque in memory of Richard Crale, a fine Australian novelist who had died in mid-career some five years earlier. On the following Tuesday, mission accomplished, they all depart. In *The Glasshouse* we had followed a few people over considerable distances of time and place; here we explore a large number concentrated in one spot for only a few days. Here is a tighter structure, a greater intensity, the possibility of a greater novel. That it misses greatness owes more to its handling than to its conception. But it is a fine book, the best since *A House Is Built* and vastly different, far more sophisticated.

We have already seen that the basic attitude of M. Barnard Eldershaw is irony: in *A House Is Built* and *Green Memory,* irony of theme; in *The Glasshouse,* irony of detail. In *Plaque with Laurel,* the most ironic of the novels, we are served a large measure of both. In details the irony remains for the most part gentle though unmistakable—subtle, even muted, but nonetheless telling. In theme it presents an indictment of the treatment of genius—not only by the Philistines, which was the cry of most Australian writers, but by writers themselves. These Canberra Pilgrims do not assay a high percentage of the gold of human kindness.

The first major theme, the evanescence of fame and the futility of attempting to commemorate it, is admirably suited to

the Barnard-Eldershaw irony. Imogen Tarrant, the woman
Crale had loved in his maturity, reflects of the Conference members that "For most of them it's only a jaunt."[29] Ida, his incom-
patible and obtuse widow, finds it "odd that Dick should have
a monument in Canberra. It's all so unlike him. He'd think it
very queer himself."[30] Bachelor Jim Walters, who had been
Crale's closest friend and was now the moving spirit of this
effort to perpetuate his memory, was forced to recognize at the
ceremony that "To set up a memorial to Richard could have only
a ritual value." Edgar Bunce, the glib Minister who did the
actual unveiling of the plaque with laurel,

> stood in Jim's mind now for that great morass of indifference and
> stupidity in which Richard's memory would sink. Where was Richard's
> memory now? To Ida Crale he was her children's father who had
> failed them; to Imogen he was her lover who had died for her; . . .
> to most of the people at the Conference he was some one they
> "ought to read" but hadn't "got around to yet." They were willing
> enough to pay him a tribute that cost them nothing.[31]

Accompanying this Ozymandian futility is a second theme,
handled with less irony, more sympathy. Attending the Conference honoring the dead Richard Crale is his living counter-
part in literary reputation and personal tragedy, Owen Sale.
Crale had borne into middle life the horrible memory of a well-
intentioned misjudgment he had made as an officer during the
First World War, an error that had cost the lives of many of his
men; Sale feels an equally crushing, equally innocent responsibility for the suicide of his wife. Having met Crale and later
read his books, Sale recognizes their "mystic fellowship," not of
guilt but of circumstance. Owen enunciates it for both: "It is
worse, far worse, to do harm unwittingly than wittingly. It makes
you one with all cruelty and pain. When you will a cruelty it
remains just a concrete action, but when you do it without
willing it it has no end. . . . You become guilty of all cruelty, a
part of the meaningless terror that stands behind life."[32]
So many fulminations against the common fate of the two men
lie scattered throughout a hundred and fifty pages of the novel
as to leave no doubt of Sale's feeling of identity with Crale—
no need, certainly, for the added assurance of the similarity of
surnames. Whether or not that sense of brotherhood is given

sufficient support by the novel is another matter. Both men were cut down by bad luck rather than bad intentions, true, but the circumstances and the men's reactions to them differed sharply. Richard's fate was played, for one thing, in a far larger arena; as a loved and trusted officer he failed his men by thinking as a man instead of obeying as part of a military machine (a "tragic flaw" worked out on a relatively epic scale), and his losses were large, and public. Owen, on the domestic front, appears to have killed his wife (by causing her to kill herself) with kindness after he had been sinned against: "Anyone would say he had been magnanimous forgiving her, taking her back, but she hadn't been able to bear the prison of his magnanimity and his forgiveness."[33] Further, Richard learns to live with his past; his writing gift, Jim gratefully finds, is unimpaired; he knows some personal solace for a while in Imogen's love; and he dies a more or less "natural death" of pneumonia. Owen, on the other hand, emerges from what must surely be regarded as a paler experience in the whole spectrum of human misfortune, to complete aridity of talent, an unsolaceable loneliness, and a self-inflicted end.

It may be argued, of course, that Owen is the lesser man, but it does not appear to have been the authors' purpose to make him so. Rather, they stress the irony of a group of people neglecting one lonely, guilt-ridden, gifted writer in life while they busily go through the motions of honoring another, long safely dead. During the major address of the Conference on the first day, Jim reflects on brotherhood in what is the authors' major statement of the Crale-Sale theme: "How easily, now that he was dead and could make no claim upon them, brotherhood flowed out to Richard. How ready every one was to forgive his tragic failures, to see him in the heroic guise of misunderstood genius! But how little patience they had with Sale's too obvious and embarrassing misery."[34]

Yet neither tragedy could be blamed on others; both men suffered from self-exile rather than ostracism, were the victims of their own natures rather than of a callous world. The conferees weren't killers, though they numbered a few vultures. After the news of Owen's death comes, writer Miriam Blume reminds aspiring writer Alison George,

"Now is your chance for a scoop. Why aren't you at the telephone?"

Alison gulped, "Oh, I couldn't!" The wretched child seemed always to be trying to gulp down her gooseberry eyes. "Do you think I could? Really?"

"Of course," said Miriam, in a most matter-of-fact tone. She had already sold the story to one of the dailies. Others had probably done the same. Alison scuttled away.[35]

Actually, the worst that could be said of the Conference as a whole in regard to both men would be a paraphrase of Willa Cather's remark about her Archbishop—that what time they failed to spend in honoring the memory of Richard Crale, they devoted to the neglect of Owen Sale.

Considerable dramatic use is made of Owen's death, not that it is ever in doubt. Owen is a doomed man from the time we first see his ravaged face—doomed if for no other reason than that the authors' plan requires that his feet, set firmly in Richard's fated footprints, follow them to the end. They keep us conscious of the fact through event and dialogue, metaphor and symbol. Death is foreshadowed when Jim Walters, having accidentally interrupted Owen in an early attempt to bolt to the hills, gives him a ride in the "dicky-seat," on which his tall figure perched "like a man in a tumbril."[36] Death is sighted in the conversation of tour members in a churchyard about the possibility of drowning in the trickle that was the Molonglo River. And death breathes through the last reported incident in Owen's life. Walking through the Canberra countryside he is joined by two dogs whose companionship pleases him—until they start a rabbit. It is imperative that Owen "save this one small creature from the cruelty of nature."[37] Instead, his confused efforts drive it (ironically) toward the dogs, who instantly rip it apart. Owen flees in horror, to seek out his own end.

This bit of symbolism is of course a minor replaying of the theme of Crale's and Sale's larger well-intentioned but ill-consequenced acts, for both the ultimate evil. Not all the king's horses and all the king's men, to say nothing of a hotel full of conferees, could divert Owen from suicide this time. Comrade Boyle reflects to Ailsa, the sensitive young poet, "It was his life that was tragic, not his death....His death itself was not so awful. It must have been a sort of consummation. He drowned himself in three feet of water, you know. A man would have to be in an ecstasy to do that."[38]

Major ironies of theme are bolstered by irony of incident and detail. Several events stand out for the deftness of their handling. One is the wedding of elderly, twice-married Mrs. Helen Josephson, writer of sentimental little stories, and didactic Connolly Moate, carefully planned to take financial advantage of the Conference and its members (eager bride, reluctant guests). When many of the attendant festivities, though not the wedding itself, were swept away by the manhunt, Helen "was so disappointed. Everything was spoiled. She felt only exasperation for Owen Sale, the cause of it all."[39]

More typical of Conference affairs is the major lecture delivered on the first day by Professor Ambrose Everton Standish, M.A. (Oxon), Acting-Professor of English at the University of Sydney, an event that enables M. Barnard Eldershaw gleefully to expose the foibles of chairmen, speakers, and audiences alike, the world over. There is no heavy-handed satire here, no Sinclair Lewis wielding a hatchet; quite enough to report such an event as it might actually have occurred. When the little professor finally got the floor, he uttered many trenchant truths about literature, distinguishing at length between craft and trade, praising the creative writer and damning the journalist, his editor, and all their works. The noticeably thin applause was later explained to him: " 'My dear fellow,' said the President impressively, 'most of them were journalists.' "[40]

Plaque with Laurel is an admirably constructed book, the straight story line being skillfully interrupted by increasingly detailed flashbacks to the earlier history of Richard Crale until by the end he has been fully developed to us from several points of view, as to a lesser extent has Sale. The assistant secretary's dutiful slipping of change-of-schedule notices under the guests' doors, late the first evening, provides an excuse at this early stage for accounts of what some of the more important guests are doing and thinking. Skillful too is the handling of the set of circumstances that enables Jim—and the reader—to listen to the consecutive, lengthy, and complementary assessments of Crale by his mistress and his widow. Equally well handled is the later dramatic alternation of scenes from the mock gaiety of the women at the Josephson-Moate nuptials to the deadly earnest-

ness of the men fanned out over the surrounding hills in an
effort to find alive the missing Owen Sale.

The greatest weakness of the book, technically, is the difficulty put in the reader's way by the multiplicity of characters. A
few we meet on the road to Canberra—a couple of dozen, in fact,
in the first few pages, Others are introduced that night at dinner
through the device of Jim's pointing them out to Imogen. The
cast already numbers thirty-two when she protests, "Stop, Jim!
I've reached saturation-point. It's like reading a florist's cata-
logue or a cookery-book."[41] The reader agrees, but the intro-
ductions go on. That a considerable number of characters are
necessary is not to be denied, part of the purpose of the book
being to show the variety of shapes and sizes in which the soul
of the Australian writer abides. But two expedients suggest themselves. One is a greater use of the scarce anonymous character,
uttering a variety of points of view as "an editor," "a lady in
pince-nez," "a genial little man in thick spectacles," so that the
reader profits by the speech with no compulsion to remember the
speaker. Another is a greater development of character among
those who are identified. Many of the named conferees fail to
emerge as individuals; others make a beginning but are sufficiently forgotten before they reappear, perhaps a hundred pages
down the line, to escape recognition even on a second reading.
One needs a directory.

Against this criticism let it be said that those minor characters
who do emerge, do so clearly, through dramatic as well as
descriptive means. How easily we recognize Doris Jones by her
raucous coltishness from the time we first see her nudging her
seatmate on the bus to Canberra, and learn that "She had been
nudging him all day, so that he was sore down one side and
very cross."[42] How well we know Mrs. Norton, Senior Vice-
President of the Guild, who, invited to ride to Canberra in the
President's car with the chief guest of honor, Mrs. Crale, had
"brought two old friends, for she could not bear to see seating
accommodation in a car wasted."[43] Her numerous attempts as
elder stateswoman to mother the Conference put quite in character her crowning remark after hagridden Owen Sale's suicide,
"Poor, poor boy! If only he had come to me!"[44] Amy Ledwidge, the
over-zealous assistant secretary, is always recognizable, whether
she is "producing lists on creased, anxious-looking pieces of

paper"[45] or worshipping her complacent superior, Secretary Percy Jones. So is Percy himself, in his calm, selfish acceptance of her adoration, most neatly revealed when, after ordering a double whisky from a passing waiter, he turns belatedly to his faithful companion. " 'How about you, Amy?' he said when the man had gone. 'Would you like a drink?' "[46]

In *The Glasshouse*, as we earlier noted, the authors had gained some experience in the portrayal of the shifting interrelationships of a number of transient individuals as they settle down for a time into a whole. There it was a dozen passengers and a few crewmen on a long cruise, and *The Glasshouse* makes relatively simple work of the job, being as much concerned with Stirling Armstrong's fictional background work on the rest as individuals, as with the drama of their actual life-in-common on shipboard. But in *Plaque with Laurel* the group life often transcends the individual in importance, and the authors' portrayal of it shows keen perceptions of the many-threaded fabric of even a temporary social structure.

Six months after publication Marjorie wrote to Vance Palmer, " 'Plaque' has fallen quite flat. Very few people appear to have read it and fewer still have felt any interest."[47] Published in London like the previous novels, the book was never reprinted in England, and there was no Australian edition. With as much first-rate writing as it contains, one is justified in wondering why.

Like *The Glasshouse,* it is a book in which the parts are greater than the whole. Excellent as the description, the characterization, and the construction are, they do not quite cohere into a first-rate novel (it was not even a favorite of its authors). But many second-raters have created more stir, sold more copies. The larger reason for its lack of success must be extracted, I would guess, from the complex of publication and reading-public problems that the Australian writer then faced and to some extent still faces. Here are novelists Australian to the core who write of other Australians in their native setting—but for want of an interested Australian editor, the book is published (like so many of this period) in England. But it is not the kind of Australian novel that the English public had come to expect: no convicts, no bushrangers, not even a kangaroo. About what happened at an Australian writers' conference, probably few Englishmen could have cared less.

Then the book is shipped back to the land of its origins to be sold by Australian booksellers among the many other products of the English presses. Again, it is an Australian book but on a limited subject; the number of Australians who would be interested in a writers' conference is even less than the number of English. The Australian reader was still ranking English novels *per se* ahead of his own, and if he read an Australian one, he was looking (at least significant numbers of him were) for bushrangers too. The reader tuned to the name of M. Barnard Eldershaw by *A House Is Built* still hoped for more loaves of optimistic national history, and, handed *Plaque with Laurel,* he dismissed it as a stone.

The subject of *Plaque with Laurel* was too atypical, too remote from ordinary life, from the experience of the "dinkum Aussie" bookbuyer. Those best equipped to appreciate the book, the Australian writers, may well have looked askance at a treatment which did not take altogether seriously their tiny sensitive minority. Not only the subject stood in the way (and conceivably few Australians got past it to appraise the broader theme), but there was the style. The Australian is noted for his sardonic humor, but it is of a broader sort. This irony was too delicate, this satire too subtle, for the average Australian palate of the 1930's. Like Marjorie's short stories (p. 80), this was sophisticated writing in an unsophisticated time and place.

Barnard and Eldershaw were disappointed but undismayed. They had shown in each succeeding novel, especially in these latest two, that they were experimentalists, more interested in trying out their powers on a variety of projects than in a cheap success. For a variety of reasons the greatest experiment of all, their fifth and last novel, did not appear for another decade.

III   Tomorrow and Tomorrow

During 1937 most of the Barnard-Eldershaw energies had been spent on a history (*Phillip of Australia*) and a book of criticism (*Essays in Australian Fiction*), both published the following year. But the writers could never stay long or far from the thought of a novel, and *Plaque with Laurel* had now been out for nearly a year. It is not surprising, then, to learn from the Barnard-Palmer correspondence in December that "We feel some symptoms of a new novel coming on—something well in the future, the death of the civilization after this when all the things we piously hope for have been accomplished."[48]

This small seed was to blossom into their fifth novel, *Tomorrow and Tomorrow*, but the germination was agonizingly slow. During the next three years the team was busy with two more histories (*The Life and Times of Captain John Piper* and *My Australia*, both 1939), Marjorie with her first (*Macquarie's World*, 1941). It was a period filled with rumors and threats of war, then a "phony war," and finally war itself. A letter to Nettie in April 1941 is important for the state of mind in which Marjorie was shortly—at long last—to begin the writing of this final novel.

Of the war it is fruitless to say anything. When I think of it, which is practically all the time, my heart is molten with grief and anger. There's one thing which keeps twisting in my mind like a corkscrew—that 1st batallion A.I.F. [Australian Imperial Force] was 75% unemployed men. I'm going to write a book—for the first time in my life, a book. And it's going to be called "Tomorrow and Tomorrow and Tomorrow." Can you make anything of that?[49]

Although it would be another half dozen frustrating years before publication, at last the start was to be made. In early May Marjorie reported to Vance on her shift from history to fiction in a passage that gives us an interesting glimpse into her working quarters:

The rather surgical looking bridge table covered with a towel is erected at the foot of my bed again *and* the towel lies nice and flat, no bulwarks of notes, no clumps of encyclopedias, no chronologies draped on the bed rail, nothing but two small stacks of paper, one written on and one plain. We've taken the hideous plunge into the new novel and it is getting under way. I'm feeling as one does feel in those early morose stages of a novel.[50]

But almost immediately a serious new problem faced the collaborators: Flora, increasingly dissatisfied with her teaching post, left it for work with the Commonwealth Government which necessitated her moving to Canberra. Marjorie naturally had mixed feelings: "I think it is a Good Thing for her but makes the world look a bit hollow from this end. We're not going to let a little thing like distance interfere with collaboration."[51] But inevitably it did.

Tomorrow and Tomorrow being their most important novel as well as the last book of any kind to be published under their joint names, it behooves us to look as closely as we can at the workings of the collaboration on it. A quarter of a century later Marjorie, never prone to discuss shares in the partnership, admitted to me frankly that while they planned and discussed the book together, she herself did all the writing. This is credible, since with her greater leisure she had apparently done far more than half of the actual composition of the two novels that preceded it and, as we shall see later, much of the writing as well as the research of the three intervening histories as well. Her fullest statement on the subject appears in a 1970 article on how *Tomorrow and Tomorrow* came to be written, in which she uses the first person singular entirely, disposing of Flora in the following paragraph:

> This novel was to be written in collaboration with Flora Eldershaw. We often discussed it but from the first I think she was sceptical about the viability of the idea. She did not feel the same compulsion as I did to write it. The collaboration broke down almost from the beginning, not from any quarrel, disagreement, or failure of friendship but by reason of war and geography. Flora left Sydney, at first for Canberra and later for Melbourne. She was extremely busy. So was I. We were both drawn into the war effort. We saw one another only at rare intervals, letter writing was almost impossible. I went on alone and the book was to suffer from the lack, most particularly, of her critical judgment.[52]

Well and good, but a little at odds with the contemporary record. The book that had been started in May was reported in early December as "coming on and should be finished by the end of the year"—thanks to the "amazing bit of luck"[53] of Marjorie's having just had ten days with Flora in her Canberra flat. True, part of the luck was her being able to work solidly all day (at home her time was badly interrupted). And Flora was presumably at work, but it is hard to believe that evenings and the weekend didn't provide some opportunity for the two to continue to shape together the now nearly finished book.

Actually it wasn't completed for another two years, largely owing to Marjorie's going back to library work the following spring. But Flora, who in the meantime had left Canberra for

Melbourne, now returned to Sydney for a time. "It's lovely to have her back," Marjorie wrote, but confesses, "There's a lot of work in front of her here, I fear—the novel, the novel."[54] She estimated it as three-quarters written now, and Flora started reading it aloud to Marjorie and to Frank Davidson "to get a birdseye view of it so far";[55] but before she finished, Marjorie was taken to the hospital with pneumonia. One of Flora's relatively rare surviving letters to Nettie Palmer, written in July while Marjorie was still hospitalized, records that "Saturday and Sunday were nice and I got on with the novel."[56] What she was doing with it she doesn't specify—presumably shaping.

Flora's only other surviving comment on the book is in an undated letter to Vance which internal evidence places sometime in 1947, the year the novel appeared. Speaking of a delay encountered by one of his plays, she reflects: "I'm afraid you're much more philosophic and resilient about these long delays than I. I feel nothing but a sick distaste for 'Tomorrow...' and wish we'd never written it."[57] Whoever did what, and how much, it was apparently regarded by all concerned as appropriate that the book should appear under the name M. Barnard Eldershaw, with the royalties shared equally.

If the above suggests that the collaboration did not completely "break down" as early as Marjorie remembered in 1970, there is no doubt that she did the writing itself and found in it both comfort and suffering. Soon after she started, she wrote to Vance of the making of books in one of her characteristically vivid flashes: "... they're a horrid torment but they're something to lean up against in a crumbling world—or is it like trying to hang a picture on a fly?"[58] At one point "It was stuck, the whole middle part—the works so to speak—was a blank. Now it has come unstuck and in the last two days I've built up the whole skeleton. [This would have been the kind of difficulty in which she would have missed Flora's supporting decisiveness. Now she could get on with the writing.] I'm in a predatory frame of mind roving round seeking what I may devour—literally snatching features off people's faces and succulent morsels from all over the place. I'd tear down the sky and drag it into my den to nourish this book."[59]

The chief impediment to the writing was of her own making— her return to work early in 1942 to the Public Library, where she divided her time between cataloguing and writing a series of fifty lectures on the "Australian Cultural Background" for use in the Library School.[60] Her reasons for going back to work at this time are not wholly clear; they appear to have ranged from some financial uncertainty stemming from her father's death, something over a year earlier, to a compulsion to be more directly involved in a society at war. Of her dissatisfactions a letter to Nettie leaves no doubt. The novel remained "an unattainable anguish." For a pittance, she complained, "the Public Service Board thinks it can buy the whole of me—the library assistant *and* the writer, my working day and my leisure." She was looking for something better paid and less demanding: "Leisure *not* for sale at any figure."[61] She soon got the pay by going to CSIRO's library connected with its National Standards and Radio Physics Laboratories, but found the work even more demanding. What part-time writer could fail to grieve for her over this succinctly related incident: "Novel lies idle. Picked it up at the week end, spent desperate hours trying to remember the point of a half written episode. Hounded it down late on Sunday night. Too weary even to feel relief."[62]

Not until 1944—some seven years after its conception, three after the writing began—was this novel, the closest to Marjorie's heart of anything she had been involved in, ready for the publisher. With the war still on, publishing decisions were hard to come by. In August she laments, "The novel 'Tomorrow' (what a prophetic name) hangs suspended in nothingness. It is getting a look in its eye like a dead albatross."[63] In December, writing of "the continuing tragedy of our times," she adds, "I'm beginning to think we painted too rosy a picture in 'Tomorrow.' One tries to outstrip catastrophe by plotting a point beyond its reach (so as to have the comfort of being wrong), then the event makes one look like a fatuous optimist."[64]

In September 1947 the book finally appeared in Melbourne— the first and only one of the five MBE novels to find an Australian publisher. But even publication had its disappointments. The title had been "shorn of one tomorrow," to Marjorie's great annoyance, and more important changes in the text had been made without her knowledge or consent.[65] Various parties were given for the authors by way of celebration, but Marjorie herself "marked the occasion with a sombre look." Her chief thought was "five years old—time it was rewritten. It just makes me feel I have a skin too few."[66]

Tomorrow and Tomorrow is a complex book, in form and content, the setting divided between a very real twentieth century and an imaginary twenty-fourth. Structurally the twenty-fourth is a device for presenting the twentieth: Knarf, the writer of the future, reads his novel of the past to his friend Ord in a single day in the manner of Conrad's giving Marlowe a chance to tell his novel-length stories to an evening gathering of like-minded men. As in Conrad, occasional returns to the circumstances of the story-telling keep the reader conscious of the background against which the telling occurs. But here the returns are far more frequent, generally longer, for the account of twenty-fourth-century life is not just a framing device but a story in itself which plays a vital part in the author's commentary on life. Of the five sections into which the novel is divided, three (the first, third, and fifth) recount this future; in addition, more than a score of brief returns to the twenty-fourth century break the two intervening sections that cover the twentieth. As to length, however, the future is treated much more briefly, occupying less than a third of the total book. Still, it has its own plot, setting, characters, readable in themselves though more important as an ideological counterpoint to the realistic novel about the twentieth century.

Running to nearly five hundred pages, *Tomorrow and Tomorrow* is appreciably longer than any of its predecessors, and necessarily so to handle all of its complications. The story of the twentieth century is in itself divided into past and future—the very real past of the depressed 1930's and the warring 1940's from which it was written, and an imagined future that begins during World War II and leads ultimately to the four-centuries-distant framing story.

With all this complexity, misinterpretations of the authors' intentions have been inevitable. He who reads and runs sees the book as a simple contrast between the life we have recently known and the authors' version of a very different future. Those who only trot discover the past to be bad, assume the future, being different, to be good, and proceed to classify the book with literature's socialistic utopias. But *Tomorrow and Tomorrow* needs to be taken at a slow walk, with frequent pauses to look with attention at the details. So read, something else emerges.

Take the title. Even with the third "Tomorrow" omitted by the publisher, the source is clear. The forematter devotes a page, without comment, to this familiar five-line quotation:

> Tomorrow, and tomorrow, and tomorrow,
> Creeps in this petty pace from day to day,
> To the last syllable of recorded time;
> And all our yesterdays have lighted fools
> The way to dusty death.   —Macbeth

Where in this passage or in its larger context in Shakespeare lies the optimistically utopian dream? As a result of the Depression and the war which for the British Empire immediately followed it, man's fate was resting heavily on the authors' spirits (as it had on Macbeth's) as they finally sat down to give their views a local habitation and a name through this novel. But the world for them was no simplistic division between Good and Bad. As thinking women they must, like Housman, "put hands upon their hearts," not wave them. Their families and their jobs had provided them with the warmth of basic financial security even during the Depression, but being sensitive they were very conscious of what that period had meant to their nation. Some of their own writer friends were among the thousands of Australians forced onto the demoralizing dole.

This was no time to admire capitalism; but it was not consequently a time of certainty, for everyone, that any of the other isms—socialism, communism—would necessarily succeed where it had failed. Writing *Tomorrow and Tomorrow* was a soul-searching, mind-probing task. Its basic "ideology" is only a profound love for—pity for—mankind, and a deep-seated antagonism toward any and all systems or events that work him woe.

The history of man in relation to the Australian continent is presented in several sections. The "First People," the Aborigines, had reached a successful agreement with the land: "They lived in it according to its terms without changing it or penetrating it."[67] But by the twenty-fourth century they had been completely destroyed or absorbed; "their docile blood had mingled without trace."[68] In contrast to the compatibility between these men and nature, the second people, "coming after the First People, disinheriting rather than inheriting from them, had laid a different pattern on the earth."[69] The "Pioneers," the English, opened the land to civilized settlement: "With courage and endurance they had pioneered the land, only to ruin it with greed and lack of forethought."[70] These became the Australians as we know them, who continued to live "in a perpetual high gale of unreason."[71] Their life in the twentieth century is drawn with a sensitive realism, but during World War II, when the book is being written, reality is replaced by imagination, which looks ahead to an outcome that had not yet occurred and to paint one that was not likely to. In this fantasy the Australians, victims of their political and economic ineptitudes, scatter and die following the conflict, to be replaced by yet a third people.

About the origins and arrival of these we know nothing save that their names are alien to the English ear (Oriental, it is hinted), but we find them firmly established in the twenty-fourth century on a revitalized and fruitful Australian continent which at first sight appears to be a utopia. This third people, as the writer Knarf, one of their number, reflects, "don't know peace because we take it for granted."[72] They have completely tamed both man and nature—or so it appears. The Riverina of the twentieth century (the area in which Flora Eldershaw was reared and which Marjorie Barnard grew to love so deeply) has become the Tenth Commune (under a system which, according to Knarf, arrogantly divided the earth into squares with a ruler), a region of irrigated orchards and gardens through which the once destructive Murrumbidgee River now flows "quiet and full between canal-like banks."[73] Engineering has tamed nature, laws have tamed man. For the first time in human history, a golden age of peace and plenty.

Had the authors written only their twentieth-century story, they could be ranked with John Steinbeck in America and Kylie Tennant and Leonard Mann in Australia as realistic documenters of the common man's struggle through the Great Depression. Their central figure is Harry Munster, a well-meaning, hard-working Everyman striving to raise a family despite the dual handicaps of a lazy, selfish wife and an economic system that goes increasingly askew. Through his wife he is drawn from his hope for economic independence as a poultry farmer to an unsympathetic city; through the Depression he comes to know every indignity from joblessness to hawking borrowed goods around the countryside to the final depth of the dole.

As the catastrophe of war alleviates the catastrophe of Depression, Harry, now middle-aged, finds employment and the comfort of a girl-mistress, only to die at the point where the book leaves factual background for fictional: in the bombing of Sydney presented as occurring in the latter years of the war. If he is a rather superior Everyman intellectually, his sufferings and defeats move us the more as he tries to puzzle his way out of adverse circumstances entirely beyond his control.

The twentieth century, as portrayed here, is thus a time of grinding poverty followed by senseless war, both the more telling for being presented by writer-historian Knarf from his background of twenty-fourth-century comfort and calm. But utopia is more satisfying as goal than as attainment. Knarf, a philosopher with "the face of an individualist," finds himself at forty-seven "a prey to desolation and doubt,"[74] realizing that "Man might turn away from surfeits to pine for hard and meagre fare."[75] For him "life had been too simple. There had not been enough pain and distress, not even enough event."[76] Yet he was one of the lucky few, for he had known a lifetime of fulfillment in his writing. Most of these third people were retired at twenty-eight, after eight years of compulsory social service; only a few of the most able were admitted to the administrative and intellectual activities of the next hierarchy, from which society's leaders were chosen by lot.

Against this rigid, self-perpetuating, efficient but impersonal leadership, a youth movement is in revolt, seeking to add liberty to plenty by opening an avenue through which the force of public opinion can reach and operate in high places. Knarf's son Ren campaigns for it; Ren's friend Sfax perfects a votometer which can record the unvoiced thoughts of the people; Oran, a VIP from the Technical Bureau, comes to observe the experiment. The results are the perfection of Barnard-Eldershaw irony: not the affirmative surge that youth had worked and hoped for, not the negative preponderance that officialdom trusted in, only the foundering inertia of an indifferent majority. The hope for social change dims in the face of this apathy—and the ominous military force that we are shocked to discover has been standing by, "just in case," quietly but firmly disperses the dissidents.

Young Ren and his friends will have to wait a long time for liberty, for as his father reminds him, "The struggle will be against inertia and vested power"—against the indifference of the ruled and the self-preservation of the rulers. But the idea of liberty is so universal that with patience the indifference can presumably be overcome; what can prevail against the Establishment is left in question. "It can succeed," Knarf continues, "so long as it does not call in death against life. If you call in violence you may replace one tyranny with another. Means and end are not two separate things. They are one. Means is end becoming."[77] And so the book ends—if, as it appears, on a note of optimism that belies my reading of the title, I can only quote once more the philosophical Knarf: "If you look at history you will see that men have always preferred suffering to thinking."[78]

Of M. Barnard Eldershaw's series of experiments in novel-writing, *Tomorrow and Tomorrow* is the largest in conception, the noblest in intention; it also contains some of the finest writing. Somewhat flawed by circumstances of both writing and publication, it is nonetheless a very important book. For this reason it seems worthwhile to look in some detail at its reception. Upon publication it was widely reviewed, occasionally with both understanding and admiration, more often with the hasty, ill-informed approach that was all too typical of Australia's literary criticism. Her critics weren't accustomed to dealing with a book of this magnitude. The special problem that it offered, of course, was that it required judgment not only as fiction but as social theory, and some who admitted its excellence as a realistic picture of the present found it objectionably implausible as an image of the future.

Even the later considerations of established critics were generally disappointing. A notable exception was H. M. Green; he not only recognized it at once as "a marked advance" over the earlier Barnard-Eldershaw novels but felt it to be one of the two outstanding books of a good year.[79] (Three years later he went further by including it in a list of eight novels that he felt had been most important in the preceding dozen years.) His understanding would seem less of a feat but for the lack of it among other recognized critics. Colin Roderick, with more time for consideration, found the combination of twentieth and twenty-fourth century life in the novel hard to reconcile, feeling that the authors sought realism but found romance. Much of his attention is devoted to details that he denounces as objectionable (a little picayunish in the face of a book so large in every way). He finds that "The whole phantasmagoria of the destruction of Sydney is unreal, crazy, impossible"—a curious indictment of a fantasy of the future. "Is it then," he asks, "a satire on State socialism? Or is it an indictment of laissez-fare? It tries to be both; and where does it finish?"[80] The answers are implicit, surely, in the questions. And when he concludes that the gospel of the book is, in a nutshell, that "Harry Munster, Mr. Everyman, poor though he is in worldly goods, inherits the kingdom"[81]—one can only ask wryly, "What kingdom?" Still another critic was moved three years after the book's publication to call attention to the fact that others had "generally overlooked the subversive nature of its doctrine"—that the design "seems to be to urge the Communistic overthrow of our social and financial system."[82] One would have expected that by this time second thoughts—maybe even a second reading—would have corrected so hasty an impression.

Much of this must have been painful to Marjorie Barnard, who felt that the first law of criticism was understanding. But she was occupied with personal attacks as well. More than a score of years later she still recalled the results of *Tomorrow and Tomorrow's* appearance: "Communists accused me of being a reactionary and conservatives called me a Communist."[83] Obviously no case can be made for her as a reactionary; through the whole of her treatment of the twentieth century, her attack on the status quo in general and capitalism in particular is relentless and bitter. No more can be said for her as a Communist; it is a Communist, Sid Warren, who masterminds the violent destruction of Sydney—with more idealism than realism and with no regard for the slow but inevitable annihilation of its people in consequence. Between these extremes, maintaining a sometimes uneasy balance, sits socialism. The book's beneficient master state of the twenty-fourth century reads at first glance like a tribute to action engendered by socialistic thought. But it proves instead to be only technology triumphant, and in failing to provide opportunities for self-expression and individual fulfillment, to be even more sterile than the twentieth century with its lack of either comfort or peace.

"I have never belonged to any political party," writes Marjorie Barnard, "nor found any acceptable."[84] She rejects all the appellations that the book called down upon her—Communist, Trotskyist, fellow-traveller, reactionary, even intellectual and prophet—confessing that the philosophy in which she was educated, that of the nineteenth century liberal, was still hers "inescapably" in the 1940's despite her having found it inadequate in the 1930's.

But there are other titles. Would she refuse, one wonders, that of humanist, or of humanitarian? It is a little startling to find her rejecting so flatly the title of intellectual in connection with a book that looms so large in Australian fiction as an intellectual effort, work of a novelist who is also a historian and something of a philosopher. Her denial is credible only as we accept her own narrow definition of an intellectual approach as being distinct from an emotional and creative one. Let me suggest that in a wider sense her approach is intellectual *and* emotional and creative. Intellectual, surely, in both the framing story with its great leaps of imagination and in the vital, realistic novel within it. And emotional most surely of all, with its passionate hatred of systems like capitalism and war, its passionate love for struggling, suffering mankind. Miss Eldershaw might have carried banners; Miss Barnard sat and suffered and thought and wrote.

Tomorrow and Tomorrow is not so much the ideological treatise that it first appeared to many hasty readers as it is a compassionate book, full of sympathy and understanding and grief for humanity, especially for all thoughtful, sincere, suffering humanity. Harry Munster (Everyman) is neither praised nor blamed so much as loved and pitied. So are Bowie and Ardie and even Sid in the twentieth century story, Knarf and Ren in the twenty-fourth. If Paula and Ally in the former, Oran and Sfax in the latter, are dealt with less gently, it is that they lack sincerity and add to the sufferings of others. It is significant that compassion for Gwen, rather than love, brings death to Harry in his finest hour.

What *Tomorrow and Tomorrow* had not endured from misunderstanding, it has suffered from neglect. Take a look at Australia's burgeoning literary histories. H. M. Green continued to think well enough of it to include a thoughtful evaluation in his monumental *A History of Australian Literature* (2 vols., 1961). John K. Ewers discusses it briefly in the revised edition of his *Creative Writing in Australia* (1956). But Cecil Hadgraft in his *Australian Literature* (1960) only lists it, while devoting a couple of pages to *A House Is Built*, which even the authors admitted to be a relatively slight work. Harry Heseltine, writing of "Australian Fiction since 1920" in Geoffrey Dutton's *The Literature of Australia* (1964), gives the better-known *House* its paragraph but does not so much as mention *Tomorrow and Tomorrow*.

Nonetheless it is a book that is likely to be heard from in the future. Almost a quarter of a century after its publication, Australia's oldest and most prestigious literary quarterly carried a substantial analysis of it.[85] The appearance of this essay and its contents alike attest to the novel's increasing relevance to modern times. Marjorie Barnard's abdication of the appellation prophet, among others, may have been premature.

CHAPTER 4

Other Fiction

ALL of the five novels were the work (the shares varying, as we have seen) of the collaboration, and appeared under the name of M. Barnard Eldershaw. To that joint account we shall also credit some important historical studies (Chapter 5) and some significant critical work (Chapter 7). Flora produced no fiction under her own name; Marjorie published a number of short stories, including one collected volume, which we shall examine here. But in the bibliography of the collaboration there are a few minor items of fiction that we should first glance at, in passing.

About as "minor" as we can get is a slice of *Murder Pie* (1936), a *tour de force* that would long have been deservedly forgotten by all but the meticulous literary historian save that it still shows up occasionally on the shelves of used-book stores. Edited by another pair of women collaborators, J. L. (Jean) Ranken and Jane Clunies Ross, *Murder Pie* was the result of still further collaboration, for it was inspired by a detective novel that had sprung from the pens of not one but several British authors. For this local project sixteen chapters by as many Australian writers were decided on, and the game numbered among its players such diverse and established talents as Walter Murdoch and S. Elliott Napier, C. H. Bertie and Ethel Turner, as well as rising novelists M. Barnard Eldershaw. And so the hand was dealt, all in good fun, the editors giving it a start with Chapters 1 and 2, each of the others taking it on from where he or she found it. And be it said that when the initial six chapters arrived from divers hands, Barnard and Eldershaw managed a seventh ("The Mystery Grows") that did them credit, although it might better be listed under the heading of experience than literature. The mystery still remaining is why the book ran to several editions.

I   *Short Stories—MBE*

The glue on the binding of *Green Memory*, the second MBE novel, was scarcely set when the authors began what was to be a long and in the main a thankless struggle with the short story. Sending to Vance Palmer late in 1931 her congratulations on a newly published collection of his, Marjorie spoke feelingly of "the difficult and delicate art of short story writing,"[1] for she and Flora were trying to put together a collection to be entitled (owing to the melancholy of its contents) *But Not for Love*. To Nettie Palmer's inquiry about their progress a few months later, Marjorie replied in a passage worth quoting for its indication of their motivation and its hint of what may have been their basic difficulty:

The stories are rather long and elaborate. What we really admire and would like to write is the short story with the delicate point, but there is an inexorable power that pushes one back into one's own mental groove and will not let one escape from it. If one cannot see the minute without seeing—and far more clearly—the years that made it, one is congenitally incapable of writing short short stories. You may say, very sensibly, "Why attempt short stories?" Technically we find it a most fascinating form and we are quite pleased with some of our designs.[2]

Their London agent was unable to place the collection, Nettie read it in manuscript and was discouraging, and that was the end of *But Not for Love* but not of the Barnard-Eldershaw interest in the short story. Within two years its successor was reported as finished save for a title, but we hear no more of it. Christened or unchristened, this second group appears to have joined the first in the graveyard of stillborn manuscripts. If any exhuming was done from either, it is not recorded.

The collaboration's only published short stories appeared in periodicals later. One of them, "Shipwreck," which was published in the household magazine *Home* (p. 81), is well constructed, well written, disconcertingly slick.[3] Middle-aged Harold is en route by ship from service in Pago Pago to Sydney with his young inamorata, Mona, and his wife of twenty years, Mary, from whom he is about to be divorced. Neat turns of phrase pin him to the dissecting board and wield the scalpel. "He had fallen in love with a sort of pop, like a cork being suddenly drawn,"

and is confident that with a new wife "his youth would begin
again, the buoyant indefatigable youth of middle age." Comes
a storm, the ship runs aground on the Barrier Reef, and he
instinctively saves his wife, leaving Mona to a second officer.
Insulted, the girl throws him over, he tells Mary he has given up
the idea of a divorce—and now *she* insists on one. She had never
been happy with him, she admits, because he is dull, but she
would have gone on if his own quest for freedom hadn't given
her the idea of it. Typical MBE irony, and, save for superior
writing, typical magazine fodder.

Another MBE story, "The Plover," first appeared in the same
magazine, but the two stories happily have nothing else in
common. In a few pages this one builds up for us in leisurely
fashion a comfortable sense of familiarity with life in a station
family (like Flora's) whose numerous children all had their
appointed tasks. This is the story of the youngest child, Susan,
whose duty and privilege was to care for the aviary, a wire-
netted enclosure in the orchard where lived, thriving and content,
an assortment of once wild birds. To this collection was one day
added a plover caught by her father in the paddock—a bird that
first fascinated Susan but which she came to hate because it
would not settle down contentedly like the rest. At last its
continual efforts to free itself led her to slip out one evening
and leave open the door to the aviary, and ("for she must not
play favorites") to the canary cage as well. By morning the
canaries had emerged to become victims of the cats and the
sparrows, the freed parrots proved tame enough to return—
"only the plover, lost in its relentless dream of freedom, had
never even noticed." While she wept for the canaries, Susan
brooded over the plover's ingratitude. The story ends:

For it she had killed the canaries, their blood was on her head,
and it had all been to no purpose. She couldn't do any more for it;
if it was too stupid to take the chance she had given it, it must just
go on pacing for ever beside the wire cage, crying for ever for its
lost world.
The plover was still there when Susan went away to school, but
when she came back for her first holidays it was gone. She never
asked what had happened to it. It left a sore place in her mind
that never healed.[4]

This story was justifiably rescued from magazine oblivion by Cecil Mann in editing the first volume of the Australian short story annual *Coast to Coast 1941* (1941).[5] As a study of the child mind "The Plover" is excellent, recalling the sensitive portrayal of the brothers James and Lionel Hyde as boys in *A House Is Built*; in fact, this whole story has the same kind of humanity that warmed *A House* and keeps it still alive. Had the long apprenticeship to the short story to which the collaborators set themselves in the early thirties produced many of this caliber, it would surely have known a happier ending. Perhaps for the others they were trying to "design" stories and achieving only the artificiality of a *Green Memory*.

II   *Short Stories—MB*

According to Marjorie Barnard, she began writing at age seven—as soon as she was allowed belatedly to learn her alphabet. Her childhood efforts do not survive. Her first publication was a group of thirteen children's stories (she was, remember, an only and lonely child) called *The Ivory Gate* (1920), which she now refers to as a "dead end." She made no further effort to write stories for children, but her continuing interest in childhood is evidenced by the number of youngsters that appear in the novels and the short stories, and the credibility with which they are portrayed.

Not till the 1930's, when she was already an established novelist, did she turn again to the short story form, first with Flora, as we have seen, then alone. What led her to begin publishing stories under her own name we do not know. Perhaps Flora lost interest in the form when the two volumes that they completed in the six-year gap between their second novel and their third failed to find publishers. Perhaps Marjorie was moving into an area where Flora did not choose to work or could not. Perhaps the short story, with its concentration, did not prove a suitable genre for collaboration. Probably it was one of the issues that they settled between themselves in 1935 when Marjorie gave up work for full-time writing while Flora continued to teach. In any event M. Barnard Eldershaw appear to have written no more short stories, but Marjorie Barnard's interest in them has never flagged.

Despite her fascination with the form, the writing didn't come easily to her. At the close of 1934 she confessed to Vance Palmer, undisputed master of the craft himself, "I've positively preyed on your short stories but the secret is unstealable."[6] Early the next year she wrote to him again in what is the clearest statement we have of her approach: her stories, she explains, "don't begin life as stories or episodes at all but as ideas or angles of vision or sometimes just phrases, and have to be clothed with synthetic flesh. There's a little troubling speck of something alive in my mind and I've got to get it into a body. It never grows one of itself no matter how long I leave it."[7] This account of the genesis of her short stories should be kept in mind in looking at the stories themselves, where (fortunately) it is sometimes more honored in the breach than in the observance.

As late as 1936 she knew only frustration and discouragement in this area. She wrote to Nettie Palmer that "when I've had one of my periodic bouts of wrestling with the short story, I sometimes send the products on the rounds, safe in the knowledge that no one will take them—and they don't."[8] Frank Dalby Davison, who was later to call himself "one of the accepted short story men of the thirties,"[9] and who was a writer on whose critical judgment Marjorie came increasingly to rely, was no comfort. Of some stories that she had been wrestling with, she wrote Nettie: "Frank declares that they are 'beautifully done' but that every time I write one I 'leave life poorer than I found it.' I ought to commit suicide after that."[10] Light as his words were, they doubtless smarted a little. It must have been a special satisfaction to her that she was able to make him eat them later. But this didn't come about for some time. It was another year yet before her stories began to be published in any numbers, and several before her memorable ones appeared.

Barnard stories have since come out in a wide scattering of Australian periodicals: dailies, weeklies, monthlies, quarterlies, yearlies.[11] Her main outlet was *Home,* where for several years (late 1930's and early 1940's) her work, both fiction and non-fiction, appeared with almost feature regularity. As Australian periodicals go, *Home* had a long and distinguished life (1920-1942). It advertised itself as "The Australian Journal of Quality," and the *Australian Encyclopaedia* describes it as "an admirable venture into the field of the high-class social periodical."[12]

It was heavily illustrated with art work and photographs, and carried "social and personal" notes from the various states, along with house, garden, and fashion features. Much of it, including the advertising, was aimed primarily at the woman reader.

Home had a fiction section in which appeared the work of such short story regulars as Vance Palmer, Katharine Susannah Prichard, Myra Morris, Don Edwards. It was a logical outlet for Marjorie's stories because she wrote primarily of, if not for, women—of the foibles and futilities of their lives, both social and private. Often her being a woman (and a very perceptive one) is an obvious advantage; sometimes, when her characters' lives impinge on the greater world of men and affairs, she is a little ill at ease. Many of her stories, like many of Wordsworth's poems, could well be forgotten; at least two are among the finest that Australian literature possesses, acknowledged classics that continue to be reprinted in anthology after anthology.

Before we look at what the Barnard stories are, let us notice what they are not, for one of their virtues is that they broke with the Lawson tradition, or the *Bulletin* pattern—the Great Australian Short Story which had come into being in the late 1800's with A. G. Stephens as midwife and which now, more than a half century later, was beginning to suffer as serious literature from close to a half century of overproduction. The setting was the outback, the spirit militantly, even jingoistically, Australian, even before the several states became a nation. Action was of the essence, characters were exaggerated, theme was obvious. These were "real life" stories, even after the life they portrayed had begun to yield to an urbanization that put more than half of Australia's sparse population into her half-dozen capital cities. Except in the hands of a few masters, from Henry Lawson to Gavin Casey, they tended to be simple, superficial, and obvious. Most were written by men (in contrast to the early Australian novel, which as we have seen was an essentially feminine art, like the English novel of the same period), and when a Barbara Baynton came along, she merely put the familiar materials to more sombre and violent uses than were customary. When the typical women short story writers appeared (the Robertsons, the Morrises, the Trists, *et al.*) with the typical women's short story, the results were only a domesticated version of the long tradition.

Into this scene, in the 1930's, stepped Marjorie Barnard, an artist with a love for the Australian continent which, as we shall see from her descriptive writing, hasn't been surpassed, but who didn't see the short story as a place for flag-waving. She was interested in humanity (when her professional duties with CSIRO required that she put together a book on radar just after the war, she confessed, "I'd much rather muck round with the human heart").[13] That it was Australian humanity didn't distinguish it, in her art. She was city-bred and her settings, insofar as they are discernible, are nearly always urban—Sydney, even, but save for the occasional use of a recognizable place-name, they could as well be in New York or London or Moscow, any city in which the human heart (usually a feminine one) abides, with all its capacity for pleasure and for pain.

Marjorie was a realist in a far truer sense than the "slice of life" writers had been. Not for her the sentimentality, the happy ending stuck on like a bouquet of plastic flowers. She was too honest, too intelligent, too much the dedicated artist to speak other than the truth as she saw it, even if it was painful. And it usually was. As she herself once noted, "Someone always gets hurt in my stories, don't they?"[14] In literature, her defense against pain was irony. She wrote to Vance Palmer in 1937, "Art can be put on like a shirt—irony can be a sort of shelter that you offer what you write about rather than a shelter for yourself."[15]

In 1943 her first and only collection of stories appeared, named for the finest story in the group, "The Persimmon Tree" (*The Persimmon Tree and Other Stories*).[16] As its nineteen stories presumably represent her choice of what she had published up to that time, it seems fair to confine our examination to these and the few she published thereafter. One of those that she thought highly enough of to give the greater permanence of hard covers was her first story in *Home*, "The Woman Who Did the Right Thing"[17]—not a great story, not her best, but for several reasons deserving of a close look. For one thing it illustrates the break with the Australian short story tradition; for another, it has many of the characteristics that are common to most of her stories.

One is brevity. Her long and previously fruitless struggle with the short story had taught her to waste no words, a lesson she sometimes followed to excess. Another is firm structure. The action in "The Woman" is simple, falling into three clear-cut parts: Barbara on her way to a party, attending the party, leaving the party. In the first and longest section (but only four small pages), we learn through her thoughts as she walks through Sydney's Botanic Gardens to her hostess's flat in Macquarie Street that she is five years a widow, is approaching forty, and has been on the brink of an affair with Murray, a married music teacher whose wife Phoebe doesn't understand him. Barbara is desperately in love, but has "done the right thing" by breaking off to protect Murray from the inevitably difficult consequences of a consummation. In the second section (two pages) she overhears at the party a conversation indicating that Murray (who, it appears, has been playing around throughout the entire two decades of his married life) is currently inseparable from a twenty-year-old girl pupil. In the third section (one page) Barbara leaves the party abruptly and returns to walk in the Gardens "while her thoughts raced down their own dark channels and a slow black tide of bitter regret and disappointment welled up in her heart. 'For nothing, for nothing,' she said over and over again to herself. . . . She wanted love, not Murray, only love. She had thrown it away for nothing." To complete this "well-made short story" comes the long-threatening rain which had earlier concerned her for her hat; but now, " 'My hat is ruined,' she thought, 'and I don't even care.' She could not imagine that she would ever want a hat again, or buy one or do any of the small commonplace, cheerful things of which her life had been made up."[18]

Prominent here is the note of irony—the noble resolution, the painful self-sacrificing decision, made "for nothing." The concentration on a woman (long a lesser breed in Australian fiction as in Australian life) is conspicuous too. So is the lack of overt action, the climax occurring in the mind and heart of the central character rather than in any conflict between characters. The story has as the weakness of its strength a reliance on a long initial exposition to detail the character's inner state. There is not even dialogue, save for the overheard chatter of the unidentified women at the party. The point of the story comes through, all right, briefly and neatly, but with a quick flash of intellectual perception rather than the pull at the heart that the same theme, more fully and roundly developed, might have accomplished. It is as though the author's long apprenticeship had left her with a kind of glib technique that has muted feeling. One is reminded of her earlier confession that "I can tick out people with some of the deadly facility of a taxi meter ticking off sixpences" and her consequent fear: "I've a lurking suspicion that anything so facile is not honest or soon won't be."[19] A still shorter, slighter, later story, "The Party," on the same theme (save that here instead of "doing the right thing" herself, the woman has apparently been jilted) strengthens this regrettable assumption.

Most of the stories in *The Persimmon Tree* center around women, as many of the titles indicate: In "The Wrong Hat" a woman in a hat shop enjoys a brief illusion of youth before being brought face to face with age; in "Beauty Is Strength" a woman in a beauty parlor, having just learned of her husband's unfaithfulness, gains new confidence for the task of winning him back. Nearly all of these stories have urban settings. Our only ventures into the bush are with an unadjusted city girl ("The Bride Elect"), and through the recollections of a homesick country child ("Dialogue at the Ballet"). Our only venture abroad ("Fighting in Vienna") recalls Marjorie's later conclusion that Patrick White's second novel was less real because set in England instead of "the country of his youth" (p. 163). Most of the stories follow simple patterns to inevitable, usually ironic, conclusions. Only one ("The Dressmaker"), which verges on melodrama, is a story within a story.

One is reminded by many of these of Marjorie's repeated emphasis on the importance of form over content, of her mention of the "synthetic flesh" with which her stories, beginning as ideas, had to be clothed (p. 81). And one wonders if she didn't lose warmth thereby, as Hawthorne did in trying to breathe life into the moral concepts with which he started. The most human of these stories is "The New Dress," in which a young girl's valiant effort to look especially nice spoiled her equally young lover's plans for their big day. Instead of a pat magazine ending or an ironic conclusion, we get a very honest and touching final paragraph: "A few minutes later they parted in what looked like offended silence, but was only the natural confusion of their young hearts."[20]

Interestingly, Marjorie's few stories with men protagonists

tend to be among her most original, most genuine. "The Lottery" is reminiscent of MBE's slick "Shipwreck" in its concluding revelation of a middle-aged wife's long-suppressed desire to leave home, but the character of the well-intentioned but selfishly obtuse husband is a very human drawing. "Say Goodbye and Mean It," a later story that Nettie Palmer gave more permanent form to when she edited *Coast to Coast 1949-50* (1951),[21] has so much technical proficiency that reviewer Ken Levis damned it with the faint praise of capable storytelling of the "magazine" type,[22] but the brash young male protagonist, unrepentant betrayer of financial trust, is fully and convincingly shown. The hero of "Sunday" is one of Marjorie's most sympathetically drawn characters (perhaps because he is a fellow writer?) as he struggles to escape, for his soul's and his art's sake, from the threefold net of comfortable home, hovering mother, aspiring sweetheart. There is nothing "slick" about this story; the author has created her characters rather than manufacturing them to specifications. "Speak to Me," which poet Douglas Stewart chose for his *Coast to Coast 1945* (1946), is an account of a bereft father—a surgeon called to operate on the eyes of a deaf-mute accident victim. The action verges on the melodramatic, but the narrative (in the first person) is beautifully and movingly written. A long introductory paragraph opens with words reflecting the author's own lifelong experience with insomnia: "Since I have been sleeping badly—thin, meagre sleep like an old, shrunk blanket that never quite covers my tired mind, under which I lie, tense, cramped and unresting, or long hours without sleep at all in the *terra incognita* of the night in which nothing exists but the ticking of the clock and the whirring, concentric stillness of my own droughty brain . . ."[23]

Many of Marjorie's stories suffer from brevity; the reader just isn't given enough time or details, in a half-dozen small pages, more or less, to enable him to become sufficiently involved. This is conspicuous in the superior impact of "Beauty Is Strength," thought highly enough of by Vance Palmer to be reprinted in his *Coast to Coast 1944* (1945), over its quarter-size companion piece, "The Wrong Hat," and a leisurely pace is one of the strengths of "Sunday." So it is in Marjorie's most recently published story, "Tree without Earth," certainly one of her finest, appearing after a long drought in Clement Semmler's *Coast to*

Coast 1965-66 (1966). Here she allowed herself space in which to develop the richly textured family life of a young couple with two small daughters trying to adjust, during the Christmas season, to the recent death of a still smaller son. Marjorie has said that she meant this as a study in maternal grief, which it is; yet the mother shuts herself off so self-indulgently with her sorrow that the reader's sympathy tends to shift to the father, who bears the double burden of his own loss and his wife's withdrawal. There is no "synthetic flesh" here—it is all painfully human. The whole is profoundly moving, with no hint of the studied competence that engendered the marring note of artificiality in some of her earlier efforts. This is one of her best, if not quite of the very first rank that she achieved twice in her life with "The Persimmon Tree" and "Dry Spell."

One no sooner reaches the conclusion that brevity is a detriment to story writing than it is given the lie by these two, both short, both superlative. "The Persimmon Tree" (title story of the collected volume) has recently been anthologized yet again—in a book of "modern" Australian short stories, despite its quarter century, and rightly so.[24] Not until Patrick White was there an author who came farther from the Australian tradition—more deeply into psychological nuance. The story lingers in the memory long after reading, for it is a delicate one that raises faint, unsolved questions that continue to tease the mind.

It is difficult to touch, even to touch on it, without rubbing off some of its sheen. It is narrated in the first person by a woman who, she tells us in the opening sentence, "saw the spring come once and I won't forget it," a woman recovering from a long winter illness, whose "mind was transparent and tender as new skin. Everything that happened, even the commonest things, seemed to be happening for the first time, and had a delicate hollow ring like music played in an empty auditorium." It is with this sensitivity that she rejoices to find the window opposite her own always closed, lest her privacy might have been "flawed"; with this sensitivity that she begins to notice, as she watches the comings and goings in the street below, a handsome solitary woman of her own age, whose air of self-sufficiency moves her to "a faint, very faint, envy of anyone who appeared to have her life so perfectly under control."

Came a warm day and at last the opposing window is slightly

open; came another, and on its sill a row of persimmons was set
out to ripen in the sun. "Shaped like a young woman's breasts,
their deep, rich, golden-orange colour" reminds the observer of
the persimmon grove of her childhood home that "In the autumn
blazed deep red, taking your breath away. . . . Why did I always
think of autumn in springtime?" And why these, ripening in
spring—"Fruit out of season?" The woman who gathers them in
later in the day and who soon starts bulbs growing in a bowl on
the sill is the one whose self-sufficiency she has been admiring.

Now the narrator occasionally passes her in the street but
with no sign of recognition, no effort to learn her name.

She was a lonely woman and so was I. That was a barrier, not a
link. Lonely women have something to guard. I was not exactly
lonely. I had stood my life on a shelf, that was all. I could have
had a dozen friends round me all day long. But there wasn't a friend
that I loved and trusted above all the others, no lover, secret or
declared. She had, I suppose, some secret nutrient on which she drew.

Her window was open all day long now, as spring advanced.

The shadow pattern on my wall was intricate and rich. It was no
longer an austere winter pattern as it had been at first. . . . I used
to lie looking at the shadow when I rested in the afternoon. I was
always tired then and so more permeable to impressions. I'd think
about the buds, how pale and tender they were, but how implacable.
The way an unborn child is implacable. If man's world were in
ashes the spring would still come. I watched the moving pattern
and my heart stirred with it in frail, half-sweet melancholy.

Then comes an afternoon when the woman stands just behind
the curtains in a wrap as if from her bath, looks out long, slowly
raises her arms, and her gown drops, leaving her naked, scarcely distinguishable through the veil of the curtains. "I turned
away. The shadow of the burgeoning bough was on the white
wall. I thought my heart would break."[25]

Only that, and nothing more— a rare and fragile flower indeed
to be found abloom in the prosaic paddock of the Australian
short story.

The other indisputable Barnard classic, "Dry Spell," is as
different from both this one and her typical short story as if it
had been written by quite another hand. It is worth examining

because of its content, its quality, and its success in winning at last from Frank Dalby Davison his startled, reluctant, but unqualified praise. At Easter time in 1938, Marjorie had gone over the mountains with Flora to O'Connell, an "almost imperceptible village" a few miles from Bathurst, to find it suffering from the excessive dryness of the Australian autumn. She reported to Nettie: "We had a look at the drought. The country is burnt brown and purple but is still flickering with grasshoppers (what they eat I don't know; it isn't grass for there is none). The sheep dig all day with their forefeet for grass roots. But the country is still beautiful."[26] This trip (and probably others like it) must have made a particularly strong impression on a Sydney woman who had spent most of her life with the generous waters of Sydney Harbor spread out in view from her verandah. Here may have been conceived the story "Dry Spell," a fantasy that presages parts of *Tomorrow and Tomorrow*.

"It was the third waterless summer, and the heat had come down like a steel shutter over the city." The opening paragraphs are a searing picture of the country, the suburbs, the city following such deprivation. The narrator, an unnamed man, is walking into Sydney along Anzac Parade from a compulsion to reach the sea. "The trees were black, and their leaves made a little dry sound like ghostly butter pats. There were no soft, rounded sounds in the night, only dry brittle ones, and the pavement was gritty under my feet. My lips tasted of dust as they always did. The torrid street lamps were like sores on the night." He finds himself among a wave of swagmen—oldtimers accustomed to "doing a perish"[27] in the outback—and as he realizes that now "the track runs through the city," he "felt coldly sick." In Macquarie Place he finds himself talking with a man in white breeches, a tailcoat, and a three-cornered hat—no less a personage than a ghostly Captain-General Phillip, founder of the colony, who assures him that worse has happened before, and that "If I could hang on surely you could." But the narrator wants no comfort, having become reconciled to the inevitable. "The country was coming to take its vengeance on the city.... Then nothing.... Come quickly. All ugliness, all corruption will be burned away." When the rain starts falling, he refuses to believe, then grieves as he stares at the drops. "Out on the roads, that pattern was tangling the feet of the perishing men, turning them back. Nothing would come of it now. Nothing would save us. We must take up the burden of remaking our world."[28]

Of these two masterpieces, "The Persimmon Tree," elusive, exotic, has the greater universality. But "Dry Spell" is the apotheosis of difficulties and doggedness peculiarly Australian.

III   Drama—MBE

There is evidence in the Barnard-Palmer correspondence of the youthful M. Barnard Eldershaw's having attempted to break into the writing of drama, but apparently only one play, written for radio, succeeded, and that at a considerably later date. This is "The Watch on the Headland," which in the 1940's won a prize in an A.B.C. competition, was broadcast several times on the national program, and has had several appearances in print over the years. The subject was a natural one for these creative historians who had by this time done the research for a book-length study of the life of the early colony.

The action, more psychological than overt, takes place on a January afternoon just two years after the First Fleet landed. The scene is South Head, at the mouth of Sydney Harbor, where to raise the morale of the almost starving young settlement, a permanent watch has been set to signal the arrival of the Second Fleet—in ignorance of the fact that it will not appear to relieve the colony for yet another six months. Three of the half dozen characters are historic: Phillip, Watkin Tench, and John Hunter; three fictitious: Midshipman Southwell, Gunner Phelim O'Byrne from the Sirius, and a girl convict, Letty. The play opens with Letty bringing O'Byrne, on watch, his ration and the information that Phillip is coming to inspect his post. The heavy discouragement in the little colony has bred rumors that England never intended to send help and that the officers have a hidden ship on which they will sail away, leaving the rest to die. Letty had known eight months on a transport, coming out, but now her only fear is of being left on this remote continent. The dialogue is lively, if wry. Says she, "I'd go to the ends of the earth with you, Phelim." Says he, "Sure, that's just where you are now." Midshipman Southwell, preceding Phillip's party, arrives to ask, "Is everything in order, gunner?" "Ay, sir," O'Byrne replies. "There's the flagstaff, there's the ocean, there's the harbour.

Everything in order, sir." Ordered to put on his jacket, he protests, "There's no back to it, sir." Southwell reassures him: "You'll
have no occasion to turn your back on His Excellency."

When the notables arrive, Hunter is urging the Governor to
give the colony up—eat the livestock and seed and take the convicts by turns to islands in the Pacific. But Phillip, who still
dreams dreams, won't consider letting go of what may prove to
be the "fairest possession of the Crown." Suddenly the overwrought gunner shouts, "Ship!" Even Tench thought he saw
one. But it was only a hallucination, the result of clouds and
desire; ship there was none. Letty says bitterly of Phillip after
he leaves South Head, "God's curse on him! It's him that keeps
us here to starve or die." The play ends with O'Byrne's moving
reply: "Aye, God's curse *is* on him. He's the loneliest wan of us
all."[29]

For a brief play with sound its only medium, "The Watch on
the Headland" is extremely effective. The vigorous dialogue is
highly individualized, by character and dialect. The writers
succeeded in bringing together in little space and at a dramatic
moment a variety of First Fleeters with an equal variety of
reactions to the colony's dire predicament—and in flashing an
understanding portrait of Phillip himself, most lonely, most
sorely tried, and ultimately most renowned of all Australia's
early leaders. With its use of actual figures as characters, the
play is truly historical, whereas their first two works of fiction,
using history only as a background, were by MBE's own definition (p. 139) only "period novels." And so "The Watch on the
Headland" leads us naturally into a consideration of the works
of the collaborators that are not fiction at all but the result of
scholarly research.

CHAPTER 5

The Histories—MBE

MARJORIE Barnard once remarked to me that she considers an author's thirties to be the most productive period in his artistic life. Her own productivity, then, was a little belated. She had just entered her thirties when *A House Is Built* was written and published, and in the following decade she co-authored three more novels that found publishers and a considerable number of short stories that didn't. But in her early forties there came a great flood of major and minor publications, some the continuing work of the collaboration, some her own, in all the fields for which both the team and she were to be known: fiction, history, and criticism. True, the fiction was minor (short stories but no novels), and, save for one book, the criticism was largely reviews. But the histories of this period are among the first and finest works in their field; it may well prove to be for them that the name of Eldershaw, and certainly of Barnard, will be best remembered. And (as both would have wished) remembered for literature as well as history.

The extent of a teacher's influence is never measurable, but as I have mentioned before, both Barnard and Eldershaw, while brilliant undergraduate students at the University of Sydney, came under the spell of George Arnold Wood, professor of history there. His influence, which marked them for life, was discernible in their early novels and now flowered in three major historical studies: *Phillip of Australia* (1938), *The Life and Times of Captain John Piper* and *My Australia* (both 1939).

I Phillip of Australia

Late in 1936, their third novel published and the writing of their fourth complete, we find the partners "teetering on the edge of a decision whether we'll break into biography or not. We have our eye on Phillip ... and his times."[1] The decision in

92

Phillip's favor was momentous: it started M. Barnard Eldershaw on the road to the past that was to put far more historical figures than fictional characters into their literary futures.

As soon as they had sent to a prospective publisher the troublesome manuscript of critical essays that, as we shall see in Chapter 7, had been nagging at them for a couple of years, they started to work. To Marjorie, of course, fell the weight of the research, since she remained free from routine employment while Flora was still tied to her teaching. Early in 1937 Marjorie began spending all her days in the Mitchell Library in Sydney among its vast amounts of material connected with Phillip's career— some of it, facsimiles very hard on the eyes. But as always, the decision and the first plunge were the most difficult; with these behind her, she could settle down to a long period of tedious reading, serene in the knowledge that at the end lay a book.

Her speed as a writer of novels, which we have already noted, was equalled by her speed in research. Within a couple of months she was able to report to Vance Palmer: "At present I'm a machine for writing a book on Phillip. . . . The research is finished, the first sorting and classification of notes made and the first chapter almost finished."[2] But this was no novel, to be dashed off at top speed in the heat of inspiration. And added to the natural difficulties of writing creatively from research notes, there was the strain of world events, to which we have earlier seen her to be very sensitive. At the end of July 1937 she wrote to Nettie Palmer: "The Deutschland incident occurred in the middle of our struggle to get the book finished. I never felt so utterly futile. To be writing a book on Phillip when our whole world was dying."[3] But the manuscript had nonetheless been completed and sent to London to the publisher of the four MBE novels. Dedicated appropriately by these two former students to George Arnold Wood, *Phillip of Australia* appeared early in 1938.

This year was an important one for Australia, and widely acclaimed (especially in New South Wales), as it was the Sesquicentennial of the arrival of the English under Phillip's command to found a permanent settlement in Sydney Cove. Much was done to commemorate the event, by publication as well as public function. Dyed-in-the-merino Miles Franklin chose to view the whole proceedings with a most jaundiced eye, recording them with Dymphna Cusack in the satirical novel *Pioneers on Parade* (1939). But Barnard and Eldershaw laid aside their own gift of irony and served the cause well. Both were members of the thirty-member Women's Advisory Council and worked on the Women's Executive Committee for Australia's 150th Anniversary Celebration. For it, in honor of the occasion, Flora edited *The Peaceful Army* (Marjorie chose the title), subtitled "A Memorial to the Pioneer Women of Australia, 1788-1938" (1938), an anthology of essays and poems of the women, by the women, and for the women of Australia. Such prominent writers as Dame Mary Gilmore, Miles Franklin, Eleanor Dark, Kylie Tennant, Helen Simpson, and Kathleen Monypenny were represented. M. Barnard Eldershaw contributed a charming account of "The Happy Pioneer—Elizabeth Macarthur," the redoubtable wife of the early settler responsible for founding Australia's wool industry, who herself successfully ran the largest landholding then existent in Australia, during the nine years that her husband John was an exile in England for his connection with the Bligh affair. This was a pleasant sample of the greater historical studies on which the team of novelists was now embarked.

Although *Phillip of Australia* was published in England, its appearance was appropriately timed to coincide with the Sesquicentennial. Its contents are less accurately indicated by the title than by the subtitle, "An Account of the Settlement at Sydney Cove 1788-92," for important as Captain Arthur Phillip was to that beginning, the book is far more a history of the young colony than a biography of its Governor. It makes admirable reading for anyone who wishes to acquaint himself with the circumstances of the founding of Australia, for it is gratifyingly broad in scope and conveniently analytical in approach.

In a "Prome" of considerable length, the authors give us the background of English politics and penal practices that led to the idea of the First Fleet and its formation; in the two succeeding chapters they relate chronologically the long and arduous voyage and the initial stages of the settlement. Then the organization leaves the chronological for the topical, for the authors "found it convenient, a plan inherent in the material, to tell the story of the settlement in chronological order up to a point when all the main issues are started, and then to disentangle them, following each through the five years of Phillip's government.

The issues fall into two main groups: establishment and expansion."[4] Establishment is treated in successive chapters entitled "The Struggle for Existence," "Justice and the Convicts," "The Church"; expansion in "Parties of Pleasure" (actually, exploration), "Natives," and "Norfolk Island."

Such a thoughtful analytical approach, such careful organization is not always congenial to the creative mind, but it is as strong a feature of the Barnard-Eldershaw histories as we shall find it to be of their criticism. The ability to analyze goes farther, however, than organization. The authors not only see their subject clearly but see it whole; they are not content to relate but must interpret. Much of the relation is anthological, for they drew heavily, as their appended bibliography indicates, on original sources, notably on the journals and letters of men of the First Fleet (many of which still exist in manuscript only), and they developed their account at sufficient length to allow for voluminous though never tiresome quotation. But they did more.

Phillip of Australia is a book about the founding of Australia by a pair of Australians, but as we have seen in their fiction, the authors are by no means limited, as so many of their literary countrymen have been, to a narrowly continental view. Of far more importance to Australian history than the details of their fascinating "Account of the Settlement" is their ability not only to see the forest in spite of the trees but to understand and explain its ecology. The settlement was not an Australian phenomenon, not even a strictly British one, but a product of the century in which it occurred. This was the Age of Reason, and reason is both the strength and the weakness of Arthur Phillip, who governed the settlement during its critical first five years. This was also the age of complacency, a quality that showed itself in the apathy, inertia, and indolence against which Phillip was continually forced to struggle, both in Government and in individuals. Illuminated by these twin floodlights on the times, the causes for the settlement of Australia emerge clearly and meaningfully, its difficulties fall into perspective.

The 18th century was an indolent century; the inertia of self-satisfaction was upon England. All the events of her history at this time had to wrestle with this inertia to be born; it shaped the course of events, so negative in its essence that it became a positive force. . . .

The American Colonies were lost through this heavy indolence of spirit, this thick, impenetrable indifference, and the national reaction to the loss was peevish rather than passionate.[5]

If the founding of Australia was shaped ideologically by this inertia, it was through the loss of these Colonies that it became a practical suggestion, made first as a means of settling dispossessed American Loyalists, second as a means of ridding England of the rapid accumulation of convicts who could no longer be disposed of across the Atlantic. It was Matra, a Loyalist member of the *Endeavor*'s crew when Captain Cook discovered and explored Australia's east coast in 1770, who first proposed settling his people in this "New Holland"; but it was typical of Governmental apathy that "Delay dragged gently on" and that before any action was taken, the outcasts had settled in Nova Scotia. "Things often settle themselves," the authors remark, "if you take no notice." This left the South Pacific open to the transportation of convicts; that they were ultimately sent, however, was less a result of constructive planning than of its lack: a clearcut example of inertia being "so negative in its essence that it became a force." There was no principle involved; even the harshness of the times was, the authors feel, a product of "moral inertia, not of fanatical righteousness."[6]

The reasons for the choice of the middle-aged undistinguished Captain Arthur Phillip, R.N., as Captain-General of the expedition to New South Wales and Governor of the new settlement to be established there are not altogether clear, but

If Sydney [Lord Sydney of the Home Office] chose Phillip because he thought him a man of mediocrity and complaisance suited to the undertaking, who would, under the vaguest orders, play the part of one of the contractors under the Act, he was very much mistaken in his man.

Phillip was a man of outstanding ability, an unusual man in his own or any day. He had that steadiness of mind that can embrace the most trivial detail without losing sight of the main issues; he had imaginative grasp allied with the most uncompromising common sense; he was completely honest. Lord Sydney met a granite wall of competence under his Captain-General's quiet exterior. In the months that followed his appointment he forged not only the practical details but the theory of the undertaking. He conceived a "Colony of Disgracefuls" as an empire. Out of the Government's indifference—its will that did not extend beyond the riddance of troublesome subjects and some vague commercial aspirations—he forged something positive. He took a criminal folly and made of it a reputable and enduring settlement.... Phillip lifted the whole conception on to a new basis; he transcended the whole drift of his times and made in theory first, in practice after, of his project something that was not intended by all the powers that had charge of it. Their indifference was Phillip's opportunity.[7]

Many of his plans didn't work; he adapted as necessary, and "was able to hold through every vicissitude his belief in New South Wales as a free country, a land of redemption, an Empire with a splendid future."[8]

Phillip was a most fortunate if largely fortuitous choice—the only first-rate piece of equipment, it appears, in the entire First Fleet. The eleven ships, collected somewhat at random, had a total tonnage of less than four thousand to carry nearly a thousand people and their supplies on a trip halfway round the world to an unexplored destination. Some were such poor sailers as to slow down the entire fleet. All were inadequately equipped. Despite Phillip's repeated postponements in the interest of supplies, the expedition left without clothing for the women convicts, ammunition for the accompanying marines, or even records of the convicts.

Yet the expedition, more than eight months en route, lost only 1 of 212 marines, only 24 of 775 convicts,[9] a far better record than some later transports achieved. The explanation lay in Phillip's good management. But as Captain-General of the expedition, Phillip as a naval man was in his element; now, as Governor of the new settlement, he had to learn as he went along. "Phillip's difficulties were overwhelming. There were the difficulties inherent in the country, the difficulties inherent in his colonizing material, and the difficulties forced on him by Government."[10] All of these are presented in convincing and fascinating detail.

As for the first, "The new country met the settlers, not with dangers, but with privations and discomforts—a deep but unobtrusive resistance."[11] As for the Government, Phillip was sometimes restricted by his orders as well as instructed by them, and his voluminous reports met with little understanding or response. As for his colonists, the Marines stood on their military

dignity when asked to help with the settling in and disrupted
the community with their constant quarrels. But the big problem was of course the convicts. Phillip had asked for able men,
largely artisans, for this First Fleet; official apathy had provided
him with "the aged, the infirm, the untrained, and the inedu-
cable scum of the streets."[12]

Over all the other problems of a new settlement and tending
to warp or obscure them, in those early years, was the struggle
for survival with its consequent pressure to steal. Phillip rigor-
ously dealt out the same rations to soldier and convict alike.
"But it was not injustice or inequality that drove men to steal;
it was hunger, absolute and unqualified."[13] This fact inevitably
shaped the concept of justice in the community. "On the one side
was hunger, gnawing and desperate. On the other, the urgent
need of society to be protected from itself, to save some future
from the ravening maw of the present." Thus death became the
penalty for a petty food theft, while the rape of an eight-year-old
girl merited only exile to Norfolk Island. In this "We see justice
conceived as a social, not an individual act. . . . Justice was in
the making under new conditions."[14]

As history, *Phillip of Australia* offers thorough research in primary materials, well-documented, clearly organized, thoughtfully
interpreted. In style it is easily recognizable as Barnard-Eldershaw's by the reader of their fiction. Although a work of research
rather than imagination, it includes something of the enlighten-
ing descriptions, the illuminating observations, the subtle irony
that one has learned to admire in the novels. At the beginning of
Chapter II, "Settlement," the voyage having ended, the authors
interpose before the disembarkation a five-page section (obviously, and unfortunately, too long to quote) on the new-old
continent that no one in the First Fleet had set eyes on before.
As a description of the landscape of Australia, a presentation of
its problems, and an evocation of its spirit, this ranks with the
best of such writing that either M. Barnard Eldershaw or Barnard has done, and at their best it would be difficult indeed
to find anyone who surpasses them.

There are flashes of the familiar irony, as in Captain Hunter's
discovery that the Governor at Teneriffe (a stop enroute) was
pleasant and polite—"with an Englishman's surprise at a for-
eigner's virtue";[15] in the parenthetical comment on Phillip's

ardent wish for more artisans among the convicts: "Unhappily, the skilled tradesmen got into gaol less frequently than the useless vagabonds";[16] and in this later reflection: "Convicts are not as a body remarkable for their self-control; otherwise a great many of them would not be convicts. Long coercion must have robbed most of these convicts of what they originally had. Self-restraint is a quite unnecessary trait when there is no free will."[17]

Irony abounds in the account of that grumbling, self-centered man of God, Chaplain Johnson, who brought out a library of four thousand volumes of religious works to lend to the convicts, many of whom could not read. At anchor in Rio, "The Reverend Richard Johnson preached in the *Lady Penrhyn* on the text 'They that go down to the sea in ships'—a mild and benevolent choice as something minatory out of Revelation was more in his line."[18] A happier choice surely than the one for his famous first service on Australian soil when, for a truly captive audience, ostracized probably forever from home and set down forcibly in the middle of an unpromising wilderness, "The text chosen, without benefit of humour, was 'What shall I render unto the Lord for all his benefits towards me?' "[19] It is Johnson who, asked by the Select Committee on Transportation in its famous investigation of 1812 whether the colony produced reformation in its convict inhabitants, "made the somewhat professional and interested reply: 'I think that if a clergyman were sent to the country with a proper salary, a great deal of good might be done.' "[20]

We have already noted the clarity of the basic organization of the book—its departure from the chronological, after the Proem and the first three chapters, in the interests of another logicality that is easier to follow. Other departures are made, as one might expect from good fiction writers, for suspense. We are told, long before the settlement suspects it, that it will be an incredible two-and-a-half years from the first landing before a combination of accident and apathy relaxes its grip long enough to let any more supplies arrive from England. We are also given some warning, as the passengers are not, that their new land will resemble not the famous Rio they had enjoyed so much on the way out, but the relatively forbidding Cape, where "they were brought face to face, whether they knew it or not, with the recalcitrant quality of the new world they were going to colonize, and where, like a single ominous stroke on a bell, they saw in action those cruelties which developed where one section of the community is subject and helpless."[21]

To anyone with the mildest interest in Australian history, *Phillip of Australia* makes enthralling reading. Only occasionally do the details quoted from various sources pour in too thickly to be completely integrated. For the most part they are kept firmly under control of the authors' theme and purpose.

II   The Life and Times of Captain John Piper

Writing to Nettie Palmer late in June 1938, Marjorie Barnard spoke of her friend's admitted hoarding of letters as "reprehensible"—a facetious remark that gave her an opening to discuss the new Barnard-Eldershaw literary project, a second history.

I speak as one who knows for I am at present engaged in a struggle with the Piper Correspondence, three huge volumes of it, in no sort of order, and all sorts of crabbed or spidery handwritings. I don't suppose Captain Piper ever threw away a letter, I don't suppose there was a wastebasket in his house. Half the documents don't mean a thing when they have been quarried out. The reason for this industry is the Australian Limited Editions Society. They have commissioned us to make them a book from original resources on the life of Captain John Piper. He arrived here four years after the foundation of the settlement and his youngest daughter died in 1905—what a span. He was an entirely amiable gentleman who knew everyone and never did any harm in the world—just went bankrupt every now and then. Nothing in himself but interesting as a focal point. I really must do some hard thinking about the soft Captain P. . . . Was very glad to get the commission as I don't seem able to come at any creative work and Teenie is too busy with a thousand things to drag me bodily into it.[22]

This project was remarkable for several reasons even before its appearance a year later as *The Life and Times of Captain John Piper* (1939) in a format so magnificent as to be both admired and regretted by its researcher. It was its authors' first big commission, and as such a gratifying recognition by the editors of these limited editions of the soundness of *Phillip of Australia,* which with all its virtues had had a rather half-hearted reception by the public a few months before. Moreover, it was a tribute to the style in which *Phillip* was written, for sound is as important as sense when the words are to be immortalized on handmade paper bound in full calf, and no footnote addict of a historian could be expected to turn the trick. And finally, it would be the first MBE book to be published in Australia (the first of general interest, that is; *Essays in Australian Fiction,* reluctantly published by the Melbourne University Press earlier in the year after agonizing delays, was a work of literary criticism little known or read). By October the manuscript was ready to be revised and typed; by the beginning of November it had been sent to the printer. The whole enterprise had been completed in less than six months, in keeping with its major writer's belief that such projects do not, like fruitcake and whisky, improve with age.

To Vance Palmer Marjorie wrote in one of her inimitable similies: "I feel the usual depression that comes at the end of a book. What, in any case, is the good of writing for a limited edition? The printing and the binding overlie the book like a sow her piglets. No one cares what the book is about, it's only published for collectors and connoisseurs of fine printing."[23] This "usual depression" disappeared shortly, dispelled by the excitement of yet another commission (p. 108). But had it persisted, it would surely have dissipated like a morning fog before the brilliance of the finished book that was finally put into her hands some sixteen months later. Early in 1940 she was able to report, with an obvious gratification marred by only one reservation,

"The Life and Times of Captain Piper" has arrived in all its glory. It really is sumptuous in maroon calf (a calf to every three volumes which is wicked), handmade Dutch paper, decorations by Adrien Feint and a very attractive lucid type. It is an exceedingly handsome job [which no one can yet deny] and we are sad to think that our friends, at the price, are very unlikely to see it. The printer, Ben Waite, has taken a year to spread himself and is very puffed up about it.[24]

She modestly doesn't add that the contents did the format justice—that the text was worthy to stand alone, minus all these bookmakers' embellishments. It is a pity that it has never had the chance—never been reprinted in more available form and numbers, as Marjorie's own later book on Macquarie for the same Society was to be, repeatedly. *Piper,* with only 350 signed copies, remains a very scarce collectors' item.

In content the book is briefer than *Phillip,* broader in scope but with less depth of treatment. The bibliography is no less impressively primary than before, and quoted passages are frequent; but the authors move more freely, the atmosphere is less scholarly, the style more relaxed and personal.

The choice of Captain Piper, a historical unknown compared to Governor Phillip, as a subject for a reasonably full-length study requires some explanation. Piper came out to Australia as an Ensign of nineteen in Major Francis Grose's New South Wales Corps—a group that certainly gathered no great glory to its name. He held numerous military and civil posts throughout his life but cut a greater figure, it appears, in Sydney's growing society. Why, then, honor him? Less because of his singularity than his typicality, less for the accomplishments of his life than for its length. Reaching Australia in 1792, Piper remained there until his death in 1851 at age 78. Thus his adult life, like that of Elizabeth Macarthur (p. 94), one of his early intimates, covered the first critical sixty years of Australian history, "a period of miraculous growth and change," in circumstance from bare existence to the Gold Rush, in geography from Sydney Cove to the broad plains beyond the long-uncrossed Blue Mountains. "His life transcends its own bounds because he was an emblem of his times," the authors state in their foreword; and then, putting it analogically, "He gives the measure of an epoch just as the little figure in the corner of a drawing shows its scale."[25]

In *Phillip* the major problem was subsistence; in *Piper* it had become acquisition. Of the first colonizers, only the convicts, in despair, "looked upon themselves as permanent inhabitants";[26] for the rest it was "a hasty gathering of gold and silver before flight," for they

saw the Colony as a Lady Bountiful; they assumed that their act of grace in landing on her shores should and would be rewarded automatically, that civilization was a seed that once planted in this grateful soil would grow by magic into a tree bearing golden apples. There were men, pleasant and blameless in themselves, who believed they had a right to the whole contents of the cornucopia by virtue of their race, their class, the accumulated civilization of their fore-

fathers, the might of the British navy and other extraneous circumstances independent of any personal effort. Captain John Piper was
the doyen of these dreamers.... He was the hero of a romance
that did not exist.[27]

Piper being a more pervading figure in his "Life and Times"
than Phillip in the "Account of the Settlement," his story is presented as a simple chronology. Three headings suffice to en-
compass his career. "Tattoo" covers his experiences while a member of the N.S.W. Corps; "Carnival" his social and economic
success in Sydney; and "Pastorale" his removal to Bathhurst after
the decline of his fortunes.

After what is casually dismissed as "a tedious voyage" aboard
the transport *Pitt*, Ensign Piper reached the new land. His approach to Australia gives the authors the opportunity for one
of those moving descriptions of the Australian continent that
they do so well:

For days, or weeks if the winds were contrary, the great curve of
the continent hung, an anonymous entity on the port bow, like the
shoulder of a dead leviathan thrust out of the sea. Now it was a
grey smear on the horizon, now brown headlands and dark escarp-
ments caught between the glittering blue of the Pacific and the
flawless blue of midsummer skies, white rocks like snow, dark thick
vegetation, never a sign of life, opaque and blank. The white cottage
on South Head, where watch was kept, was the first human habitation
seen since Cape Town. Entering Port Jackson was like passing
through the grey rind of the continent into another world. Beyond
the ancient sea-bitten headlands the sunken valley of the harbour
carved the land into a long, many-branched estuary, safe from
anything the sea or wind could do. On the port side the land rose
to a steep ridge, bay followed bay in endless variety and succession,
each with its crescent of sand, the water shading out from crystal
through green to blue, patched with purple where the reedy rocks
lay in the shallows. On the headlands the trees grew down to the
laughing water. To starboard the land opened out into wider bays
and deeper indentations stretching out of sight, and the land, thickly
timbered, rose more gradually. It was six miles in a westerly direction
to the anchorage in the cove, past small tight green islands and the
bare rock called Pinchgut, where prisoners were occasionally sent
to contemplate their sins on a diet of bread and water, an exile
within an exile, past low sandy country and a reedy bay where the
colonists cut rushes for their thatches, to a squarish bay scooped

out of a headland that fell away on either side in a succession of anchorages.

The little settlement lay within the arms of the cove.[28]

The modern traveler who is fortunate enough to approach southeastern Australia by ship will find the entrance and the harbor little changed. But in 1792 the little settlement where now the great city of Sydney flings its red-tiled roofs across the enclosing hills "still looked, four years after the foundation, like a temporary encampment."[29] Far from following the blueprint of Phillip's dream of a dignified city called Albion, the place "had been wholly shaped by necessity."[30] But it was settled, was shaped. By the time the *Pitt* arrived, "a sail was still a major event," but "Women no longer wept in the streets, nor did men, speechless with emotion, clasp one another by the hand, as when the first ship of the second fleet was sighted"[31] two years before.

The worst was over. Out of Phillip's boundless strength and courage, and despite his poor human material, his mortifying lack of supplies, a colony had been firmly established—and now lay awaiting exploitation by Ensign Piper's Corps. It had not long to wait. Before the necessities were unloaded, the master of the *Pitt* cleared £4,000 by selling (with Phillip's reluctant approval) merchandise that he had brought as a speculation. "The whole quality and tone of life in Australia was changed in a few weeks," for Major Grose, not only head of the newly arrived Corps but now Lieutenant-Governor of New South Wales, had "accepted a current heresy handed down from the Spanish conquerors of the Americas, that a colony was a natural source of unearned wealth and an appropriate field for unlimited privilege."[32] One could hardly expect a twenty-year-old ensign to disagree with his commanding officer.

Piper was stationed at Norfolk Island during the worst of the struggle between the Corps and Governor Bligh that culminated in the Rum Rebellion, but he naturally sided with the Corps. For one thing, he had become an intimate of "the most forceful man in the colony," John McArthur, whose attractive home "would almost appear to him as proof of the essential rightness of John McArthur's policies."[33] When in 1810 the Corps was relieved, Piper, now a captain, chose to resign and remain. Although it had not yet greatly enriched him personally, he cast his lot with the new world. End "Tattoo," begin "Carnival."

By this time "Australia was already making money, but like a beehive was being systematically robbed."[34] Now, however, Macquarie was Governor, with specific orders to end the abuses of the "Rum Corps" who by trade monopolies had, during the two decades since Phillip's departure, been doing the robbing. This Macquarie set out to do by favoring as a class the convicts who had completed their sentences to become free men, "for only from among these men at that time could an owning class with a permanent stake in the country be raised up." The emancipists "were the tourniquet which he applied to stop the gold hemorrhage."[35]

Yet for Piper it was only now that the gold began to flow. Never having had much means or talent for the machinations of the Corps, he returned from a home leave in 1814 to a good civil job with the Government, thus expediently becoming a Governor's man against the old New South Wales aristocracy. On Point Piper, renamed for him when he was given a grant for a permanent official residence there, he erected "the finest mansion in Sydney with one of the finest views in the world."[36] He survived the recall of Macquarie and his replacement by Brisbane, and through grant and purchase came to own so much property, to do so much entertaining in the grand style, that he was aptly called by one of his admiring friends "the Prince of Australia." His golden age lasted twelve years.

Piper had prospered under Macquarie, flourished under Brisbane; in 1826, with the coming of Darling, he rapidly declined. He had sadly overreached himself, both as manager of his own affairs and as chairman of the directors of the Bank of New South Wales. Forced to liquidate in a time of falling values, he found that his property, "so easily acquired," had to be sacrificed. Failing in a suicide attempt over his mismanagement of public affairs, he was dismissed "from the service that he had always looked on as a prerogative rather than as a duty."[37] End "Carnival," enter "Pastorale."

Our interest in Piper, throughout, is less with his life than his times. Overshadowing his personal fortunes and misfortunes in those early years of the nineteenth century is the enormous geographic expansion of the colony. For the ruined Piper there chanced to be the saving grace of a two-thousand-acre grant in the Bathurst area (which had now been settled for more than a decade), and to it in 1857, aged 54, he moved his household. "Crossing the mountains Captain Piper was marching west with progress. Circumstance had made him follow the trend of life: when the military caste held sway he was a soldier; when Macquarie changed the military colony into a civil state he was a civil officer; as the great pastoral age dawned he set his face westward and became a pioneer."[38]

He spent three years building his homestead at Alloway Bank, where life "is a curiously unreal world looked at from the perspective of almost a century. It floats like a transparency over the eternal plains. . . . Australia was not allowed to deflect these girls [Piper's daughters] by one jot from the genteel fiction of a young lady's life originating in an England they had never seen. They lived a fiction and their parents lived a fiction."[39] In fact, they entertained governors. But Piper, with his openhandedness and his poor business sense, managed to get into financial trouble again even in the good years, the 1830's; in the bad, the 1840's, he failed. The "house" he had built, unlike James Hyde's, lay in financial ruin.

But he was not alone. His role is still that of the typical, not the singular, for there was a serious general depression. A young country, Australia was to be restored. But for an old man, John Piper, there was no recovery. A pity, for he had already lived three lives in the history of his adopted land: soldier, officeholder, pastoral pioneer; no doubt the Gold Rush would have provided a welcome further adventure had he survived.

If Piper himself, for all his amiability, his generosity, even his honesty, is not a heroic figure, it is that he was chosen for the role not of hero but of, within the narrow limits of his time and his circle, Everyman. Of his life is made a thread on which are strung the otherwise scattered events of Australia's first half century; his personal participation in the three major occupations in the colony during his lifetime gives form and interest to bare historical fact.

Although much of *Piper* is a study in human pretension, it is related with little of the authors' favorite tool, irony. It is as though the amiability of their central character has moved the authors themselves to an unwonted gentleness, and their attitude is less caustic than perceptive. The New South Wales Corps learns "the monotony of garrison duty where there is no enemy and no relaxation,"[40] and even in the social life centered on Norfolk Island, at Government House there were "always the same guests, the same dearth of ladies, the same topics of conversation."[41] The neat turn of phrase is not missing: Phillip "denied his officers privilege as he denied the convicts license,"[42] and he segregated his flock "as much to save the convicts from the marines and their rum ration as the marines from the convicts."[43] There is no waste of words when Piper's character and course of action are summed up as his "amiable extravagance."[44]

The book as a whole is most notable for its descriptive power. All cooking was done outdoors in the early settlement, and "when the evening meal was prepared, Sydney glowed with five hundred points of light, the dark land starred like the sky above it."[45] Explorers repeatedly attempting to scale the Blue Mountains were "turned back by a silence and loneliness that penetrated the last walls of the spirit."[46] However romantic Piper's view of life, the authors see beneath to the reality; in the 20's the rich river flats of the Hawkesbury were an Eden of plenty, "But however idyllic the Hawkesbury looked, horror and menace were not far away, the blood-stained triangles and the fear of floods."[47] And Port Macquarie, a convict settlement for secondary punishment, was "a great clot of misery and bitterness . . . outside the moral law."[48]

Conspicuous always is the authors' awareness of the land. This is reflected in a description of the Piper homestead at Alloway Bank that has the added virtue of doing for the unique quality of Australian light what her painters long despaired of:

It stood on a hill overlooking the river flats, a wide gentle view of undulating land almost treeless where the colours flowed under the grass season by season and light painted the great canvas anew every hour. In the middle distance, to the right there rose one steep little hill, flat topped, thickly timbered, dark and romantic on the pale-coloured plain—Stewart's Mount. Another, higher, called Bald Hill, was bare and almost lost in the swimming light. The plain was rimmed by mountains always blue but changing from one shade deeper than the sky to slate and from frail evanescence to stark permanence. Alloway Bank stood well back in this big shallow bowl with three-quarters of the plain stretched out in front. Everything that stirred upon the plain was visible from the house, the flash of the sun on a gentleman's carriage, the twinkling of gig wheels, horsemen riding across the paddocks, bullock teams on the red roads, the coming and going at Ranken's mill on the river, coloured dots that were grazing cattle. At night the darkness and the silence seemed to stretch away for ever.[49]

Both MBE and MB often expressed and defended the opinion that history is a creative art.[50] *The Life and Times of Captain John Piper* is, in content as well as format, artists' history.

III My Australia

While *Piper* was still being beautified by printer Ben Waite, another gratifying commission appeared, this time from England. Jarrolds of London asked the Misses Barnard and Eldershaw to do a book on Australia for a series which already included volumes on England, Ireland, Wales, and Scotland—a "free essay" of about eighty thousand words. When this new offer was dropped into the mailbox, the depression suffered when *Piper* was finished a couple of months before flew right out of the window. On New Year's Eve, 1938, Marjorie wrote to Vance Palmer a letter that reveals not only her reaction to the offer but also her place in the collaboration and her dedicated but diffident attitude toward her craft:

I know after Piper I swore I'd see myself in hell before I took another commission but this—this stirs me to the backbone. I held my breath till Teenie decided and yesterday cabled acceptance. The snag is the time, the publisher wants the ms. by June. I've offered August. I'll have three weeks thinking it over and then I'll drown myself in it. I'm a little afraid telling you about this, feel my excitement break in foam against your steadiness, realize it's a job to which I haven't much right, not the right of knowledge or major accomplishment and in the interest of the job itself should perhaps have turned it down.[51]

Part of her diffidence arose, no doubt, from an Australian's recognition of the importance of having her native land well represented in a series otherwise devoted to the homeland, the British Isles. Part of her excitement as certainly sprang from the honor of having received the offer; part of it was as unquestionably her habitual response to the challenge of a new writing task. Yet another part, we can guess, may have been less obvious even to herself but no less real—a sense of being respectably saved, for another few months, from facing up to the more creative work for which she had resigned her job nearly four years earlier—from the short stories that she was intermittently struggling with, from the novel that she felt she should be gestating.

Immediately after the new year began, she went back to "reading steadily at the Mitchell"[52] for the new book. By the end of March it had been blocked out into the four parts (no simple chronological pattern this time) of which it was finally composed: (1) the new world (Australia as a field of social experiment; (2) the old world (the earth and its indigenous products; (3) the dispossessed (the aboriginals); and (4) towards an Australian culture. By the middle of April the writing had begun. By late August, with it well out of her hands, Marjorie was suffering from the doubts that always grew with the work. "Our book is within a couple of weeks of publication. The thought of it gives me a feeling of guilt and distress."[53]

Neither emotion was called for; the book was excellent, and so successful that a second cheaper edition was published in 1943, and a new and revised one in 1951 to bring the work up to date after World War II. The editors of a routine series must have been gratified to open a manuscript whose first chapter began:

Australia has a short history and a long legend. The last continent to be discovered, it had long hung, insubstantial as a wreath of cloud, on the horizon of man's imagination. In the south, the cartographers said, there must be a land mass to balance Europe and Asia in the north, else the world would lose its equilibrium. So, abhorring a vacuum, they drew in whatever shapes pleased them. Up across the broken bridge of the East Indies to Cathay and India and at last to the Mediterranean, carried on the lips of sailors and travellers, there must have come some faint breath of the reality, for at Rome in A.D. 150 Lucian was talking of marsupials—animals who "use their bellies for pockets." In a legend of a legend Ulysses sailed to the South Land and in the history of Chaldea there are traces of a voyage.[54]

This beginning—information clarified by succinct analysis and enriched by lyrical overtones—is well sustained throughout the book. That imagination will illumine fact is indicated by the appearance before the first chapter, even before the Prologue, of Marjorie's four-page "A Mask of Australia for Inaudible

Voices" which had earlier appeared in the magazine *Home*.[55] In it, in the dawn, "The Continent speaks with many voices, sometimes singly, sometimes in chorus, out of its infinite variety,"[56] voices that detail poetically the varied and changeless beauty of this land—its hidden mineral wealth, its animals, birds, insects. The Chorus of the Trees adds its note for the flora. Then the Herald of the Future asks about man, and a sleeping black man rises, backed by his shadowy Past and shadowy Future. His Past remembers the white Asian ancestry that he has forgotten; his future foretells his conquest by white men to come. The black man listens as incredulously as does the Continent when the Herald of the Future details its imminent conquest as well. "I have conquered one race. I shall conquer another," the Continent asserts. But the Herald replies, "They will come to you at last in love and humbleness. They will learn of you and follow in your ways. You will conquer them, but not by force. They will love and honour and serve you. They will take your strength and secret power, and raise it to another plane. You will be a hearth and a home to a new race."[57] And the sun rises on the scene of Captain Phillip's taking formal possession of the land with a hoisted flag and a fired salute. As the authors put it so well later in the book, "The process of the conquest of the white race by Australia had begun."[58]

This mask strikes a poetic note that will be well sustained in *My Australia;* the Prologue that follows promises the clear vision and the keen analysis of Australia that we have found in the earlier histories. It opens:

> Obscured neither by the holy dust of antiquity nor by irrelevant pageantry, the movements of Australian history through its brief century and a half are clearly articulated. It is pre-eminently a social history jointed upon economic issues. Rum, wool, gold succeeded one another as key commodities and, in a widening world, the claims of labour became the crux of Australian political life. Like the pillars of Hercules, the two great issues of Markets and the Standard of Living flank this modern story.[59]

This paragraph summarizes the first third of the book, the "New World," which is a brief, readable history of Australia—social, economic, and finally political—from the undiscovered continent to the time of writing. It is a masterpiece of condensation and clarity, a tribute like *Phillip* to the creative minds which could deal analytically with great masses of fact without becoming dull. The authors trace in turn the effects on Australia's inception of three distant revolutions: the American, which led to England's founding a convict colony there; the French, which distracted her from her original plan for a peasant community of small landowners and permitted the Rum Corps to fatten on the ruin of Phillip's work; and the Industrial, which allowed big investors to profit by England's need for Australia's raw materials. They trace too the pattern of the three oligarchies (Rum Corps, pastoralists, and financiers) which have existed within the two periods of experimentation into which they found Australian history to fall: experiment from without (from the founding of the colony to the discovery of gold in 1850), when various schemes proposed for her failed; and from within (from 1850 to and overrunning the Great War of 1914), when her own schemes for herself largely succeeded.

Most illuminating are the writers' analyses of the enormous changes in Australian life that were the effects (direct and indirect) of that inner phenomenon, the Gold Rush; of a much later but only slightly lesser watershed in Australian history, the outer phenomenon which was to become known as World War I; of the "main lines of the terrestrial conflict" for the settlers: water (its scarcity), distance (its immensity), vegetation (the abundance of the many-specied eucalypts and the "pyrrhic victory" gained over them by ringbarking).[60] But the most telling analysis of all is that of a more elusive subject—the Australian character. Here is the penultimate paragraph of *My Australia*:

Circumstance and history have fostered independence in the Australian character—but independence of action rather than of thought. Versatility in practical affairs, handiness on a large scale, willingness to experiment in anything from taking down an engine to setting up new machinery of government, independence of the individual within the consent of the group seem to be national qualities. We produce men of action, be they artists, aviators, cricketers, engineers, politicians, not philosophers nor theoreticians. We have contributed much to practice in many spheres, but little to theory. Distances and the slow earth have made us tolerant and, in a way, sluggish, sluggish certainly where we are not involved, have bred a sardonic humour and a natural distrust of the garrulous.

Quick to change, but slow to revolution, we have been impatient in a peaceful sort of way. The seasons have kept us sober. A good standard of living, a free-and-easy mode of manners, a nation-wide passion for sport, have kept the people together. Misfits tend to go elsewhere. Misfits unhappily include many people of outstanding ability. We export brains. The solidarity of the population in the past has tended to make it stolid—except when it is a question of sport—and the man or woman of specialized capacities is apt to find no public or too narrow a sphere at home, so promptly quits it. Many Australians have distinguished themselves in the great world. Their loss makes the future more difficult and the population the poorer. While brains leak away it is difficult to build up a public opinion which will make Australia appreciative of its brains. It is nearer to being the Paradise of the average man, but it sets that average high.[61]

This picture of the "Australian genius," still valid, was especially remarkable in its time for its honest objectivity, its lack of either an intellectual's prejudice or an Australian's chauvinism.

Being written as a timely guide, *My Australia* has of course not proved timeless (as the accounts of Phillip's and Piper's long completed times are) in either the original or the revised edition. The history of the opening "New World" third of the book remains valid; it is the later and larger of the book's two major sections, "Old World," that has suffered from the passing of a third of a century. In this second section chronological treatment is abandoned for the spatial and the topical. First the continent itself is presented in detail in an east-west movement. Most of the material on the country itself is still sound, but many details of the capital cities have naturally been outdated by the intervening years. There is still too much truth, however, in the frank admission that "The hapless ugliness of an Australian township [town] has to be seen to be believed . . . it has nothing to do with poverty except of the imagination."[62]

The authors may often be unhappy over what Australians have done to their country, but they are as always at their inspired best in describing the continent itself. When the first white settlers finally got beyond the coasts in the nineteenth century, they found that "The untouched interior stretched as far as the imagination could reach, wild, rough country most of it, well grassed after rains, brown and bare in the dry spells, a silence that was continent-wide, blue skies, the fairest on earth, light dry air, distances piled on distances."[63] The native flora and fauna come in for detailed attention, for "Australia is a wonder book that is only half read."[64] Imports are discussed also: undesirable ones like rabbits, starlings, prickly pear; desirable ones like sheep, cattle, horses (in whose honor two full pages are quoted from their friend Frank Davison's *The Wells of Beersheba* (p. 153). For areas that the authors do not know personally, they quote freely from what as literary critics they were to designate as "the landscape writers." Considering the variety of sources from which the authors' knowledge of the continent must have come, it is remarkable that they were able to mold them all into so consistently readable a whole. Even statistics come to life in their telling.

The excellent section on "The Dispossessed" (the aborigines) is not invalidated by the fact that many of the areas of the life of these "First People" have seen improvement since, and that the lowering birthrate the authors decry has taken a sharp jump upward. It is still profoundly true of the early settlers that as white men they

did not stop to think that the black man held, not in his mind perhaps, but in his habits and instincts, the key to the strange locked continent on whose doors they were battering; the aborigine knew it as flora and fauna knew it, he was a tree that felt and spoke. It entered their heads that they might teach him something, but that they might learn from him, never. . . . He was the possible link between the new-comer and the earth, but he was disregarded and dispossessed.[65]

The final section of the book, "Towards an Australian Culture," is particularly illuminating. It begins with a generalized discussion of why the English culture that the settlers brought with them could not suffice. "Culture is a very perishable commodity. It cannot be transplanted, for it must have one foot in the soil and the other in the spirit of the race. . . . We have what we carry in our blood, the past that had been kneaded into us, but for the present and future it becomes not an end but an influence. Art and letters produced overseas can never again give full satisfaction to the Australian."[66] Imitations of the English produced in Australia did not suffice; true Australian culture originated with the bushman, whose life was closest to the new

earth. One of the results is that "To this day Australian culture
has remained very largely a matter of individual, not communal
effort."[67] Thus architecture and drama, which require cooperation
and capital, have done poorly; painting and literature, both individual efforts, well. Capsule histories of these two arts follow.
In a discussion of contemporary Australian novels Barnard and
Eldershaw modestly omit all of theirs, but they do include "our
own *Phillip of Australia*" as one piece of evidence that "the
serious historical book" is on the increase,[68] and in an appended
"Short Selected Bibliography" they list, among a dozen Australian novels, their *Plaque with Laurel,* a revealing choice.

The Palmers, on whose judgment both Marjorie and Flora
heavily relied, liked *My Australia* well enough to wire their congratulations, whereas the authors had been steeled for their
"very patent disappointment."[69] But even after Douglas Stewart's
"pious review" of the book in the *Bulletin,* Marjorie is "still not
happy. I *know* the thin places, even if I've had the craft to
camouflage them."[70] They weren't apparent to the reading public,
however; the booksellers' stocks of the book disappeared in a
single day. Friends joined the authors in a congratulatory party,
and Vance Palmer spoke so kindly of the book on his Sunday
radio broadcast that Marjorie "Felt a sort of bulging in my
imagination as I listened. This book seems to have got away from
us, to be something totally different now from what it was when
we finished it."[71] They can hardly be blamed for enjoying the
sweet taste of success again, having known so little of it after
their first novel. It had been ten years since *A House Is Built* had
taught them its savor.

CHAPTER 6

The Histories—MB

I Macquarie's World

WHEN Marjorie Barnard freed herself from steady employment in 1935, she indicated that apart from the novel and the critical essays that the collaboration was working on at that time, she expected to strike out on her own. The first full-length work published under her name alone did not appear for a half-dozen years. It was *Macquarie's World* (1941), another history.

This, thanks to the quality of *Piper*, was another commission from the Australian Limited Editions Society. Why, after producing three substantial historical studies in three years, the collaboration was abandoned for this fourth, we can only guess. It appears that Marjorie had done most of the research, much of the writing, for the earlier books. Perhaps Flora had begun to lack the necessary interest, as she had always lacked the necessary time, or felt that she could not continue to take half the credit for a role that may have become increasingly advisory. She was still in Sydney at the time, and this was not yet the end of the collaboration; but it does indicate that Marjorie had gained enough self-confidence to strike out on her own.

She failed, however, to find the excitement in this book—in either prospect or preparation—that she had known in the earlier ones. Again we can only guess the cause. Perhaps she missed Flora's support, or found the period less congenial. Or as an essentially creative writer she may have begun to weary of the steady grind of research, or to feel the mental and physical strain at which she had been working (three substantial volumes in two years besides other lesser preoccupations). Certainly she had become increasingly exhausted spiritually, first by rumors of war, then by war itself. "It lays the mind waste to watch the concrete working out of that pitiless logic we grasped in the abstract a year ago," she wrote in mid-1940.[1]

It is at this time that we first hear of the new project in a letter to Vance Palmer, in which she admitted of it that "It will be good to be back in the Mitchell pretending that I'm doing something and going somewhere."[2] Three months later, to Nettie, "I'm still pushing Macquarie up hill. The book will have to be a roaring comedy. Nobody had a sense of humor apparently in those days with the result that it is the funniest page of history I ever turned."[3] By December she was writing that "I have come to the job with a very unwilling mind and the tedium of this first clerical part has nearly driven me mad."[4] But the research was done, the classifying was in process, and she was about ready to write. The trouble was, as she admitted in January, that "After a long period of aridity I'm ready to write again, a book, but unfortunately not this Macquarie book."[5] Judging from the date, this would have been among the early birthpangs of the fifth MBE novel, *Tomorrow and Tomorrow* (pp. 64-65).

When in April 1941 *Macquarie's World* was finally finished, Marjorie's usual period of doubt was rather one of boredom. "I'm trying to scrape it off my mind. That sounds something like a furred tongue and that's just how I feel about it. Some day —maybe—the Australian Limited Editions Society will bring it out and divers people will pay £2.2 for its beautiful typography and nobody whose opinion I value will read it."[6] Even when the first copy reached her (an edition limited, like *Piper*, to 350 signed copies) she was disappointed. It was "beautifully printed and bound in grey cloth and maroon leather," but the illustrations (numerous full page drawings by Frank Medworth) were "the very scratchy kind with blobs of strident colour popped on just any where. The printer, Ben Waite, rings me up and we moan together softly over our ruined masterpiece."[7] It must have been comforting to the author later that while *Piper* remains to this day difficult of access in its faultless limited edition, *Macquarie* escaped through the kind offices of the Melbourne University Press of the wider world—in ordinary cloth in 1946 (with a second edition in 1949) and in paper in 1961, the offensive illustrations replaced in all of these larger MUP editions with maps and line drawings by Douglas Annand, who had illustrated some of her earlier work in the magazine *Home*. As late as 1971 it appeared yet again in hard covers, republished by Sydney's Angus & Robertson.

.

In organizing her material, Marjorie largely abandoned the chronological for the topical, as had been done in *Phillip*, using even more chapters (Macquarie's world, a later one, being more complex): Two for the place (town and bush), four for the people (convicts, officers, settlers and traders, aborigines). But with a novelist's sense of the dramatic she inverted the remaining chronology so that the first chapter, "The Exile," pictures Macquarie's departure, a defeat that the remainder of the book sets out to explain.

The author had shown so little enthusiasm for this book in the making that we might expect to find the quality of the writing affected, but it isn't. There has been no falling off from the previous books in breadth of concept, clarity of organization, sensitivity of understanding, or beauty of style. We have to look at the title page to remind ourselves that this is the work of Barnard, not of Barnard and Eldershaw.

The setting is strictly limited to Macquarie's antipodean world: in space, Sydney and the widening settlements spreading out from it; in time, from his landing in 1810 to assume the governorship to his reluctant departure a dozen years later. Of his past we are told little save that his appointment was something of an accident, owing to his having been second in command of the Australia-bound 73rd Regiment when his commanding officer, the governor-designate, fell ill. Of his future we are told nothing at all—a fact that one reviewer of the book complained of, since it leaves us with no inkling of such vindication as Macquarie found in England. Only by implication do we learn of the Rum Rebellion itself—the uprising of the N.S.W. Corps officers against the preceding governor, Bligh. All of these limitations serve the purpose of concentrating our full attention on the character of the new governor, the problems he faced, and his successes and failures in shaping his new world.

During the research for *Piper* Marjorie had written to Nettie Palmer, "I know the Sydney of the 1820's better than I know the Sydney of today."[8] Now she strips off another decade and reveals the town of the 1810's to us, street by street and building by building. Her fascination remains for an area that she and Flora had already used briefly (and as of later dates) in their first two novels, "the tumble of fortuitous and dilapidated cabins called the Rocks."

Liberty as perverse as the Black Mass reigned there. It was a human jungle, every second house a tavern, licensed or unlicensed, haunt of sailors, haven of runaway convicts. Huts and houses were built at all angles, finding such lodgment as they could on the rocky terrain, lanes wound between them, tumbling down steps from level to level, running to ground in dark culs-de-sac. Unlighted, undrained, unpatrolled, this was a dark and tortuous patch upon the plain and open town.[9]

But there were brighter spots, such as the Government Domain, a "gentle natural wilderness" that Mrs. Macquarie enjoyed, and gardens full of English flowers, for "homesickness makes gardeners."[10]

In this "kept city" (a drain which the Colonial Office increasingly resented), "society, though small, had as many circles as Dante's Inferno."[11] Wealth rather than birth was important ("Only convicts brought their pasts with them from England"), even though the sources of the wealth (rum, trading monopolies) were questionable. "Freedom was a cloak that covered many sins," and "The presence of a subject people [the convicts] ... heightened every man's opinion of himself and gave him by contrast a most pleasing illusion of immaculacy."[12] An emancipist (a freed convict) might become rich but he couldn't be accepted socially.

Sydney was "a seething place of opportunity and despair" following no clear-cut policy for long.

Phillip conceived it as a future town owned and controlled entirely by Government, the necessary nucleus of a hinterland cut up into neat little farms owned by a reformed, grateful and self-supporting peasantry. The New South Wales Corps turned it into a fortress of private privilege, a brigand's tower from which the country-side could be marauded and then held. Macquarie gathered it back into the hands of Government and began to mould it to his own ideas of elegance and use ... The three outlooks, Phillip's, the Corps', and Macquarie's, co-existed. Phillip's view, modified, was now that of the Colonial Office. The Corps was gone, but its heirs, the Pure Merinos, the exclusionists, the Old Hands, continued tenaciously to hold their ideal of a free field for privilege. All three, the Colonial Office, the Old Hands, Macquarie, looked on Sydney and simultaneously said, "Mine."[13]

The "bush" was a far larger area than the town, and growing. In 1813, during Macquarie's governorship, the Blue Mountains, which had hitherto limited the settlement to a narrow coastal strip, were finally crossed. Two years later a road was built, opening the way to the vast unknown interior of the Australian continent. But "The story of the New Country is not Macquarie's story at all. It comes into this narrative only as a knocking on the door."[14] Fortunately, for Macquarie would have found it an unsatisfactory part of his world. Partly his commendable desire to encourage the emancipists, partly his love of neatness and order, led him to prefer the modest, docile farmers to the powerful, wide-ranging pastoralists.

New South Wales had never been a classless society; the First Fleet was sharply divided into two groups, the ruling military and the ruled convicts, whom even Phillip had learned to segregate. These two continued into Macquarie's world, save that the military was now joined by numerous civil officers. There was a growing judiciary to prescribe and enforce the English law, directors of the all-important Commissary, medical men, chaplains, and others. "The civil service was a curious hotch-potch of confusion. It was made up almost entirely of irregularities."[15] There were problems of pay, problems of perquisites, problems of jurisdiction, problems of outside loyalties—and most of all, problems of privilege. "It was Macquarie's business to clear up both the iniquity and the muddle. He proceeded to the best of his ability, and by means of proclamations and general orders to do so. He did not completely succeed; the thing was too ingrained and universal."[16]

The author makes no attempt to paint these ruling officials, civil or military, in any brighter colors than the record provides. However, her picture of the ruled, the convicts, is a more cheerful one than we are accustomed to. The fiction of these early times naturally dramatized the brutality of both the system and the men: brutal lashings from the masters and brutal retaliations from the slaves. Here is stressed the hopeful side of the picture, all the more promising when held up for comparison with what life would have been for many of these victims of the transportation system had they remained victims of English society instead.

When Phillip arrived with the first two groups of rulers and ruled to start taking over the Australian continent, he found a third, the aborigines, already in possession. Marjorie has been accused of being a little hard on Macquarie in this book, but she makes clear his limitation here. When of an evening he sometimes went across the great harbor to watch a corroboree, "He saw nothing but the artless caperings of the childlike savage in those rites so old and deep in the blood that the men who danced them and were stirred by them had forgotten their explicit meaning centuries ago."[17] His good will and love of order led to attempts to educate their children, settle their adults, but when these failed he laid it to ingratitude, and tried no more. He was not the first Englishman in Australia who failed to recognize that the cultural gap between the two people was too wide to be bridged quickly by even the best intentions.

Three of the classes to whom Marjorie devotes chapters—officers, convicts, and aborigines—were commonplaces in Phillip's world, now a quarter of a century gone. Others, lumped under "Settlers and Traders," were Macquarie's special problems. With her usual care in classification, the author presents four groups of settlers. The first were the gentlemen, a class divided into two subclasses: the Old Hands, officers of the N.S.W. Corps who had known privilege so early that they felt themselves to be a kind of aristocracy, and men of wealth more recently arrived and bent on getting wealthier. The second main group were free but poor men who came out as immigrants and received small grants for their trouble. The third were the emancipists, who received less. From these two had sprung the fourth, the "cornstalks," the first generation of native-born white Australians, who were just beginning to come of age during Macquarie's regime.[18] The gentlemen settlers were the graziers, whom Macquarie distrusted ("they had broken his predecessors, three of them").[19] The emancipists, with their lesser grants, were necessarily farmers; it was these who had suffered discrimination and whom Macquarie was determined, not altogether unselfishly, to promote. The traders, too, were usually emancipists, and were Macquarie's main support (he had forced the officer class, both civil and military, out of this area).

These were the principal inhabitants of Macquarie's world.

Macquarie arrived on 1 January 1810 to take charge of the settlement; on 1 December 1821 Brisbane formally succeeded him as Governor. The author as exactly dates the moment of division between "Halcyon," the period of Macquarie's happy productivity, and "Storm," the period of his decline and defeat: 28 July 1814.

What had he accomplished in that first four-and-a-half years? He had fallen heir to the job by accident, as we have seen, with no administrative experience or expectations outside the hierarchy of the army. After an almost eight months' voyage out of England, he had arrived in Sydney empowered to dismiss the usurping government and revoke all its appointments and grants. He proceeded to clear away the effects of the Rum Rebellion. He put the colony on a sounder economic base, even establishing a bank in Sydney against the instructions of his superiors in London. He cut down on the number of licensed public houses, encouraged marriage and church attendance, established schools. But most conspicuously he changed the face of Sydney. Douglas Annand's maps in the end papers of the unlimited 1946 edition of the book—Sydney in 1811 at the front, Sydney in 1821 at the back—are worth a close comparative study; they might be called Macquarie's finest memorial. But even they do not tell the full tale of the streets improved, roads built, public buildings erected. The Governor was not a modest man, but it was no empty boast when he said, " 'I found New South Wales a gaol and left it a colony; I found a population of idle prisoners, paupers and paid officials, and left a large free community thriving in the produce of flocks and the labour of convicts.' "[20]

His decline was not, of course, a matter of a single day. The 28th day of July 1814 only marked the arrival in Sydney of the Judge of the Supreme Court, Jeffery Hart Bent. Bent was by no means the first man with whom Macquarie had failed to agree (he was too wrapped up in his concept of his own absolute power, we are told, to bother to be tactful); but it was Bent who became "the rallying point for every discontent in the Colony." More, he irritated Macquarie to the point where the Governor "had to offset the threats to his power by ever more high-handed expression of it."[21]

Bent was ultimately recalled, but there were others. Chaplain Samuel Marsden, for one, was a continual thorn. Macquarie, never able to take criticism, over-reacted to the discovery of a petition to the House of Commons, bearing a number of signatures, concerning his arbitrary manner of government, and he took prompt if illegal revenge. "It was a saturnalia of abuse."[22] It would be incorrect to say that complaints on both sides flew back and forth between Australia and England, for one of the great problems for all was the long weary months required for an exchange of communications. In 1817 Macquarie was crushed by a series of critical dispatches from Lord Bathurst. One related to Macquarie's extravagant building schemes, which had multiplied under convict architect Francis Greenway. "His building plans," the author believes, "were a form of compensation. They grew in magnitude in proportion as he was defeated on other fronts."[23] Others concerned themselves with the increasing numbers of complaints about Macquarie's governorship. The Governor's wounded reaction was to offer his resignation, which Lord Bathurst for the time disregarded.

But in 1819 Commissioner Bigge was sent out to look into the whole situation. The echoes of the thirteen-gun salute that welcomed him had scarcely died away before he and the Governor were at swords' points. When in 1820 Macquarie once more sent in his resignation, it was accepted, and at the end of 1821 the wheels of Government had ground him out a successor. In early 1822 Macquarie sailed to England. We have come full circle, back to the opening chapter "The Exile."

Marjorie lays not a little of Macquarie's defeat on his character: his lack of humor and tact, his vanity, his stubbornness, his passion for details and his confidence in the efficacy of yet more rules and regulations. But she also sees him as caught in a change of policy by the Colonial Office. The original notion of Australia had been of a dumping ground for criminals, which led to the vision of a community of peasant landholders who would become self-supporting. But "Wool had changed the status of the colony. Australia was too good to be wasted on a parcel of rogues. It could be a valuable source of raw material and the money earned by the export of wool would be spent buying British manufactures."[24] The small landholders were useless here; the concern for the emancipists, whom Macquarie had backed so strongly, disappeared. The landed gentry, once reprimanded and restrained in their pursuit of personal profit, must now be encouraged for the profit of the English. Macquarie was out of date.

One reviewer of *Macquarie's World* felt that Miss Barnard's "dispassionate scholarly objectiveness could not rid itself of something approximating to a subconscious antagonism for her chief character."[25] True, she showed no fondness for him, finding in him none of the greatness of Phillip nor the charm of Piper, but she did give him full credit for his accomplishments, and what credit she could find for his personality: "Here, clear to see, are the permanent strands of his character: the delight, sometimes beneficial, sometimes merely fussy, in reorganization; the impulse to tidy and docket; the will to favour but the inability to cooperate; the precipitancy; the patent honesty, good intentions and energy."[26]

II *Minor Historical Writing*

From the late 1930's on, Marjorie Barnard published a considerable number of minor books, commentaries, and articles on a variety of historical Australian subjects, mostly on commission now that her reputation as a writer of history was firmly established. One of the most charming is a capsule history first published in 1943 by Ure Smith, achieving a second edition (with some post-war revisions) in 1949 as the first of his Miniature Series. It is dedicated to Marjorie's great good friends John and Effie Tierney (he, the "Brian James" of Australian rural fiction), and opens with a poem "To the Australian People" by another writer she had come to know and admire greatly, Leonard Mann.

This little book was a reworking of "This Australia," an article of Marjorie's that had appeared in the *Home Annual* back in 1937. and included many of the original "decorations" by Douglas Annand. It must have been an easy research assignment for one of the authors of *My Australia*. Her chief task was to cut Australia's familiar history down to fit the size and spirit of an attractive little gift book (the first edition ran to only a few dozen generously decorated small pages of large print). "Australian history has a zodiac of its own,"[27] she announced, and proceeded to present her subject as a half-dozen periods, to each of which she assigned a dominant symbol. Thus the sign of the first five years (Phillip's regime) was the Cooking Pot, followed by the Rum Bottle, the Whale, the Golden Fleece (all self-explanatory), then the Mace (the long constitutional period) and the Sword (Australia's military involvement with the greater world from 1914 on). The sections are skillfully interlaced, an organic whole, and the beauty of the prose is sustained throughout. The result is *Australian Outline*.

Four years later Marjorie wrote the historical commentary for a large collection of excellent drawings, some in color, by Sydney Ure Smith, artist as well as publisher; these were issued in soft cover as *The Sydney Book* (1947). In even so small and secondary a role, her style never failed her. In the beginning "The austerity of the coast silently shouldered the little settlement into the one spot where it could hope to survive."[28] It was on "the untouched harbour—the brilliant living water trapped in the land, the shores dark with alien and monotonous trees, the little secret beaches, the silence, the foreign sky, the effulgent light."[29] There "For fifty years the face of the settlement was turned to the sea, in homesickness, in hope and in expectation of profit."[30]

Her commentary is entitled "Sydney: A Triptych." On the theory that every city is a palimpsest on which the past has been written in successive layers, she finds first Phillip's Sydney, of which only place names remain, since greedy private enterprise following his governorship had preferred building personal fortunes to erecting his hoped-for Albion; then Macquarie's Sydney, with new plans and enough accomplishments so that it still "lies buried, like a foundation stone, in the Sydney of today";[31] and finally Queen Victoria's Sydney, that which grew (Macquarie's being the last attempt to plan) when the means to build unfortunately arrived at a low ebb in Anglo-Saxon taste, leaving Victorian architecture predominating in an ornate gloom through which a few of Macquarie's simple Georgian relics still shine.

Commissions of this sort became more numerous (what other Australian writer with such a combination of historical knowledge and stylistic flair?). Some time after Marjorie had begun the research for her monumental *History* (p. 130), she did another small book on her native city, *Sydney, the Story of a City* (1956), for the Melbourne University Press—not so small as *The Sydney Book,* and this time with illustrations (mostly half-page or smaller reproductions of early drawings and later photographs) generous but subsidiary to the text. Like *Australian Outline* (except that this limited itself to the city that

that only started with), it covered the whole sweep of history from its beginning in 1788 to the time of writing. This stretch is neatly emphasized by the end papers, the front a drawing of Sydney Cove in 1788, the back a photograph from the air of "Sydney Today." Another enlivening feature is the heading of each of the eleven chronologically arranged chapters with one or two appropriate quotations: from that great mine of information the *Historical Records of Australia,* the Sydney *Morning Herald,* Anthony Trollope, and other sources old and new. Abandoning her usual excess of modesty, the author even uses two quotations of her own: one from *Australian Outline,* one from *Tomorrow and Tomorrow.*

A remarkable thing about these numerous historical works, large and small, put out over more than a quarter of a century, is that often as they cover the same ground, they never repeat themselves. The same facts, the same reflections even, are given a new fillip by refreshingly new expression. One sensitive to style quickly comes to recognize the Barnard hand, but through its continual freshness rather than its repetitions.

Three more small commissions appeared, like the huge *History,* in the early sixties, but required little additional research, only a fresh approach, since all involved Macquarie's long-familiar world. The first and last were of pamphlet form and size: *Australia's First Architect: Francis Greenway* (1961) for the Australian Landmarks series, and *Lachlan Macquarie* (1964) for the Great Australians. The latter is not just a greatly condensed version of *Macquarie's World;* it includes Macquarie's ancestry and early experience, as the book did not. It is the one Barnard production that one wouldn't easily recognize by its style; this is owing, presumably, less to the writer's exhaustion from the long labor of the long *History* than to the demands of the series editor for a kind of textbookish simplicity. Its thirty pages make an interesting comparison with the longer book in tone. Of the first crossing of the Blue Mountains we read, in the *World,* in the lyric prose that flows so naturally from the Barnard pen, "it was the silence of the ridges that proved the worst obstacle. It closed in about the little party like water, it struck upon their hearts like fear."[32] In the same material in *Lachlan Macquarie* only a glimmer remains: "Lack of water and of fodder for the horses were

serious handicaps, but the silence that brooded over the untouched bush put an even greater strain on the party."[33]

Much the most elegantly garbed of all these minor commissions is Max DuPain's *Georgian Architecture in Australia* (1963).
This beautiful quarto, copyrighted by the National Trust of
Australia, grew out of the 1962 exhibition put on by its Women's
Committee with the title "No Time to Spare," emphasizing the
importance of saving what remains of the country's scant Georgian heritage. The striking photographs are DuPain's, the task of
writing brief social histories of the areas concerned (only New
South Wales and Tasmania were settled early enough to know
the Georgian influence) was turned over to Marjorie Barnard
and Daniel Thomas, respectively. To fully appreciate the Barnard
style, one has only to compare Marjorie's fulfillment of the
assignment with the knowledgeable but graceless paragraphs
of her co-author. She acknowledges with gratitude the loan of
research done by Miss Rachel Roxburgh (Georgian architecture
being a specialty beyond the easy command of a scholar of the
general history of the Macquarie period); but her use of the
loan is typically her own.

"History is the remembered past; old buildings are visible
history."[34] Here the palimpsest of *The Sydney Book* is read backward and in greater detail. "Behind the facade of modern Sydney
there are other submerged cities adding another dimension to
the present. If you peel back the years, you come on city after
city, Sydney in the building boom between the wars, the more
tranquil Edwardian city, Queen Victoria's Sydney, Macquarie's
Sydney, and at the bottom of the pack the last vestiges of
Phillip's Sydney."[35] She has only a dozen pages here in which
to pack the social history of New South Wales, but there is no
sense of haste or even compression. Instead, there is the mellow-
ness of a lifetime of confident artistry, as in her opening generalization:

> History is a creative art. Memory is fallible, interpretation an
> ever-changing spotlight, fashion and reaction powerful influences.
> Memorials in brick and stone, more limited, more exact in their
> implications, are less variable and less at the mercy of human
> frailties, other than neglect. These are scattered through our history
> marking here a public enterprise and there the life of a family.
> It is as if stones, like words that have lain a long time in the

language, absorb associations, gather lustre from a thousand suns, to become in the course of time more than stones, till even what was commonplace takes on to the eye of the beholder a new grace.[36]

In addition to these publications in book form, Marjorie occasionally contributed nonfiction as well as fiction to a number of Australian periodicals. Her most frequent outlet for both was that glossy family monthly *Home* which, as we have already seen (p. 81), carried many of her published short stories in the late 1930's and early 1940's. In *Home* appeared a number of her historical sketches, also, most of them during 1938. Editor Sydney Ure Smith had entertained at one time a grandiose plan for a Sesquicentennial issue that year which Marjorie was to have written almost entirely. Although the publishers cancelled it as too expensive, they did use a good deal of her material during that period of concentration on the nation's beginnings.

The first issue of the year, the cover of which carried a portrait of Captain Phillip and proclaimed "Australia's 150th Anniversary, 1788-1938," included her essay on the career and character of this "First Australian," about whom she had just written at book-length with Flora and whom she records here as one "who had all the virtues and none of the graces."[37] A single later issue carried two of her contributions: a beautifully produced first appearance of the dramatic "A Mask of Australia," which was to reappear the following year as an introduction to the book *My Australia* (p. 108); and "Prelude to History" which, beginning "History is far more than the lives of great men," summarizes the 150 years of Australia's past in order to raise questions about her future. Notable here is her paragraph on the deep inner meaning of the word *bush* as used in her native land to denote the interior:

Bush means something to the Australian that no other word can mean. It belittles a vastness, is full of dry familiarity, covers a whole world of sights and sounds and scents, efforts and triumphs. It means to us perhaps more than any other word in the language. A small, dull stab of a word, it sums up the peculiar quality of our national pride. Without parade, it is almost a secret word, a password, a sign.[38]

The most substantial Barnard contribution to *Home* was "Historic Muster" (ultimately subtitled "Personages of Austra-

lian History who have contributed to the making of the nation").
This feature, which ran through nine consecutive monthly
issues,[39] was made up of thumbnail biographies (many with
photographs) of several dozen prominent Australians from various periods, areas, and vocations. It is strange to find among
them only one woman—Elizabeth Macarthur, whose career MBE
celebrated the same year in *The Peaceful Army* (p. 94); Caroline Chisholm, to the hastiest glance, looms larger than some
of the men that appear toward the bottom of the barrel.[40] At
first sight it seems strange too that no creative writers are included, but this omission is somewhat rectified by the appearance in the *Home Annual* of the same year of a Barnard article
"Pen and Brush," which celebrates ten early authors—five poets
and five writers of fiction—but again no women. (Among the
dozen artists one—Adelaide Ironside—was included, although
she became an expatriate at age 24.)

The last two installments of "Historic Muster" do leave the
numerous statesmen and explorers for such groups as printers,
editors, journalists, churchmen, men of learning. This last cate-
gory gives a devoted student an opportunity to pay tribute
to her old professor, George Arnold Wood, as the exemplar of
"Scholarship—new style."

> George Arnold Wood, sometime Challis Professor of History at
> the University of Sydney, was an Englishman by birth, an Australian
> by conviction, a sound scholar, a Liberal to the marrow, a teacher
> whose sympathy with and understanding of youth made him a great
> spiritual force in the university. He never divorced scholarship from
> life. To him the future was even more important than the past.
> In him the homely virtues were raised to their highest. He was
> husband, father, citizen, friend. He had the moral courage to face
> obloquy for a principle. Life could not bribe nor intimidate him.
> He was quietly steadfast in a simple goodness that nothing could
> wear away. His life was a benison, and the tragedy of his death a
> cruel weal across the face of life.[41]

That this concludes with one of the very few overwritten lines
in all the poetic Barnard prose may be owing to and excused by
the depth of the genuine feeling behind it.

To one interested in literature as well as history, "Vice-Regal
Guests" ranks with "A Mask of Australia" as the most creative
of these numerous contributions to *Home* during 1938. Both

owe a debt to Marjorie's interest in fantasy, which was to flower in the story "Dry Spell" (p. 88) and the novel *Tomorrow and Tomorrow* (p. 64). The subtitle here is "Being a record of proceedings at an official phantom gathering in Sydney during the recent celebrations." No invitations had been issued to the early discoverers of the continent—Malay, Spanish, Portuguese, Dutch—but in a great amphitheatre beside the harbor are seated, in chronological order following discoverer Captain Cook and his botanist shipmate, Joseph Banks, all of Australia's governors, notably the first dozen of New South Wales. Their conversations and their memories constitute a very human if slight review of the first eighty years of that colony and the men who controlled it. Cook chats with Banks about his own later death in Hawaii; Hunter, who gave so much, got so little, sits brooding over the past; Bligh boasts to King of his handling of the Rum Corps; Macquarie is "glad they hadn't invited Bigge" (p. 122); Bourke reflects thoughtfully to Gibbs that the Self-Government Act of 1842 was the "beginning of real autonomy and the beginning of the end of our power," while their successors Fitzroy and Denison quarrel over which of *them* brought in the new order. Phillip saw them all: his successors, the governors of New South Wales and of the other states and the Commonwealth, as the performance began, and "The pageant of Australia unwound before their eyes."[42] This minor drama prepares us for the excellent MBE "The Watch on the Headland" (p. 90) several years later.

Marjorie also published occasionally in *Australia, National Journal*, another of the Ure Smith productions, and several small things of hers were anthologized in the *Australia Week-end Books* edited from it by Smith and Gwen Morton Spencer. The longest and most significant of these, "Parade of Women," also has a dramatic quality.[43] Nine dates from 1791 to 1940 head brief flashes purporting to come from sources that vary from diary, letter, and reminiscence to tombstone. These present a sampling of Australian history through the eyes of her women: a convict girl trying to escape; the wife of a Rum Corps officer revelling in their special privileges; a pastoralist's wife enjoying prosperity, suffering distance; an immigrant girl arriving under Caroline Chisholm's protective wing; pioneer women self-reliant through all trials; a woman whose devotion to her husband held her fast through World War I but dissipated before the even more catastrophic depression; and last, "voices of women" uttering, in the face of World War II, scattered remarks ranging from sublimity to ridiculousness. A journalistic *tour de force* but bearing the unmistakable marks of the historian-novelist's hand and brain that shaped it. Even when Marjorie Barnard turned out minor pieces, there was no let-down in the quality of her writing.

III   A History of Australia

For one who has always thought of herself as first a writer of fiction, Marjorie Barnard has devoted an amazing quantity of time and pages to history. If this has sometimes seemed a loss to her, a sacrifice of her creative energies to lesser projects, it has been a boon to Australian historical literature. In fiction she met with varying success; in history she has unfailingly achieved.

Her other historical works, major and minor, were but preludes to the monumental *A History of Australia,* which appeared in 1962 after years of research and writing; it is as though all that had gone before were rocks quarried for the construction of this final definitive tower, some eight years abuilding. The author might have said, as George Eliot did of her greatest effort, that she began it as a young woman, finished it as an old. For it started, I suppose, in Professor Wood's history lectures, or even earlier, perhaps—whenever she first became conscious of her love affair with Australia; when she finished it, she was sixty-five.

Marjorie Barnard has never spared herself. In mid-life she began to have warnings of what was to become a serious vision problem later. Yet she undertook this gigantic task in full knowledge of what it would cost—in sight, in time, in interruption of the more creative fiction to which she still aspired. The true measure of the labor involved in the *History* lies not in the book itself, physically massive as it is with its seven hundred large pages of fine print. It lies rather in the appended bibliography, sixteen pages full of sources both primary and secondary, with at least most of which we can be sure she had made herself thoroughly familiar (as witness the extensive array of reference notes at the end of each of the twenty-four chapters). The *His-*

torical Records of Australia alone cover an appalling number of shelves in the Mitchell Library. Then there were countless letters, diaries, and other documents to decipher. And (despite the several names she includes in her "Acknowledgements"), she worked virtually alone. By this time, mercifully, she had ceased to type her own finished copy for the publisher; but she still painstakingly handwrote the entire manuscript.

With the early years of Australia's history Marjorie was of course already reasonably familiar through her researches for the books on Phillip, Piper, and Macquarie. *My Australia* had covered the entire sweep—as far as the middle of the twentieth century in its revised edition. But that had been a relatively brief telling. Now the author goes back to the beginnings and the pre-beginnings: here the discovery of Australia starts not with Captain Cook but with the speculations of the early Greeks, Christians, and Arabs; the system of transportation not with 1788 but with 1597. Here the Gold Rush no longer begins with Hargraves's finds in 1851 but with a convict named Daley who in 1788, the first year of the settlement, "seeded" a clod of earth with some fragments of old gold—and was rewarded, when the hoax was discovered, with three hundred lashes instead of the pardon he had dreamed of.

No history, even of so young a nation as Australia, could be truly definitive, but this big volume is the closest to it that has yet appeared. Even so the author is necessarily torn between what to include, what to omit. She closes a long chapter on the land and its handling with the remark that "The full story of this belongs more to science and economics, but in any history of Australia a space must be kept for it, for it is vital to the history of the whole."[44] Space must of course be kept for the early explorers, too, but being a novelist at heart, she doesn't attempt to summarize the accomplishments of them all; instead she concentrates (in a chapter "Voyage in the Bush") on the career of Hamilton Hume. Hume she chose not because he was best known, certainly, but because his 1824-25 journey from Lake George to Port Phillip "is very closely woven into the general pattern of Australian life and history," and "had an interesting prelude and a tragi-comic codicil."[45] At the end of her detailed chapter on the depression and its consequent social experiments, she reminds us that "These are only a spot check on developments between the wars, they are representative, not definitive."[46]

She has an eye for the telling detail. An account of legal procedures in the young colony is illumined by this observation on a largely convict society: "Trial by jury was impossible for lack of jurors, since under English law a man once condemned could not sit on a jury."[47] Sometimes she piles detail upon detail very effectively. Of the building of Australia's railroads in the days before Federation, she writes:

There was no general plan even within a colony, and each colony existed as if in a vacuum. One result was . . . the break of gauge between the different colonies which has proved so harassing, particularly in war-time. New South Wales used the standard gauge of 4 feet 8½ inches, Victoria and South Australia the more comfortable one of 5 feet 3 inches, and Queensland a narrower one. [3 feet 6 inches, for economy. These facts were enough to prompt visiting Mark Twain's caustic remark on the apathy of the intellect that must have been responsible for them; but Marjorie continues with further damning evidence:] As if this were not enough, subsidiary lines in the same systems had different gauges. At one time South Australia could boast six different gauges, Victoria and New South Wales four each, Queensland three and Tasmania two.[48]

The organization of material in this comprehensive *History,* as in *Phillip* and *Macquarie,* is partly chronological, partly topical, pauses in the flow of time being made occasionally in order to explore at length a particular subject. Here the author explains and justifies her mixture of methods as dictated by the demands of the material:

History cannot be written, without confusion, in strict chronological order. . . . The historian, in his search for the modicum of truth allowed him by the circumstance of handling something in continual flux, must be given a certain latitude. Some threads of the narrative, as for instance the history of the savings-bank movement in Australia, are best followed from beginning to end at one time, other and larger phases must be followed through until they reach a natural pause, to be picked up again later in a different context. In a word, the historian must handle his material as he sees fit and that will rarely be arbitrarily.[49]

Actually the best chapters in the book are the topical, where one subject is studied at some length: those on "The Dark

People" (the aborigines), the explorer Hume, and "The System: a Retrospect"—an account of the entire program of transportation and treatment of convicts, which ultimately (in the mid-nineteenth century) ended in a whimper. These and others could be read with profit and pleasure as separate essays, but they serve their larger purpose of giving depth to the whole.

The entire book is to be credited not only for its multitude of particulars but for its broad generalizations. It opens with a memorable statement of the crux of Australia's peculiar situation: "If you would read history, and most particularly Australian history, study your atlas, for in the long run geography maketh man. It presents him with gifts and problems, and his history is the story of how he takes advantage of the one and grapples with the other; it moulds his way of life."[50] We have seen earlier how much was added to *Phillip* by the initial perspective which explains Australia's beginnings not just against the broader background of England but as part of the eighteenth century. Here the chapter on Australia's discovery begins:

> Now for a little while we must cast our net over a great ocean and a long period of time. It is a matter of perspective. In writing or reading the history of Australia, or of any other country for that matter, it is easier and simpler to look on it as individual and separated from the rest of the world, as if it were a short story complete in itself and not only a chapter in a long and ever growing volume. Any such limited outlook would lead to distortion. It is not enough to say that Australia was discovered by Captain Cook in 1770. The finding of Australia was part of a pattern of world expansion, an integral part of the exploration of the Pacific, and it is a story that goes back a long way in time.[51]

With her, we go too.

Australia is the country in which the visitor is far less often asked, "How do you like Australia?" than "Don't you love it?" Marjorie is aware of the pitfalls in the path of one writing a history of his native land. In a discussion of recent developments toward the close of the book, she begins: "This is a subject that the wary historian approaches with caution. It would be so easy, and with the best will in the world, to write advertising copy, to point to successes and ignore failures and muddles." But honesty forces her to add, "There have been plenty of all three," and to distribute her attention among them.[52]

Despite her breadth of vision, Marjorie Barnard is unmistakably Australian in many of her points of view. Her analysis of the reasons behind what she calls their "unfortunately named" White Australian Policy (the instrument mainly responsible for federation) shows her usual clarity: added to eugenic considerations, the triple fears of racial problems, a lowered standard of living, and even extermination. This last she bends over backward to discuss objectively, but she naturally views with alarm the increasing militant and nationalistic populations in the area of Australia:

> The threat from the Near North of infiltration, of conquest, of annihilation, is a fact. The atlas proclaims it. It is not so much a moral, political, or economic issue as a matter of geography. We are their Near South, we are at a different, but not necessarily superior, stage of development. We not unnaturally want to retain our own traditions. Our pride and our European outlook forbid a compromise or a sharing. This is not a moral judgment but a statement of fact.[53]

Yet when she comes to the aboriginal problem, she feels that "The mixing of bloods and that alone can bridge the gap between the Stone Age and the present."[54] With no regret at all, apparently, for the loss of a discrete race, no understanding that some, at least, of the aborigines have pride too and "not unnaturally" want to maintain *their* traditions, their identity, she closes her discussion with the suggestion that "The most practical thing that those who criticize native policy could do would be to marry an aboriginal, bring up their half-caste children to marry white again, and so assist nature's remedy of assimilation."[55] All this with no discernible note of irony.

The appearance of *A History of Australia* did not meet with universal acclaim. There were undoubtedly some professional historians who resented that this comprehensive work had been turned over to an essentially "creative" writer instead of to one of their own number. There were others capable of pointing out errors in the book—almost inevitable in handling such masses of material. (Angus and Robertson, Sydney publishers who had commissioned the book, brought out a second edition the year after publication, making corrections possible; it has been reprinted regularly since.) But if the professionals might have done a more accurate job, would it have been as readable? Would the road finally built to connect Alice Springs and Darwin have been described as "a military road at perpetual attention, straight as a ramrod"?[56] Marjorie was historian enough to be skeptical of her sources. She warns:

> Students of Australian history must guard against the natural mistake of believing that reforms and panaceas outlined by governors and others came into operation as planned. The *Historical Records of Australia,* whilst probably the soundest source of information, still put a formal gloze on the situation that really existed. They are sometimes no more than a record of good intentions and rational thinking. The colony was not famous for its rationality. There were so many interested parties pulling in opposite directions, so much undisguised human nature and no very strong tradition. The over-all pattern tended to be chaotic.[57]

It must be admitted of *A History* that the style is not as consistently excellent as that of the earlier shorter works; no wonder, with so much territory to cover, such masses of fact to be marshalled, so much impersonal detail to be included. There is a tendency in places to the too short sentence and the too short paragraph of some of the other later Barnard writing. This usually occurs here where the matter is dull with fact; as she herself remarked, "Dates and figures make bony reading."[58] But often she breaks out in her familiar best, as in this analogy with which she opens her account of Hume's explorations:

> The bush was like the sea, a rooted, tideless sea. It presented to the first settlers the same anonymity, wild and strange. Its dangers, more passive, were just as real. It closed like water over those who penetrated it. It went on and on across a continent as unlimited as an ocean. A specialized knowledge was needed to navigate it, but it could not be learnt at a marine college.[59]

Marjorie manages to get in a good word for her own profession, writing frankly in a brief "Envoi" of "literature rather than of painting or of any of the other arts, because I know more about it."[60] Even here, however, she doesn't "write advertising copy" (p. 133). Earlier, discussing among other social experiments the origin and functions of the Commonwealth Literary Fund, she concluded that its most important aspect was "the public assertion that the writer is of value to the community."[61]

Those who deny the existence of an Australian literature (and it is shocking how many Australians still do, or at least express surprise on hearing that there is one) must in consequence, she affirmed, deny the existence of an Australian nation. She repeated here her theory of the folklore origins of the native literature—a theory mentioned in *My Australia* and expanded on, as we shall see, in several of her critical works. But she admits freely that for the first hundred years of the less than two hundred years of Australian history, "there was no Australian literature, only writing in Australia."[62]

She might have reminded us of how exact that hundred-year figure is. For the *Bulletin*, that extraordinary periodical to which she gives extensive credit for having been the first to foster "not only native material, but the vernacular,"[63] began publication in 1888—exactly a century after Phillip landed, from the dozen ships of the First Fleet, his fifteen hundred convicts and marines —the momentous beginning event in any "History of Australia."

CHAPTER 7

Criticism–MBE

I Early Critical Writing

IN any literature, particularly a youthful one like Australia's, many writers play more than one role: pinch a novelist and you will hear a poet squeal—or likelier, a short story writer or a critic. Barnard and Eldershaw wrote no poetry, published very few short stories, but their experience in planning novels and bringing them to completion inevitably armed and inspired them to do battle on the critical front. Before their natal year as collaborators was out, they had published a substantial pair of expository pieces in a Sydney newspaper, both bearing on the type of novel that had so suddenly made their pseudonym something to conjure with. From that time on, they contributed considerable nourishment to the sadly ill-fed corpus of Australian literary criticism. The culmination was their *Essays in Australian Fiction* (1938), not only one of the earliest collections of its kind to appear in Australia but still one of few, still admired, still often referred to and quoted from.

How the essentially creative mind, working subjectively by inspiration, by intuition, through particularization can also function successfully in so disparate an activity as criticism is always a source of wonderment, even though it often happens. The artist puts on his other hat (or perhaps turns inside out the one he has been wearing) and presto! he is now calm, objective, analytical, measured—ready to arrive intellectually at generalizations. Here are Barnard and Eldershaw beginning an essay on one of their contemporary novelists:

When the hardy critic lays an author's works upon the table in chronological order for the purpose of reviewing them, the first thing he looks for is movement. There may be development, progression, elaboration—or repetition. Development may be defined as growth in the organic sense, a maturing that is compatible with the most radical change so that the latest book may be as different yet as naturally evolved from the first as a frog from a tadpole. Progression is a more logical but less organic movement; it admits of change, but it is of a more specific order, a change that is literary and intellectual rather than personal and emotional. The difference between the first and the last will be no more than the difference between the child and the man. In elaboration the movement is slowed down, the growth is lateral. The author's talents show neither change nor increase, only increased elaboration. They are produced gradually to their logical conclusions. All that is in the last book was in the first, but in a more rudimentary form. Elaboration is the intelligent exploitation of the author's capacities by himself; it is lateral growth. The roots are unaffected, the original supplies neither increased nor diminished. Repetition is stationary; here is no development, progression or elaboration, only permutations of theme and style. The author has accepted a formula and sticks to it. This may come early or late in an author's career, from subjective or objective causes. If it comes early it is from inward poverty and an unwillingness to recognize that he is a one-book man; if it comes late it is the tragedy of a man who has outlived himself, the tragedy of impotence. Talents must grow in one way or another or cease. This is as workable a classification as one can get, I think. It comes near at least to the crux.[1]

Here is the logical, analytical, almost scientific mind at work. Here is objectivity—definition, classification, enumeration, cause and effect. The vividness of metaphor has yielded to the clarity of analogy. The authors' generalization complete, the specimen to be examined may now be anesthetized upon the table while they seek deductively to demonstrate its place in the diagrammatic scheme.

The competence and confidence revealed in that long quotation from their *Essays* had been built up through several years of apprenticeship to the trade of literary theorizing. Their first published articles, appearing in the Sydney *Morning Herald* late in their *annus mirabilis*, 1929, were obviously suggested if not actually commissioned by the nature of their best-seller. "The Period Novel, an Infinity of Problems" and "The Genetic Novel Has a Wide Field," each running in two weekly installments,[2] already indicate what more ambitious critical writing was later to confirm: that M. Barnard Eldershaw could think and write cogently as well as creatively.

The first examines the then current popularity of the period novel among both writers and readers. Causes and results are analyzed, definitions are advanced, telling phrases abound: the period novelist can give us romance unhindered by the disillusionment that in a modern setting "would hamper his tale, deflate his eloquence, and tarnish his magnificence."[3] Of the many appeals of this type of novel, the one that drew them to it was that "A period is a place where a writer can be alone with his characters." A passage analyzing their technique in *A House Is Built* closes with "A better foil for a story of growth than the pruderies and absurdities, the reticences and vanities of the Victorian era, could not be found."[4]

In the second of these articles the authors point out numerous contrasts between the episodic novel, a cross-section of life covering a few crowded hours, requiring invention, and the genetic novel, a linear section spread out over years, as *A House* was, requiring a sense of finality. "One of our reviewers," they confess, "after criticizing the end of *A House Is Built,* remarked philosophically, 'It had to end somewhere.'" They include an interesting sidelight on the story in its first appearance:

We had no intention of setting forth the quartermaster as the principal character. It was the *Bulletin* serial by its title [*The Quartermaster*] and excisions that did that. It is the rise and fall of the Hyde family as a complex unity that we tried to delineate. There is no hero or heroine. That one character receives more attention than another is due only to the natural inequality of man. Maud slips out of the narrative early, not because she was not a vital part of our plan, but because she was happy, and there is always less to be said about happy people.[5]

These two essays are interesting not only for the light they throw on the first Barnard-Eldershaw novel but as a sample of their early expository prose. The first starts out a little overlearnedly, as though its authors, literary unknowns who had only recently awakened to find themselves famous, were not yet entirely at ease in their new importance, but it picks up. The second is less successful than the first—less spontaneous and freeflowing, on the whole, more complex and studied. But the material in both shows the results of remarkably wide reading, the thought is clear and logical, and the illustrations are expressed with the sparkle, the caustic wit that stops just short of cruelty, which was to become almost a trademark of their style. Scott's kind of historical novel is described as "something between a moral lesson and a trip to the zoo"; Donn Byrne, a figure in the romantic revival, decorates his books with mannerisms that "show like tinsel in the cold light of the 20th century."[6] The genetic novel of cause and effect is dangerous because it is too facile—we can hear the pieces click as they fit together; in May Sinclair's novels "The click is positively deafening."[7]

Six months later (June 1930) at the 7th Annual Dinner of the Australian English Association in Sydney, the customary toast to Australian literature included mention of the fact that the most outstanding recent works in fiction were by women, two of whom were guests of the Association on this occasion—Miss Barnard and Miss Eldershaw. The builders of the *House* replied with appropriate expressions of their confidence in the future of Australian literature, Miss Eldershaw (as one would expect) first and at the greater length. The following year she was invited to deliver a major address to the organization, in 1935 a second, both of which we shall look at a little later because of their bearing on the published *Essays* (p. 144).

It was Flora, as the "shop window" of the pair, who nominally took on the early speaking engagements and editorial jobs, but we can be sure that the results were the work of the pair. It was Flora who in 1933 (after they had added a second faintly historical novel to their list) appeared before the prestigious Royal Australian Historical Society with a very penetrating address on "History as the Raw Material of Literature."[8] Here they find most Australian novels to be set in the present because the Australian past is not very satisfactory as literary material. Its brevity precludes the long vistas needed, and more important, contributes to the nation's lack of historic sense. With no violent divisions, no local wars, no invasions, no bitter wrongs, no lost provinces, no hereditary enemy to brood on, no historical monuments, the Australian isn't in the habit of looking backward (although the Royal Australian Historical Sociey, founded in 1901, they gracefully acknowledge as a beginning). The national past of social experiment and mass progress lends itself less well to the historical novelist than would spectacular deeds. Another century, they feel, may change the picture. (In the meantime we are reminded that in their final novel, *Tomorrow and Tomorrow*, they themselves gained the "long vista" required for perspective only by projecting themselves four centuries into a fantasied future.)

"The excitement of hunting facts . . . is certainly considerable," Flora read to the group, "but facts once caught and nailed, especially historic facts, are apt to be disappointing. The only thing to do with them is to stuff them with fancy and dispose them in as lifelike a pose as can be achieved."[9] Eye-witnesses, they feel, are most prejudiced. George Arnold Wood, whose two engrossing books *The Discovery of Australia* and *The Voyage of the Endeavor* had appeared in the previous decade, was surely in their devoted minds when they wrote that history is a creative art, for the historian creates history (in the light of his own personality and imagination) out of the jumble of events. The greater his creative powers, the more convincing his story. "Therefore the most credible historians are likely to be the least accurate."[10]

They decide that "Perhaps realism is normally a reaction to romanticism—the subject must be sugared first before it can be salted."[11] Barnard and Eldershaw certainly leaned more to salt than to sugar. The reading of history, they had earlier concluded, gives "an unparalleled vantage point for contemplating the irony of existence."[12] Among the numerous advantages they find in taking raw material from history, the last mentioned but certainly not the least in their consideration is that it affords such rich material for irony.

To these several reflections on history in literature, the two young critics were later to add some on geography that reached a wider audience. "The Landscape Writers" appeared in Australia's leading literary quarterly, *Meanjin*, in 1952 under Flora's name, but it was from MBE's common store of ideas and had actually been put into shape earlier by Marjorie. They take no credit for the title, adapted "from what has been called the 'landscape school of writing,'"[13] but this essay was to give the term a wide circulation. Their thesis is that "Geography maketh the man, for geography is his context, fashions his habits, postulates his necessities and out of his habits and necessities arise his reactions, historic and cultural." In Australia the settlers had to adjust to a strange new land, and "In one sense, the history of Australian literature is an account of our embodiment of the effect of geography, social and physical, upon literature."[14]

Australian literature began at the folk stage, they find, and the folklore element persists, for as fiction writers branched away from it, it found a new outlet through the landscape writers. These return to the soil, most of them to give travelers' accounts of the still undiscovered continent. Amazingly, "Their books in general, in number and popularity, eclipse all other forms of writing in Australia today. Even in the present difficult state of Australian publishing and writing, in its search for publication the descriptive book, almost alone, finds a ready response and audience"[15]—not always as a reward of merit, since many are badly written, but because "they give a romantic vision of a world with which many men secretly or openly want to identify themselves, the unique Australian world that is the possession and kingdom of our imagination. We, a small people, can say: 'We have this strange, this antique, still virgin world; it is ours.' "[16]

Numerous landscape writers are mentioned: R. B. Plowman, Myrtle White, Alan Marshall, George Farwell, Colin Simpson, Elyne Mitchell, William Hatfield; and for the aborigines, William Harney and scientists like Professor A. P. Elkin, Dr. Phyllis Kaberry, Ronald and Catherine Berndt. But the essay chooses two exemplars of the landscape's many to review in detail, with long quotations: *Hard Liberty* (1938) by Fred Blakeley, a bushman born and bred, and the now better-known *Flying Fox and Drifting Sand* (1947) by Francis Ratcliffe, an economic biologist from England, who "had Australia like a sort of beneficent malaria" and whose style improves in the report of his second visit as it "takes on a good coat of sunburn."[17]

It is unfortunate that at least one reprinting of this memorable Australian essay reproduces it only in part (without mention of the fact), omitting among others the final paragraph, in which enthusiasm for landscape writing is tempered by an important reservation made by two essentially creative writers:

Fed from many sources, history and folk lore, the love of the miraculous or the unknown, science, or just the workaday life moulded to the needs of the soil, the stream of landscape books flows on. There is much in them for which we are grateful, to bring us a deeper knowledge and understanding of Australian life, its difficulties and rewards. Our only danger in the present depression in Australian publishing is that the descriptive book may be accepted, not as tributary and source for truly creative work in which man and his environment can be completely fused and interpenetrated, but as substitute for it.[18]

As prominent members of the Australian literary community, the pair were called upon to undertake numerous editorial jobs. In 1936 the Fellowship of Australian Writers in Sydney put out an *Australian Writers' Annual*, about a hundred pages of stories, poems, essays, cartoons, and advertising. Flora was designated editor, and most of the active and prominent Australian writers of the day contributed, including Vance and Nettie Palmer, Frank Dalby Davison, Miles Franklin, Eleanor Dark, Mary Gilmore, Tom Inglis Moore, Henrietta Drake-Brockman, Kenneth Slessor, E. Dithmack, Myra Morris, even Will Lawson, also business manager for the enterprise. Modestly, the editor included nothing from MBE or her components; but presumably the editorial on "The Future of Australian Literature" comes from that joint pen. At this date they were still able to speak of their national literature as "so young," with a future that could be told only by looking at the literature of other countries and by Australian conditions.

Most revealing is their discussion of recent changes in the "overseas habit." "Until quite recently, if the novelist did not go to England himself, his novel at least must go, for local publication was almost impossible." This had bad results, since the English publishers didn't publish primarily for the Australian market. But times were changing. "Local publication, which is now within the reach of most competent and many incompetent writers," helps—lessens the English and American influence. In just the past couple of years, they found, many books from local presses, capable of serving as Australian models, had appeared (fiction writers such as Prichard, Palmer, and Davison, and essayist Murdoch), opening the future to whatever genius might appear on the Australian scene.[19]

We have already noted Flora's later editorship of *The Peaceful Army* for the Sesquicentennial (p. 94). Almost at the end of their collaborative career, Barnard and Eldershaw were assigned the privilege and labor of putting together the sixth volume of the then annual anthology of Australian short stories, *Coast to Coast 1946* (1947), the editorship of this series being

passed around among prominent writers and editors with a
special interest in this form. *Coast to Coast,* as Marjorie was to
say in reviewing a later volume, is not to be overlooked—"It has
an historic as well as an entertainment value."[20] Barnard and
Eldershaw were no strangers to the project, an MBE story having
appeared in the first volume, MB stories in four of the previous
five; but with their usual self-effacement they included nothing
of their own in this one, although to have done so would not
have been without editorial precedent.[21]

Their inclusion of stories by their special friends—Vance Palmer, Frank Dalby Davison, and Brian James—could not be criticized as personal partiality; not only were these men leading
short story writers who were already established "regulars" in
Coast to Coast, but all had excellent stories to contribute. Other
authors they chose were equally well established in the short
story: Dal Stivens, Douglas Stewart, Don Edwards, Alan Marshall, Gavin Casey. In a series that has tended to perpetuate the
same names from year to year, MBE perhaps deserve more credit
for having introduced three new ones that were to become
justifiably well known later: E. Gollschewsky, John Morrison,
Judah Waten. That the ratio of women authors to men is lower
than usual, in this volume, is remarkable, under editors who had
recently been extolling women novelists as such (p. 148). But
we don't know, of course, what their range of choice was;
Marjorie was later to write feelingly of *Coast to Coast's* change
from an annual to a biennial after 1948: "I know from experience that the editor has to dig and dig deeply to find enough
stories of worth to fill the volume."[22] Certainly the pair worked
hard at the job; their acknowledgments, like those of Vance Palmer in the 1944 issue, suggest more editorial eclecticism than
usual: less dependence on Sydney's *Bulletin,* more periodical
variety, including one story from the *Meat Workers' Journal* of
Victoria! On the whole, *Coast to Coast 1946* is a better-than-
average collection.

II   Essays in Australian Fiction

Among Flora Eldershaw's numerous public appearances as
spokesman for the pair, two papers she delivered to the Australian English Association in Sydney are important as the genesis

of their book of criticism, *Essays in Australian Fiction.* The first, in April 1931, was "Contemporary Australian Women Writers"— one of the many pieces that come from the shared store of M. Barnard Eldershaw, into which Barnard put more writing, out of which Eldershaw did more speaking. Here they examined only two women writers (the only ones, they confessed, that they had so far formed definite opinions about)—Henry Handel Richardson and Katharine Susannah Prichard. The paper is significant as a shift from the pair's earlier theorizing about literary types (p. 138) to the examination of particular authors and books.

In September 1935 Flora delivered a second address to the same group on "Australian Literature Society Medallists." (Again the voice was the voice of Flora, but the words were the words of M. Barnard Eldershaw—more food from the common larder.) Since 1928 this Melbourne Society had been awarding an annual gold medal to the most meritorious novel of the year. This M. Barnard Eldershaw thought to be the "highest honor available to the fiction writer in Australia";[23] they consequently felt the first half dozen winners to be suitable choices for a discussion of Australian fiction. Here is the list: 1928—*The Montforts*, Martin Mills (early pen name of Martin Boyd); 1929—*Ultima Thule*, Henry Handel Richardson (the final and most popular of the trilogy *The Fortunes of Richard Mahony*); 1930—*The Passage*, Vance Palmer; 1931—*Man-Shy*, Frank Davison; 1932—*Flesh in Armor*, Leonard Mann; 1933—*Pageant*, G. B. Lancaster. Their conclusion after a close look at these first six winners was that no "Australian type" emerged—a good omen, they felt, for Australia's literary future.

Before we turn to the *Essays*, the major MBE critical work, we should glance at the climate of literary criticism in which it appeared. Since a truly Australian literature cannot be said to have flowered until the late nineteenth century, it is inevitable than an adequate body of critical writing would be a much later bloom. Nettie Palmer's prize-winning essay *Australian Literature 1900-1923* (1924) was the first attempt to deal historically with the subject. In it she remarks that "Books of essays and criticism have seldom appeared, except through some accident of academic or journalistic affairs.... Hitherto much of the best of Australian criticism, original and constructive, has only appeared in fugitive form."[24] As late as 1945 poet Kenneth Slessor was still constrained to say, "The professional critic has not so far had an easy time of it in Australia. His position has been nebulous, his means of living by his work uncertain and sometimes impossible. There have been few periodicals willing to give space to him."[25] A decade later Miles Franklin bluntly asserted that "Volumes of criticism are unattractive commercial risks."[26]

It becomes obvious that when in the 1930's Barnard and Eldershaw settled down to the painstaking job of preparing a book of critical essays for publication, they were inspired by neither tradition nor the expectation of fame and fortune. But having long been thoughtful readers, dedicated writers, and loyal Australians, they felt compelled to give what recognition they could to modern Australian fiction, what guidance they could to the writers and readers of it.

The critic of Australian literature had seldom been more than a reviewer of books, and even in this "fugitive form" he suffered from a number of maladies. One was a lack of readers, for with Australian books far less highly regarded than English and American, the number of people who wanted to read about them was few indeed. Another was the problem of a critical standard: whether, with the native literature in its infancy, it was fair to judge it by universal criteria. The critic might incline to damn the book solely because it was home-grown, or to praise it to the skies for the same reason; whichever his bent, he was sure to find it hard not to be self-conscious. Then there was the question of personalities. The Australian population was small, the literary community infinitely smaller and generally close-knit, with the result that the critic found himself faced with the books of his friends, or enemies—a consequent temptation to personal prejudice. Even if he managed to maintain complete objectivity, his praise might annoy his fellow critic, his censure affront the author—both his intimates. This was the kind of atmosphere in which M. Barnard Eldershaw girded their respective loins to enter the lists. If they were unable to extricate themselves entirely from some of these critical dilemmas, the measure of their achievement is the degree to which they succeeded.

So many references have been made to Flora's fine critical mind that it would be easy, lacking other evidence, to assign to her the leading role in all these essays into criticism, but it would be error. Marjorie has done in her own name a good deal of book reviewing and other critical writing which is clearly of a piece with the work they published jointly. It is even likely, since the *Essays* were prepared for publication after she had full time for writing, that in them her hand was most often on the pen. The one thing we know is that the collaborative process for this volume of criticism was not, as for *A House Is Built*, a matter of assigning sections to each. All of the subjects were repeatedly thrashed out between the two. This was a kind of enterprise that lent itself more readily to collaboration, certainly, than the novel, the subject matter being admirably suited to mutual mulling and the form being a number of short analytical efforts rather than an organic, creative one.

Marjorie once referred to their hope of publishing this book as something conceived "in our innocence"; the original plan was certainly more ambitious than realistic. It included a dozen sections: individual works, the work of individual writers, groups like contemporary women novelists, general subjects like the convict in fiction, general types like travel books, fiction, the short story (labelled "doubtful"). The two final sections were to be "Perhaps something on prose" and "Something on critics and criticism."[27] Needless to say, the finished book had to fall far short of this grandiose scheme. The actual work of writing and assembling the essays was fraught with the usual competitions for the authors' time followed by the usual self-doubts. The nightmare of at last coming to terms with a publisher was extraordinary; there is no room here for a detailed recounting, which would be worthy to stand as a memorial to the problems of publishing in Australia at this time, particularly of publishing something as unpopular as literary criticism. Suffice to say that it was several years after the book was first conceived before it was finally and reluctantly published, with alterations both approved and unapproved by its authors, by the Melbourne University Press in 1938.

Essays in Australian Fiction is a slight volume (fewer than two hundred pages) of only seven essays—a combination of the subjects of Flora's two earlier lectures before the Australian English Association (p. 140), with some changes. One was the omission of G. B. Lancaster (Marjorie had been aggrieved by the choice of her *Pageant* as the ALS's 1933 medal winner); another, the addition of Eleanor Dark, who since Flora's lecture had won the medal not once but twice. Also added was Christina Stead, who had begun publishing in 1934 in a strange mood and manner that had attracted the attention of critics generally and that challenged these two in particular. The most important change, however, was in scope. Save for *The Montforts*, to which the discussion of Martin Boyd was still limited, the entire works of each novelist, not just his medal winner, were thoroughly examined. The final table of contents, then, was "Two Women Novelists" (Richardson and Prichard of the first lecture), Davison, Palmer, Mann, *The Montforts*, Stead, and Dark, in that order. At one point before publication Marjorie complained of their editor's insistently calling their units "chapters," implying a continuity that did not exist, since the seven essays are entirely independent studies. I shall therefore do them no injustice if I choose my own order for examining them.

In their first essay the critics were on notably safe ground; their conclusion that both Richardson and Prichard "have an assured place in the history of Australian literature" is still unarguable. Richardson had already established her international reputation and her canon; Prichard was only mid-career, but her later work did nothing to greatly change, certainly not to disappoint, this judgment of the mid-30's. The divergent geniuses of these two, the critics felt, had become the foundations of a new era, expatriate Richardson by "vindicating Australian fiction overseas," Western Australia's Prichard by "creating a style essentially Australian."[28]

Throughout the *Essays* the authors are most concerned with the aspects of fiction in which their own excels: character, background, style. Most of their attention to Richardson is devoted to *The Fortunes of Richard Mahony*, her greatest and her most Australian work. She wins marks from them here because "Her preoccupation is not with ideas, philosophical or literary, but with her characters." Equally to her credit (as to theirs) is the fact that there are no traces of sentimentality or romanticism in this trilogy—rather, irony. They do fault her for her depiction of the Australian background (which they themselves hymn so long and lovingly): "It is not the real Australia in its varied and subtle beauty that is drawn for us but an ugly and hostile waste."[29] Later, forced to admit that Richardson is no stylist, these two ardent admirers of style concede that "this is a definite advantage in a book so intensely introspective and emotional. As the story is told largely from within, most of the prose is in character and a great deal of it is in broken sentences, the shorthand of the mind."[30]

Several times in the *Essays* the authors suggest that comparison of one author with others is unworthy of the critic; fortunately they several times practice what they preach against. Otherwise we might not have this illuminating contrast between these two women novelists:

> To turn from Henry Handel Richardson to Katharine Susannah Prichard involves a re-orientation of the mind that almost amounts to dislocation. These two are so different as to be complementary. If Richardson stands for the universal in art, Prichard stands for the individual. Richardson is taken up with what life can do to man, Prichard with what man can do with life. The one is a pessimist and fatalist, the other an optimist who does not underrate the enemy; the one is humanitarian, the other socialist.[31]

This second half of the essay centers on the four novels Prichard published between 1921 and 1930—"definitely Australian," the author being "a specialist in background" who draws from her own experience of the opal fields (*Black Opal*, 1921), the timber getters' camp (*Working Bullocks*, 1926), station life (*Coonardoo*, 1929), even a traveling circus (*Haxby's Circus*, 1930). The authors like diagrammatic devices: "Richardson's novels arranged themselves in a crescendo, Prichard's fall into a circle"—a circle of qualities rather than quality, fortunately, the fourth marking a return to the kindliness of the first after the harshness of the second and the stark tragedy of the third. "Although in no sense a sequence, the qualities of the earlier novels knit together in *Haxby's Circus*. The comradeship of *Black Opal* unites the circus folk; the vitality of *Working Bullocks*, the will to go on and to live without repining, is their backbone, too; the fidelity of *Coonardoo* . . . is in Gina."[32] There is more of such description than of criticism. In fact, to turn (if I may paraphrase the MBE paragraph quoted above) from the Barnard-Eldershaw treatment of Richardson to that of Prichard involves a conviction that the quality of the critical writing has declined with the quality of the work criticized, although the critics somewhat redeem themselves in the following:

To say that Katharine Susannah Prichard is essentially an idealist is not to accuse her of sentimentality or of the least trace of didacticism. No one is less of a sentimentalist. The world of her books is harsh and hard, but it is not hopeless. Underneath lies faith in the courage and steadfastness of man. . . . Prichard's men and women cannot be destroyed utterly . . . because they have qualities indestructible by anything that life can do to them. The brave are never wholly conquered; they still have their valour.[33]

At the time the *Essays* were written, Leonard Mann, already past forty, had published only two of the novels that were to occupy him for the next quarter of a century. These Barnard and Eldershaw view with reservations but with a hopeful fascination. That *Flesh in Armour,* the medal-winner, didn't get the attention it deserved was, they felt, owing to a public taste sated with war books from overseas. They themselves find its value difficult to assess apart from its subject matter, but conclude that if the book is not great, it at least has moments of greatness.

It is a World War I "study in dimensions"—three: the Australian army in France, one platoon of infantry in a battalion in that army, and one individual in that platoon. The accomplishment of the book is summed up in a neat one-sentence paragraph so quotable that it has been quoted: "*Flesh in Armour* records the destruction of the individual, the disintegration of the battalion, but the triumph of the army."[34] This essay goes little beyond shape and synopsis, however. We are told how important is Mann's "effort to catch and portray the likeness of the Australian soldier overseas without resort to the conventional realism, romanticism or idealism,"[35] but we don't learn much about the means he did use. More than half of the few pages devoted to this book consist of quotations, several at page length but left unanalyzed.

Human Drift, a less notable book, gets better handling. A story of the nineteenth-century gold diggings, it is nonetheless akin to *Flesh in Armour,* the same qualities of character appearing in a similar set of circumstances. But the story is so slight that "One suspects that Mann wanted to write this book and invented a narrative at a later date as a concession to the novel's convention. The story did not come first and inspire the book."[36] To authors who both practiced and admired style in its finer ramifications, Mann emerged as "anything but a stylist in the conventional sense," but though they pause to brood over some extremely awkward constructions, they find excuses for him, as they had for Richardson. "Prose and subject-matter are closely amalgamated. The prose, like the theme, is in a state of undress; the manner is moulded unconsciously to the matter."[37]

This essay on Mann is one of their shortest. By far the longest are those devoted to two other male fiction writers, Vance Palmer and Frank Dalby Davison, who each get as much space as Richardson and Prichard together. These are the two that the critics knew best personally, a fact that raises the issue of the difficulty of complete critical objectivity in Australia's small literary community.[38] Not that Vance Palmer didn't deserve a lion's share. Then in his fifties, he had been writing and publishing steadily for a quarter of a century. That he should be included in the *Essays* was inevitable and just. That the essay about him should be generous in length was natural, since even a judicious selection (his own choices) left the critics nine volumes of fiction to examine in depth. But the tone of enthusiasm in their treatment seems to stem as much from the man as the works; if he was (and few could have denied him the title) the king of Australian letters, he apparently could do little wrong.

The microscopic examination they give his writing leads the critics into stretches of rare prolixity, such as the following description of his first slim book of slight sketches (*The World of Men*, 1915):

An attitude of life is implicit in them—the right of human beings to be themselves, the intrinsic interest of life apart from its trappings, a refusal to shape and decorate that arises out of confidence in his material, reticence that is a form of respect for life, a feeling for surfaces, the texture of events, and a recognition that all events are embedded in a background of living and working.[39]

This is not the critics at their clear, succinct best, but strained as though in an effort to do honor rather than justice. So, surely, is the judgment that one of these sketches "is *in embryo* [italics mine] as fine as anything Vance Palmer has done."[40] Forced to admit disappointment in the next book on their list (*Cronulla*, 1924), they state that it "does not round out the promise of the earlier book," without acknowledging that the fault can hardly

be lack of practice, since it came nine years and several undis-
cussed novels later. And even it is excused as "not so much a commonplace light novel as an essentially sincere piece of work
masquerading as a commonplace light novel."[41] A fine dis-
tinction, surely.

They find Palmer's novels falling into two phases, the first
(which ends with *The Passage*, 1930, the winner of both the
Bulletin prize and the ALS medal) consisting of four novels
which, while showing development, remain "conventional, both
in subject-matter and treatment."[42] (Though these are a prelude
of better things to come, it seems disproportionate to have spent
25 pages—more than half of this long essay—on them.) The second phase begins with *Daybreak* and *The Swayne Family* (both
1932), and again the analysis becomes overly minute, leading to
overwriting that repels, even loses, the reader. One analogy,
seeking to explain the ups and downs of the Swayne family by
likening the shape of the story to "a wave pattern, a trough between two waves,"[43] is developed at such length that it clarifies
less than it clutters. It is something of a relief to get our feet once
more on dry ground in an excellent discussion of Palmer's statement that his purpose in writing was to set down Australian
rhythms.[44]

My excuse for having stressed some of the obvious weaknesses
of this essay is that they are rare enough in the MBE canon to
be unpleasantly conspicuous; my guess, that they appear here
because, in appraising Palmer (a greater literary figure, perhaps, than writer), the critics were under the tension of trying to
give credit whether or not credit was always due.

Frank Dalby Davison merited inclusion in the *Essays* by
virtue of an ALS medal and several published books. He was also
a close friend who needed encouragement. How else to explain,
in this volume on Australian fiction, the lengthy consideration
given to two books (*Blue Coast Caravan*, 1935, and *Caribbean
Interlude*, 1936) that are not fiction at all but travel? Not that
bulk was needed. True, Davison's output of fiction had been
slight, but after the first it was memorable and promising. And
the essay could profitably have been shorter.

The first novel (*Forever Morning*, 1931), a conventional romance, hardly seems worthy of the detailed analysis and ex-
haustive quotations allotted it.[45] Though the critics do find in

it some promise of better things to come, Davison's works fail to show the development of a Palmer, for instance, for his later fiction is not a series but several very separate, even unique, entities. Here, at the risk of sounding too enthusiastic myself, I must say that it would be difficult to overrate either his second book (*Man-Shy*, 1931) or his third (*The Wells of Beersheba*, 1933). Flatly, both are incomparable in two senses: nothing exists suitable to be compared with either, and both are intrinsically beyond compare. *Man-Shy*, "A Story of Men and Cattle," is Australian to the core, an honor to the ALS medal, and one of Australia's unquestioned, unquestionable classics. MBE only do it justice when they call it "something between a long short story and a universe."[46] And something, they might have added, between a book for children and a history of Australian pastoralism. Its heroine is a red heifer whom we follow from birth to almost the hour of her death; yet "there is no trace of sentimentality in the book."[47] And there is no trace of overwriting in this fine review.

Man-Shy is a slight book—under forty thousand words; *The Wells of Beersheba*, "A Light Horse Legend," is slighter still—around ten thousand. But here again, in so small a space, is a kind of perfection that the critics recognize and, after a few clarifying statements, let speak for itself with more quotation than comment. Like *Flesh in Armour*, it is a memorial to Australia's part in World War I, telling "of the grim and simple necessity, the watering of the horses at the Wells of Beersheba, that drove the men on to victory."[48] Yet "There is no trace of jingoism in it, but rather a sort of sculptured pride."[49]

These two, with another small book, *Children of the Dark People* ("an Australian story for young folk" recounting the natural and supernatural adventures of two aboriginal children lost in the ancient bush), are the fiction upon which at the date of the *Essays* Davison's reputation rested. Each was an original experiment, each successful—but slight. Nonetheless, MBE close this long essay with strong words: "Both in achievement and in promise Frank Davison is one of the most deeply significant figures in Australian literature today."[50] His promise unhappily was never realized; he published little more in a long life save for the voluminous, frank study of urban sex that appeared in the year of his death a third of a century later (*The White*

Thorntree, 2 vols., 1970)—hardly the fulfillment of the hopes he had raised earlier. All of this the essayists cannot be blamed for failing to foresee. The question is whether his notable but scant achievement at the time merited so long and laudatory a treatment by his friends.

The Montforts (1928), the only predominantly Australian novel by intermittently expatriate Martin Boyd, is "an Australian microcosm" which Barnard and Eldershaw found sheer joy— a family chronicle covering the better part of a century (from the early 1840's to the end of World War I) in a country that had known the white man for only a century and a half. It was the first of its kind and hasn't been superseded. Other historical novels center around the convicts, the aborigines, the winning of the land. This one is closer in subject to MBE's own *A House Is Built* (which appeared the next year), being primarily urban; but the Montfort family is larger, its origins socially higher, and it is portrayed for a generation longer with vastly more detail and a more universal intent. That all of this attains unity through their ancestress Madeleine du Remy des Baux and that it all gets packed into a single volume of three hundred and fifty pages are accomplishments which these critics duly admire.

They are even more fascinated by Boyd's philosophy of life— not, like Richardson's, that character is fate, not like Prichard's, that environment makes the man, but that an accident (like Madeleine's indiscretion in uniting her blood with the Montforts) having happened, "it becomes part of the natural law and her descendants must abide by it. The natural law works itself out in life, but behind the natural law there is neither a divine nor a moral sanction—only chance."[51]

The essay does not fail to grasp what gives the book its greater significance as an Australian chronicle—the parallel between the continuing influence of Madeleine upon the Montfort family and that of the British tradition upon the new nation, both fraught with restlessness. It is notable too for its concise rendering of the gradual emergence of an Australian spirit through four generations of originally English Montforts, and for its appreciation of Boyd's use of background: "*The Montforts* fulfills one of the first essentials of an Australian book in that it takes the Australian scene and conditions as much for granted and moves as naturally among them as an English novel takes the English scene."[52] Higher praise hath no antipodean critic than this.

There is no problem here, as with the early Davison, Palmer, and Dark of a too conventional skeleton, for *"The Montforts* refuses to fit into any of the standard pigeonholes." It is not a romance, although it has some romantic elements; not a satire, although satire is used as an astringent; not a piece of realism, being too "edited and sculptured" for that.

It is in fact a book that it is impossible to label. It is a novel of craftsmanship, of intellectual subtlety, a triumph of judgment. With its theme and treatment it might so easily have appeared invented, diagrammatic, synthetic, clever but sterile, yet it is none of these things. It is deeply imagined, a full book. And it is a mine of interest for the literary technician.[53]

This is a full review of the "full book," detailed and appreciative. What probably pleased Boyd most, if he saw it, was the thing that MBE valued most in criticism—understanding.

The essay was limited to Boyd's one thoroughly Australian novel; turning to Christina Stead, Barnard and Eldershaw choose to consider her then three novels as having brought "a new note into Australian fiction," even though only one (*Seven Poor Men of Sydney*, 1934) had an Australian setting, *The Salsburg Tales* (1934) being only slightly connected with the author's homeland, *The Beauties and the Furies* (1936) not at all.

Their usual analytical bent frames their approach to this most difficult of their subjects. The "new note" (new indeed in the Australia of 1938) they find to be composed of two qualities, richness and strangeness. The first, defined and illustrated at considerable length, lies in "sheer beauty of diction," the surest way to MBE's hearts. "The words have an imaginative bloom on them. They are a little far-fetched, a little strange, so that they prick the imagination."[54] The quality of strangeness comes out in many ways—the subject matter (most of the stories in *The Salsburg Tales* are fantastic) and in treatment. These qualities the critics find to be best expressed in the *Tales*, where they are in harmony with the theme. But *Seven Poor Men of Sydney*, set in Australia, rightly wins their closest attention. "The scene is laid in Sydney and its environs, but it is none the less a strange world for that. Familiar scenes are shown, but from a new angle, revealing curious proportions. The background is heightened, enriched from the imagination, stylized, interpenetrated by a strange light."[55] Even in a description of the harbor, "the scene is removed from us by a mannerism." They fault Stead throughout for her poor character drawing and often preposterous conversations, but here make one charming concession: "People do not talk as the characters in *Seven Poor Men of Sydney* talk, but they might if they always expressed what they felt."[56] They find it a somber book, its philosophy being "Life as it is is untenable."[57]

As for *The Beauties and the Furies*, "It is a book that does not repay close analysis." The prose they find "singularly over-ripe," making their point with this quotation: " 'Her words came dripping rarely, white and sweet, like sugar cane shreds, from her sensually swollen lips.' "[58] They close with the conclusion that beyond the story and its ornament they "could find nothing —a vacuum—which was a disappointment after the developing social outlook in *Seven Poor Men of Sydney*."[59] And so this examination of the "new note" in Australian fiction ends with a sigh.

Marjorie may have insisted to her editor that these essays had no inherent order, but actually a kind of sequence does appear in the collection—from those the authors regarded most highly to least. And Eleanor Dark is last. In only three years she had published three novels, two of them ALS medal winners. She was already popular as well as critically acclaimed. And she was still young—younger than Barnard and Eldershaw.[60] Yet even her future did not look promising to them. It is this essay on Dark that begins with the masterly analytical piece quoted on page 137, in which an author's growth is defined in descending order as development, progression, elaboration, or repetition. Dark doesn't rate high on the scale, her growth showing only elaboration.

That opening definition, applied to her works, means that "The attitude of mind and general conceptions from which the three novels spring remain static, the change and elaboration are in the technique, the vehicle."[61] The attitude that is static throughout the three novels (*Slow Dawning*, 1932; *Prelude to Christopher*, 1933; *Return to Coolami*, 1935) is a "thinly disguised romanticism." Plot, dominated by coincidence and accident, predominates. Because of the rigid construction of the stories "the characters are held as in a vise," and are similar from book to book because "they are cut to an ideal, not just fished out of life."[62] Even the backgrounds suffer from being built to specification.

These be unkind words but all too well substantiated. Yet the authors mercifully find Dark an "unwilling romantic," because she tends to veil her romanticism with other devices such as frankness, realism of detail, and a kind of scientific approach. MBE's conclusion is that Dark has, despite her flaws, added lustre through her technique to a national literature that has frequently been accused of being "bald, crude, and ingenuous."[63]

Just as one sighs that so few authors were treated in these discerning essays, so one yearns for a later examination (a kind of "Australian Fiction Revisited") that would cover the further works of these subjects. How, for instance, would the critics have reassessed Dark on the basis of those colossal later novels, *The Timeless Land* (1941) and *Storm of Time* (1948), larger in scope and execution than anything previously attempted for Australia's past? Even if they had found them colossal failures, they would surely have had to concede to the author something more than the "elaboration" allowed her here. One even wonders if this carefully built and painfully candid study may have encouraged Mrs. Dark to extend her talent.[64] This, for Marjorie, would have been a critical consummation devoutly to be wished.

Essays in Australian Fiction (which did not, as we have noted, limit itself strictly to Australia or to fiction) is a collection of sound enough judgments within its field to assure it a place in the slender canon of Australian literary criticism. It is frequently listed, frequently referred to, frequently quoted from.[65] The book had been difficult to write and almost impossible to get published. It would be pleasant to report that when it finally did appear, early in 1938, it was welcomed with open minds and pocketbooks by all of literary Australia; but that isn't what happened. Marjorie's reports to Nettie Palmer on its reception, over a period of several months, include such items as "a *very* sour notice in the Sydney *Morning Herald* which will confirm all the publisher's worst fears";[66] the fact that all their other friends "seem to think that little book of essays a delicate subject to be tactfully avoided";[67] and "We hear of them now and then but never actually meet anyone who has read them."[68] Still more telling was the publisher's report at the end of the first year—208 copies sold. There may be some comfort in the fact that the scarce copies still available in Australia's public and university libraries have doubtless attracted a far longer list of readers over the years than the book knew in its pale heyday. And more comfort, though very belated, in its being reissued—not in Australia but in the United States—in 1970.

One wishes that the original publisher had not required that the volume be so small. How welcome to any student of Australian literature would be the considered opinions of Barnard and Eldershaw—even if only as something to argue with—on some of the general topics they originally proposed (p. 147). One particularly longs for the essays "Australia in Fiction" and "Critics and Criticism" which did get as far as the editor. More individual studies would have been—would be—welcome, too. Xavier Herbert and Patrick White didn't get started quite early enough to be considered for inclusion (Marjorie was to take on the latter single-handed, years later—p. 162). Kylie Tennant and Dymphna Cusack might have had a special entree to the *Essays* as women novelists, but each had published only one novel before 1938. Norman Lindsay's early novels were available but probably uncongenial to MBE; Brian Penton's two-volume saga of nineteenth-century settlement in Queensland, appearing in the mid-30's, would have been a likelier candidate for their treatment. The most conspicuous omissions of the day would seem to be Miles Franklin and Brent of Bin Bin, each of whom was already credited with three novels (Marjorie was to make up this slight to both of them—p. 167—when it was discoverable that they were one).

But all this is only wishing. There was certainly no encouragement at the time for a larger volume, and no one can yet quarrel with the choices they made—just a little, maybe, as indicated earlier, with the proportioning of their too scant space.

CHAPTER 8

Criticism—MB

I Miscellaneous Critical Writing

FLORA Eldershaw published only an occasional book review on her own. Marjorie Barnard, on the contrary, did a good deal of critical writing, including much reviewing over many years in numerous periodicals—chiefly from the late 1940's to the early 1960's, chiefly in Australia's two leading literary quarterlies, *Meanjin* and *Southerly*, chiefly of fiction, always Australian. This was the long fallow period after the war and *Tomorrow and Tomorrow* when she published no major work until *A History of Australia*. Many of the books she reviewed do not loom very large on the literary horizon now, didn't even then, but many of the reviews are still illuminating.

MB, like MBE, developed her judgments from critical standards that required the laying down of generalizations—sometimes rather extensive opening statements against which to measure the ensuing particulars. Occasionally the tail wags the dog. More than half of her review of a popular first novel, for instance, is devoted to a history of Australian literature in order to explain the literary tradition which, inescapable by this young writer but in conflict with her own leanings, produced contradictory attitudes in her book.[1] In one of her rarer nonfiction reviews (of an Australian history) more than a third of her space develops a version of the beginnings of Australian literature which she felt should have been included.[2]

Some of her general discussions are worth preserving, both for their intrinsic soundness and for their reflections on her own literary practice. Many of these constitute small essays—on writing, criticism, literary forms, techniques, publishing—which, lifted intact from their context, throw considerable light on the literary scene and her own attitudes toward it. Only quotation can do them justice, and they are worth quoting, but as they

159

would make a small volume in themselves, we must pass them by here.

Her reviews are always enlivened by the highly figurative Barnard style. One of Astley's novels is "touched by the flying fringe of greatness";[3] Vance Palmer's works have become "the very bread of Australian fiction."[4] Sometimes her wit with words is less kind, as when she describes a novel by an established woman writer as being "gelatinous with romance,"[5] and the war neurosis of another's character as seeming to come "direct from a textbook and not a very good textbook either."[6]

She is careful to justify her judgments. A listing of the many virtues of a best-selling novel is cancelled by "But this is good journalism, not good literature."[7] Unimpressed by another impressive book, she suspects that the author doesn't know her subject—"but then neither do I. I can only fall back on the argument that it is not convincing. It is the author's job to convince the reader, however little the reader may know. The onus is on him."[8] Later, having found a book exhaustingly "laden with introspection. It is the pack the characters bear on their shoulders in their interminable journeys," she ends with, "These are hard words perhaps, but I have endeavored to evaluate the book in its own terms. It is offered to us as a serious work, not as light entertainment, so as a serious work it must be judged."[9]

Much of her minor reviewing must have been a tedious burden, but Marjorie was sustained by the continual hope that some good thing would come out of Australian fiction even though it seldom did.[10] She was usually able to find some word of hope or cheer for the worst of them and never launched a full-scale attack, in the manner of some lesser critics, just to show her own cleverness. Only occasionally was she stirred to downright unmitigated denunciation. At four novels written in the all-too-popular "Australian tradition"—the "hunk of life" school which she designates as "tough" (vs. tender), she levels this barrage: "They deal in the vernacular, nothing is glossed over, their authors would as soon be found dead as acting the role of *deus ex machina*, debunking is their trade, bad grammar their fetish. They have their clichés, of course, not the least of which is an abhorrence of anything middle-class."[11] Another book she attacked was one of the *Coast to Coast* anthologies, which she felt had a "very flimsy content," many of the twenty-six short stories included being "frail to the vanishing point."[12] Of a number of them she ventures that "A vulgarer pen than mine might have enquired . . . 'So what?' "[13]

The reader who felt that *Essays in Australian Fiction* was sometimes overly enthusiastic finds a cutting edge in frequent use in disposing of some of these later publications, nonfiction as well as fiction. A fellow historian she takes to task for his vocabulary, which moves her to a very indigenous rejoinder: "To talk of the Australian *mystique* or *ethos*, of 'frontiermen,' with the wild-west connotation that the term carries, and to name the swaggie of 'Waltzing Matilda' our 'culture hero' is, candidly, shocking to the sensibilities. Stone the crows, this is jargon."[14] Her review of an introduction to Australian fiction begins:

> This is a controversial book, not on account of heterodox opinions or theories developed, but for the lack of them. It provokes argument by the flatness of its judgments and the even spread of its omniscience. The author tells his reader a good deal but shows him very little. The introduction is brief to the point of being summary and the effect on the reader is something like what it would be if he were guest of honour at a well-attended public meeting in the local School of Arts at which all present were introduced to him in the American style with comment.[15]

She closes with the sad conviction that "In the critical field the labourers are still few."[16]

Several times Marjorie wrote multiple reviews, including two annual "Fiction Chronicles" for *Meanjin*. For one of these she went through the seven novels sent to her from the reviewer's basket and concluded, "Vintage years do not come round very often. 1956 was not a vintage year."[17] For the other, she reviewed, in a few pages, thirteen. It seems a pity to have had her eyes and her mind wasted on the mediocre in these transient reviewlets. It must have been gratifying to her, as it is to us, that she sometimes drew more challenging subjects—was able to add consideration of two of Vance Palmer's later books (*Golconda* and *Seedtime*), for example, to her appraisal of his earlier work in the *Essays*.[18] And still more gratifying to have some assignments that gave her the chance to work with a single writer at the greater length and depth of the critical essay. The most ambitious of these was a *Meanjin* article on Miles Franklin which at nearly twenty pages constituted a fair dress rehearsal for her later book-length study (p. 167).[19]

Another wrapped up the four novels of Seaforth Mackenzie, a poet and journalist whose fiction she finds a consequent mixture of "heightened sensibility and mechanic sensationalism."[20] Among these four (published over a spread of seventeen years) she finds the first (*The Young Desire It*, 1937) and the third (*Dead Men Rising*, 1951) to be excellent reflections of the impact of experience on the creative mind; the second (*Chosen People*, 1938) and the fourth (*The Refuge*, 1951) she finds to be full of literary tricks and lacking in sincerity—such a falling off as to suggest that the author had resorted to "artificial insemination of the Muse."[21] The last she dismisses neatly and accurately if a little cruelly: "Needless to say *The Refuge* is very well written. It is everything except convincing."[22]

Marjorie's greatest opportunity as a periodicals critic came in 1956 in the chance to write for *Meanjin* on Patrick White. In her most recently published book (*Miles Franklin*, 1967), she refers to Henry Handel Richardson as "probably Australia's most famous novelist to date, although Patrick White is running her close";[23] it must have been a lift to her as well as to Australian criticism that in her later years she was able to help place on White's broad, tweed-clad shoulders the mantle with which in her prime she had clothed Richardson. At the time, he needed her support far more.

It is a curious commentary on Australia's early disregard of its now unquestionably greatest novelist that Marjorie had to begin her essay on "The Four Novels of Patrick White" with the words: "Of Patrick White, the man, I know little save by deduction,"[24] and that *Meanjin*'s founder and editor, C. B. Christesen, in commissioning the essay the previous year, assumed White to be still living overseas, whereas the novelist had been back in Australia some seven years and was quietly living on a farm at Castle Hill, only a few miles from Sydney. As a result of the commission, Australia—its literary circles, at least—was to have available some solid information about both the man and the novels that had been appearing over nearly two decades in England and the United States, though largely Australian in setting.

White's first novel, *Happy Valley* (1939), had been published just ten years after MBE's first, and by the same house. The irony of the title, the name of a most unhappy Australian town, must have appealed to this critic. Step by step she feels her way cautiously through this literary phenomenon to find it "the most closely patterned, the most efficient of his books"[25] in structure; of the content, "Only the ruthless survive. The story is ugly and pathetic."[26] Hardly the typical "bush" novel—the negative initial responses of lesser Australian critics can be understood if not forgiven. *Happy Valley* Marjorie found to bear "few of the marks of a first novel";[27] *The Living and the Dead* (1941) to be in the same mold but more intricate. It too "is an unhappy book; all the characters are lost or frustrated or decadent so that it is difficult to know who are the living and who are the dead."[28] Nonetheless she finds more humor in it than in *Happy Valley*, as well as a more lucid and conventional style. That it is also less real she attributes to its being set in England. "Well as he knows England, he still moves more freely in the country of his youth. Of Australia he writes from within, though as an expatriate, seeing it always in the changing terms of memory."[29]

From the community of *Happy Valley* to the three major characters of *The Living and the Dead* to the secret life of one Theodora Goodman in *The Aunt's Story* (1948), Marjorie finds to be a journey of increasing concentration. This story "has its own painful logic, the prose is richer than in the earlier books, the imagery more striking and ingenious. This is the most imaginative and bizarre of Patrick White's novels. It has impetus and unity and is constructed with great skill." She concluded that "It is executed with great artistry and it is surprising that it is not more moving."[30] It should be noted that three years later, following a reprint of the book, she writes of it again. Now the portrait of Theodora seems to her "tender, tragic, inexorable and completed"; and after a fifth reading she concedes the book true classic stature: *"The Aunt's Story* has become for me one of those rare and inexhaustible books that reveal themselves slowly and have at each rereading something more to give."[31]

There could have been no fifth reading before she wrote of *The Tree of Man* (1955), for this, the most Australian of the four, had just become available, having been first published in the United States, then in England. She finds the first three novels but a prelude to this "story of ordinary people,"[32] the young pioneering couple Stan and Amy Parker, who live out their lives "entrapped in inarticulateness. They cannot express their feelings, but their feelings are nonetheless intense. They fumble for the meaning of life; they thirst, in their parched, inadequate lives for the moments of ecstasy and illumination."[33]

And so we come at last to the critic's concept of White's underlying philosophy. "What is the kernel of his writing? Though he has wit, the deft wit of words and the ironic and sardonic wit of situation, all his books are sombre. He writes of the frustrated and the inarticulate, of the mad and the lost ones. There is always the burden of pain."[34] By comparison with this undeniable gloom, the positive side of his philosophy is less evident, harder to grasp. She finds it best revealed in *The Tree of Man* as "the ineffable moment." Specifically, she concludes, "Poetry, music, religion are the paths that the soul, imprisoned in flesh, may take, 'the paths out of sleep.' Love is an illusion, pain a certainty but the capacity to feel pain is the mark of a human being. And pain is its own reward."[35]

Marjorie Barnard did not of course utter the last word on even the few works of White then available. She would be the first to admit it, for even in her second and longer interpretation of *The Aunt's Story* she concedes: "That, perhaps, is only one reading of this many-sided, subtle book."[36] But she can be credited with having made the first attempt by an Australian critic to write a thorough and understanding essay on this strange new genius who was rising to loom head and shoulders above the rest of Australia's writers. By the time Geoffrey Dutton made his longer study five years later, he was able to include a bibliography of eight articles on White, of which Marjorie's stands at the top not only in point of time.[37]

Later she was to review White's fifth novel, *Voss* (1957), beginning with "This is a book of extraordinary grandeur, of great impact and a most disturbing originality." Its remarkable quality "arises from its freedom from all literary and other trammels. It is an inevitable book, which few books are. There is nothing contrived." One of its virtues is that it is new. To prove her point she holds it up to each of the earlier novels in turn. The comparison of *Voss* with *The Living and the Dead* yields one of her inimitable phrases: *Voss* is much more mature, "as if its writer, who had once affected melancholy as a decor, had become marinated in it."[38] She finds the book a palimpsest containing the explorer Leichhardt, the Christ story, the erotic—certain of the existence of these strata but doubtful of their order. Again she admits to the inconclusiveness of all of her conclusions: "This is a tentative reading of the enigma. So much of the interest of the book lies in its inwardness, which can only be interpreted by readers after their kind."[39] And she closes with "*Voss* is a gadfly book that won't leave you alone—despite, in the nature of things, high reader-resistance in some quarters."[40]

Marjorie published numerous other articles on Australian literature; it isn't necessary to look at all of them in order to understand her philosophy or divine her skill. An early one, "Scribbling on the Map," is an excellent example of her ability to write clean-cut, highly readable expository prose. In it she indicates the role that both fiction and nonfiction writers play in the "discovery of Australia" by adding imaginative understanding of the continent to the earlier labors of explorers and stock men[41] —a role that both MBE and MB certainly fulfilled exceptionally well. In 1942 there appeared the first of her several capsule histories of Australian literature, "Our Literature," one of a number of radio scripts by noted writers (among them the Palmers, Frank Davison, Miles Franklin) later published in book form.[42] Here she discusses at considerable length one of her favorite theses—the growth of Australia's literature from its folklore. She also explains the development among the early men of the bush of an Australian vocabulary: "Always the harder, plainer word replaced the softer, greener one. They made an idiom that worked, and was salty and good on the tongue, humorous, a little sardonic.... It has become—it is—our literary language."[43] As if to prove her point (but likelier in deference to her radio audience) she drops into a good many Australianisms herself, to wit: Early Australian literature was not the result of conscious co-operation like the Celtic Renaissance: "our billy has boiled without being watched."[44] It is a small literature but indigenous —"as natural to our country as the gum tree." "A migrating people has never been able to carry its literature, as the aboriginal carries a fire in his canoe, from one place to another without loss or extinction."[45] Even though lost, the early epics "fertilized the paddock for what came after."[46]

Marjorie's crusade for a greater appreciation of Australia's literature went beyond her native shores. She did a very excellent and thorough article on its history for the 1950 edition of the British *Chambers's Encyclopaedia*.[47] Here she again rides the hobbyhorse of her folklore theory of the origins of Australian literature in the bush—a theme that appears so often in her critical and historical writing that we should pause to look at *Southerly's* comment (presumably by its editor, R. W. Howarth). Here we are reminded that the early ballads in Australia were not truly indigenous but "adaptations to local conditions of English and American rhymes brought out by convicts and settlers"[48] —a fact that the writer feels makes the "literary" origins of Australian literature inescapable.

Here for once scholarly honesty overcame Marjorie's usual excessive modesty and gave us a short paragraph detailing the works of MBE. She was not so bold in an essay on "Australian Literature Since 1929" done ten years later for an American quarterly that was making a survey of the world's various national literatures over the past quarter of a century.[49] The first third of this essay is devoted to the early history of Australian literature in order to make the modern era intelligible. But when she reaches it, she pays tribute to numerous greats and near greats without a mention of Barnard's, Eldershaw's or their joint existence—undue reticence surely, since she makes special mention of the historical novel, and *A House Is Built* appeared in the very year with which her assignment began, a generally recognized turning point in Australian letters. She writes at length for this American audience of the novel and the short story, but thinks that Australia's poetry has a better claim than its prose to a place in world literature. Drama is scarce because of the small market; the essay "can only be compared to snakes in Ireland," for "There is something in the national character that rejects the essay as a literary form."[50] Lack of adequate literary criticism she finds serious. "The history of Australian literature is scattered with the corpses of short-lived literary periodicals," the "brave exception" being *Meanjin*. She feels that Australian literature still has qualities of folk literature—is a corporate rather than an individual enterprise, with few outstanding figures, none of genius rank. But the whole she finds to be important and effective: "Through its creative writers, small as well as great, this vast continent is gradually being assimilated by its white settlers."[51]

II Miles Franklin

Late in 1935 Marjorie Barnard first met novelist Miles Franklin (some eighteen years her senior) and was much impressed by her wit—an impression strengthened the following year upon hearing her give "a wise and witty address" on early novelist Catherine Helen Spence.[52] That at this time Marjorie was less impressed by Miles's writing than by her person is understandable on two counts: Miles was a remarkably striking individual, and her best novels were at that time either unwritten or unclaimed. Years later (in 1955, the year after Miles's death), Marjorie devoted one of the longest and most important of her numerous critical studies in the quarterly *Meanjin* to Miles and her works;[53] another dozen years, and this beginning flowered in a book-length study, *Miles Franklin* (1967), the only one of its size on Miles, of its kind by Marjorie.

Marjorie once remarked to me half-facetiously in connection with my beginning this study shortly after she had completed hers, "*I* was lucky; *Miles* was dead." Miles was lucky, too, for she was thus spared the pain that, sensitive to criticism as she was, she would surely have felt from even as kindly and judicious a handling as Marjorie's. She would have been pleased with the tribute paid, in the opening pages, to her amazing memory and her Irish facility with words; but wounded surely to read that on the other hand "She was no philosopher, displayed little skill in constructing her books and not much originality in plot."[54]

Since Marjorie found that "Miles writing is indivisible from Miles living,"[55] she felt required to devote the first third of this critical study to her subject's background and early youth. It is surprising to find ourselves taken as far back as the days before the continent of Australia was discovered, and given several pages of the kind of survey already done so frequently and well in the critic's historical writings; but this is for perspective, for only seven generations had elapsed since Australia was still a *tabula rasa*, and Miles herself was the fifth generation of a pioneering family, her ancestor Edward Miles having come with the First Fleet.

Her biographer, as we well know by now, has a strong dose of the mental orderliness that she denies her subject. Consequently Miles's seventy-one years are neatly divided for us into four periods: ten years of childhood, ten more of adolescent rebellion, thirty as an exile, and a final twenty-one back in Australia. The childhood was spent happily in a large family in the bush. From neither the rebellion nor the adolescence did she ever fully recover. Much of the period of exile, split between the United States and England, remains shrouded in mystery, although the last half dozen years of it were both her most prolific and her best as a writer. The final two decades in Australia were relatively unproductive, unhappy.

"The trouble with a critical assessment of Miles's work is that while the memory of Miles herself still lives her writings are eclipsed by her personality,"[56] which was "full of complexities and contradictions and quirks of character."[57] Here Marjorie had two more pieces of luck. One was that having known Miles personally in her later years, she was able to give us from her own observations some telling glimpses into that personality; the other, the availability of *Childhood at Brindabella* (1963), Miles's autobiography of her formative first ten years, published posthumously.[58] Of the strange secretiveness that led Miles never to speak of her three decades abroad and to deny to the death the authorship of several of her major novels, her biographer concludes, "To be mysterious was with Miles a sort of nervous tic. It had become a meaningless habit."[59] Lecturing, she contends, appealed to Miles because "she liked people, particularly people she did not know."[60] Of Miles's final dreary period in Australia when, disillusioned and still homesick for a lost world, she had stopped writing, Marjorie queries, "Who knows exactly what Miles felt—even when she told you?"[61]

Miles was only sixteen when she wrote *My Brilliant Career*, a first novel that should hardly have been held against her save that "It is a genuine Miles Franklin. It is crude, inept, stiff, exaggerated, but it contains most of the ingredients of the later books"[62]—the mixture of romance and realism, the passionate feminism, the highly individualized vocabulary, the love for the pastoral life with its animals and singing rivers. Of the end of Miles's long creative period, forty years later, this damning conclusion is reached: "She changed very little after writing *My*

Brilliant Career. She matured but she did not alter. The same sort of raw material continued to appeal to her: she already knew her characters, her plots, her backgrounds, her periods of history."[63] One is reminded of that descending scale of movements available to the novelist, as laid down in the MBE treatment of Eleanor Dark: development, progression, elaboration, repetition (p. 137). Clearly, Miles Franklin goes a step below Mrs. Dark, to the foot of the class.

But what Miles's work lacks in variety it makes up for in volume, the themes laid down in the novel she wrote at sixteen being repeated numerously throughout her long creative period. This study covers the novels thoroughly, book by book, with synopses, generous quotations, and criticism, both Marjorie's and others'. *My Brilliant Career*, published six years after it was written, was a very successful first book but was withdrawn from circulation by Miles herself because of the storm of protest it raised among her widespread clan; they found it an invasion of their privacy, Miles found their attitude painful and humiliating. She shortly wrote a second novel to prove that the first had been fiction, but *My Career Goes Bung* didn't find a publisher for forty years. Meanwhile Miles had become what she could never forgive Henry Handel Richardson for being— an expatriate.

Marjorie provides what little information is available on Miles's activities in social work in Chicago and London, and her wartime service as orderly with the Scottish Women's Hospital Unit in Macedonia. Of this breadth of experience Miles never talked, much less wrote, however, so that only the last half dozen years of her exile, when she began writing again, are significant for this study. One of Marjorie's best chapters is "Brent of Bin Bin Steps Out of the British Museum." When the Brent books first began to appear a third of a century earlier, Marjorie had been as much in the dark as to their authorship as anyone and everyone else, even going on record with "I shall be very surprised if Brent is not an elderly man—probably a bachelor."[64] The secret will not be officially out before the time comes for the opening of Miles's private papers, but as more Brent and more Franklin books appeared, for comparison, Marjorie changed her mind. Here, with only circumstantial proof (but lots of it), she method-

ically unmasks Brent to reveal the unmistakable and impish face
of Miles.

The Brent series of five novels covers almost a century (from
1830 to 1928), but "There is no plot in the ordinary sense. The
narrative winds and loops and circles about a thousand natural
obstacles."[65] Confusingly, publication did not follow chronological order throughout. The first two, however, *Up the Country*
(1928) and *Ten Creeks Run* (1930), set in the nineteenth century, are conceded to be the best of the lot. *Back to Bool Bool*
(1931) and *Gentlemen at Gyang Gyang* (1956—posthumous) are
set in the 1920's, the decade in which they were written, and
suffer in consequence, for "Miles is never really happy writing
of the present day.... As she moved into the present she felt
more and more impelled to take a satirical view of life and hap-
penings."[66] *Cockatoos* (1954), set at the turn of the century, is
of special interest because "It is largely autobiographical and I
dare Miles to contradict me."[67] Between the heroine Ignez and
her author, innumerable parallels of ability and experience exist,
although Ignez never succeeds, never returns to Australia, as
Miles did.

While "Brent's" works were being published, so were others,
major and minor, admittedly by Miles Franklin. Only two are
significant. One of these, *Old Blastus of Bandicoot* (1931) was
not only written in England but published there. Marjorie finds
it "the perfect type book, displaying in compact form, if not at
their highest, Miles Franklin's qualities as a novelist."[68] The
other, generally regarded as her greatest, was written in Australia the year of its author's return from exile. *All That Swagger*
(1936) is a book big in size and scope—500 pages and four generations, from the 1830's to the 1930's—which Marjorie calls
"not so much a novel as a quarry from which a hundred novels
could be taken."[69] She sees it as Miles's effort to make amends
to her family. Not only is it dedicated to her paternal grand-
parents, but her grandfather was clearly the model for the
great central figure of pioneer Danny Delacey—although Marjorie
feels that "It would be a mistake to think that this novel was his
biography. It is nothing of the sort. He was the tuning fork;
Miles picked up the note from him."[70] But the book, she believes,
is the Franklin family's chronicle as truly as *Cockatoos* is Miles's
own autobiography.

An about-face from the accepted best to the accepted worst of Miles's novels brings us to *Prelude to Waking*, not published until 1950 although it had been written in 1925 and presumably owed its name to having been the first in her "second great spurt of writing." The setting, like the place of writing, is England, and "Miles was never happy when she laid her action outside Australia. . . . When she wrote of other places her ink ran thin and pale."[71] Even Marjorie can find nothing good to say about this one, although she faithfully discusses it in some detail. It is enough for us to note her caustic conclusion: "Perhaps this book had to be written to get Miles into the habit of writing again. It did not have to be published."[72]

The judgment rendered at the end of what Marjorie calls Miles's creative period (1933) was not altered by anything that came out of the two decades remaining to her. There were two collaborative efforts which Marjorie finds a surprising turn for such an individualist as Miles. One was a satirical novel that we have noted earlier (p. 94). Miles and Dymphna Cusack had met while both were contributing to Flora Eldershaw's anthology *The Peaceful Army* during the preparations for the Sesquicentennial. Each of them had "a racy sense of humour" and they " 'knocked sparks off each other' "[73] on the subject of the pretensions that bloomed during that period of ardent nationalism. Their joint rollicking *Pioneers on Parade*, like Eliza Doolittle's accent in *My Fair Lady*, is inevitably more appreciated by outsiders than by Australians. Marjorie finds it "adolescent in outlook"[74] but generously hopes "that it will continue to be read for its humour if not for its widsom."[75]

Miles's other collaboration was with Kate Baker in bringing a volume of Joseph Furphy's letters together with an explanatory text. Again, Marjorie's balanced criticism: "This is a dull book, there is no question of that, but it has preserved material that would otherwise have been lost."[76] *Joseph Furphy* as a work of literary criticism "is full of admiration mixed with some explanations and observations, but there is little analysis. Miles was not of a critical turn of mind, nor was she of the stuff from which reviewers are made. She admired or disliked books and their authors very heartily. Her reactions were generally emotional."[77]

Yet Miles's last work was criticism. From an invitation to give the Commonwealth Literary Fund series of lectures on Australian literature grew her final book, published posthumously —*Laughter, Not for a Cage* (1956), in which "Personal prejudices, favorable and unfavorable, are rife."[78] It is "biased, emotional and sometimes ill-informed." Then comes the critic's saving concession: "As reading matter it has much to recommend it. Miles had wit. She described Jane Austen as 'the full-rigged ship in a narrow-necked bottle.' There are dozens of flashes like this."[79]

At the close of her critical estimate of *All That Swagger*, Marjorie concludes: "This book has so much of life in it that it would be heartless to carp at its faults, like spoiling a friendship because of some small imperfections."[80] Perhaps I should feel the same restraint in the face of this knowledgeable, thorough, and eminently readable study of Miles's work, Marjorie's latest publication. But in spite of its many excellencies, there is a certain falling off from her earlier work in small ways. One is a tendency—noticeable also in *A History of Australia* and her most recently published short story—to short sentences, short paragraphs, that give a choppy effect quite different from the sustained fluency of her earlier prose. In her account of early Australia here, for instance, "The animals were strange enough but gentle. The aborigines were shadows flitting through the land. They and it had evolved together."[81] And "The sheep was the greatest pioneer of all. There was a market in wool. The looms of England were hungry for it."[82] Sometimes we find results before causes—not for dramatic effect but from a failure, apparently, to give a final shaping to all parts of the manuscript in relation to the rest, as when on page 38 we are told that "She [Miles] was a healthy child, except for the trouble with her back"—a trouble we are apparently expected to know about but don't hear of until page 51, when one reason given for her childhood preference for the company of adults over children is that "A curvature of the spine made rough play painful." This need for a final editing shows up in repetition, too, as when on page 52 we learn that "When Mrs. Franklin died in 1938, at a great age, Miles was overcome by grief and remorse. . . . She grieved, not because she loved her mother but because she had not." And on page 169, that when in 1938 old Mrs. Franklin died at the age of eighty-three, "Miles was stricken with remorse as well as grief. . . . When the old woman died Miles was sad because she had not been able to love her more." This kind of duplication is especially glaring in a short book.

The author has been taken to task for her admitted ignorance of whether or not Miles's First Fleet ancestor Edward Miles was a convict, when as a historian in Sydney she would have found it a natural and simple thing to check the record. Though at numerous other points Marjorie shows herself willing to venture educated guesses about the unascertainable, she shrugs this off as "not important." Such an attitude seems curiously cavalier for a biographer who admits that Edward Miles's status may have affected her subject's attitude toward the convict strain in Australia's history.

I suspect that Marjorie may have been inhibited by a reluctance to invade the family's privacy. In answering a question of mine about the use of her own letters in this study, she wrote me: "Privacy matters a lot. In my little book on Miles Franklin I was careful not to touch the things she kept hidden. I could have found out a lot of things." This opens the delicate question of a writer's responsibility to the public as well as to his material. I can understand, while I regret, the deliberate destruction of both sides of the Barnard-Eldershaw correspondence, which was probably as personal as professional. But it is hard for me to accept Marjorie's burning of the Palmers' letters to her, since they were far more professional than personal and would have provided a valuable insight into the minds of two of the most important literary figures of their time. It is fortunate for this study that the Palmers carefully preserved hers; she herself found them useful to quote from in a *Meanjin* article as recently as 1970.[83] And she was grateful for the use of Miles's letters to the Palmers, from which she uses copious, useful, and sometimes quite personal extracts in the later pages of this study.

Be it understood that any flaws in *Miles Franklin* are very minor in comparison with its virtues: its competence, its balance, its liveliness. We are fortunate to have it (it has been published in both the United States and Australia), and Miles is fortunate to have had it done by a critic as experienced and open-minded as Marjorie Barnard, for it is the first full-length study of Miles and, I would guess, likely to be the last. The papers Miles left in trust have still to be opened, as we have already noted, but her contemporaries now await with few qualms the fearful revelations of the diary with which she used to threaten them. With Brent's identity already determined beyond any reasonable as well as unreasonable doubt, it is unlikely that anything earth-shaking will be revealed. Marjorie herself has been unable to give to Miles the critic any palm for reliable judgment—only for wit; or to Miles the novelist any laurel for style and technique—only for subject matter. Miles herself, however, took out an extra insurance policy on immortality by leaving her considerable estate to create the Miles Franklin Award of £500 yearly for the best Australian novel submitted. As her own novels become increasingly dated and the charisma of her personality fades, Miles may be remembered less as the writer of her creative years or as the *enfant terrible* whose image she assiduously cultivated than as the little old lady in the old-fashioned clothes who hoarded the money she made from her novels in order to encourage later novelists into perpetuity.

Conclusion

THERE is, unfortunately, no source through which we can now learn of Flora Eldershaw and her aspirations over the years as intimately as we can come to know Marjorie Barnard through her letters to the Palmers. I find myself wondering, for instance, how deeply dedicated to writing Flora was, and whether she may have yearned to be free to devote her life to it (as Marjorie succeeded in doing over two long periods) but was prevented by the necessity of earning a living. My guess is that she did not have an overpowering creative spark, that her interests as well as her talents drew her to other activities: to lecturing, to organizational involvement, to committee work, and (in literature) to criticism rather than creativity.

But there can be no doubt of Marjorie Barnard's lifelong devotion to the Muse. If she wasn't free to write, she was yearning to be, and if she was free and the inspiration was not upon her, she suffered. She wrote criticism, much, and history, more, but she aspired above all to fiction. I was once moved by her poetic prose to ask her if she had never written poetry. "Not since I was eleven," was her reply. Even as a reader, she early confessed to Nettie Palmer, she was "not as sensitive to poetry as to prose,"[1] and verse remained one of the "blind areas"[2] of her mind. Even earlier she had dismissed the essay as a form for which she had a "peculiar regard" but of which she was "totally incapable."[3] There is no indication that her heart was particularly in the team's early attempts at drama. But the short story and the novel, especially the novel, have never ceased to be her lodestars.

The fiction of MBE and MB is notably uneven in quality but never mediocre. The short stories range from the slick to the superb, but never content themselves with the popular "Australian" pattern. Of the five novels that attained publication, only one, their first, succeeded in reaching any sizable public; yet despite its intoxicating success, they never saw it as more than a beginning, a feat to be built upon, not repeated. Hence the

175

continual experiments in both form and content, some more memorable for the attempt than for the attainment, but none content to strive for a cheap popularity.

Marjorie and Flora didn't just practice the art and the craft of fiction, they thought about it, and so made a second name for themselves as critics—writers of considered appraisals in an age that supplied Australia with far more creativity than judgment. From the drudgery of book reviewing to the tedium of judging competitions to the writing of polished critical essays and lectures, they established, both together and separately, names as widely read, concerned, and discerning critics.

History they viewed with fiction as a creative art. Their numerous historical studies, much needed, were carefully researched and admirably conceived, but they glow most brilliantly from the dusty ranks of such literature through the beauty of their style: the poetic imagination with which they lifted up even everyday events, the lyrical language with which they adorned them. I predict that whether they like it or not, their names will wear as much luster from their histories—more, perhaps—than from the fiction that was dearer to at least one of their hearts.

Although too few of their books have yet been reprinted in their entirety, the Australian literary world has already paid them the tribute of borrowing from them heavily, both fiction and nonfiction, for anthology after anthology.[4] The future is always difficult to predict, but I think that the names of Barnard and Eldershaw will be best remembered as *Australians*—as authors who, in all their writing, saw their country steadily and saw it whole, and who, seeing it, had the art to make it more intelligible to those with lesser vision. Shortly after I first met Marjorie she went into a Sydney hospital for a serious eye operation which confined her, sightless, for many tedious days. I was in Sydney at the time, not a first visit but one made infinitely more meaningful because I was soaking myself in the works of MBE and MB. I remember sending a message to Marjorie, some time before I was able to visit her, that I hoped she might find some satisfaction in knowing that while her eyes were bound, my vision was being vastly widened and deepened by what she had earlier recorded.

This was true for the city, true for the continent; true for the background, true for the present; true for the culture, true for the people. And illumination came not alone from any one kind of writing. It came from the novels—notably the first and last, but who could forget in *Green Memory* the description of the Rocks in Sydney, in *The Glasshouse* the nostalgic give-and-take of those two exiles, Stirling and the ship's doctor, in *Plaque with Laurel* the Australian countryside between Sydney and Canberra, and the atmosphere of the capital city? It came from the criticism, with its interpretation of authors, books, and purposes Australian. But most it came from the histories: the major studies and the minor, shot through with revealing passages of the sights, the sounds, the smells; the past and the present; the meaning and the purpose of that unique continent and nation that is Australia.

This is no small contribution to a country which has never understood itself, and to a world that had scarcely heard of it or cared to. It was the consummation of intelligence and love and faith working through literature but much larger than literature. If it is not what the authors dreamed of accomplishing, it is not less. And it is a secure if modest pedestal from which to face the ages.

Notes and References

Preface

1. Marjorie Barnard, *Miles Franklin*, Preface (unnumbered first page).

Chapter One

1. "A Bookful of Sunlight," Red Page of the *Bulletin*, September 28, 1901. Miss Barnard wrote of the enthusiastic review in which this appears: "This is hardly literary criticism. It was written while the impassioned nationalism of the 1890's still warmed the blood." *Miles Franklin*, p. 64.

2. Geoffrey Dutton, review of H. M. Green's *A History of Australian Literature* (2 vols., 1961), *Australian Book Review*, February, 1962, p. 49. "Prevalence" is a relative term, not to be construed as "majority." E. Morris Miller, who in his great bibliography (*Australian Literature*, 2 vols., 1940) divides writers of fiction into "Novelists" and "Women Novelists," finds, of those who began to publish between 1900 and 1930, 30 men worth discussion, 23 women.

3. Marjorie Barnard to Nettie Palmer, April 9, 1935.

4. MB to NP, April 21, 1948.

5. "Tributes to Flora Eldershaw," *Meanjin*, XV (Summer, 1956), p. 392.

6. *Ibid.*, p. 391.

7. *Ibid.*, pp. 390-91.

8. *Ibid.*, p. 391. J. B. Chifley was Australia's Prime Minister from 1945 to 1949.

9. Nettie Palmer, "Flora Eldershaw," *Walkabout*, XVI (October 1, 1950), p. 8.

10. "Tributes to Flora Eldershaw," p. 390.

11. Nettie Palmer, "Flora Eldershaw," *Walkabout*, p. 8.

12. "Tributes to Flora Eldershaw," p. 390.

13. MB to NP, February 13, 1933.

14. MB to NP, August 19, 1932.

15. MB to Vance Palmer, July 24, 1934.

16. *Meanjin*, XVIII (July, 1959), pp. 251-52. This entire issue was devoted to honoring the Palmers. Vance died that July, shortly before the issue appeared; Nettie survived him until 1964.

17. Miss Barnard has said that they had no other pseudonym. Nettie Palmer once wrote that "On one famous occasion the partnership was indicated (look at the two middle names) by a pen-name, 'Faith Sydney.'" ("Flora Eldershaw," *Walkabout*, XVI [October 1, 1950], p. 8), but I have been unable to locate this.

18. *Miles Franklin*, pp. 150-51.

19. Nettie Palmer, *Fourteen Years: Extracts from a Private Journal 1925-1939* (Melbourne, 1948), p. 128. (This and the following references are from an entry dated December 23, 1933.) An old friend of Flora's reputedly went through the book and identified her contributions with disconcerting accuracy, a feat no one else has approached.

20. *Ibid.*, p. 127.

21. *Ibid.*

22. *Ibid.*, p. 128.

23. MB to NP, March 19, 1933 (postscript).

24. MB to NP, April 4, 1933.

25. MB to NP, October 16, 1934.

26. MB to NP, April 17, 1934.

27. *Ibid.*

28. MB to NP, September 25, 1931.

29. MB to VP, January 22, 1935.

30. MB to NP, December 11, 1933.

31. Nettie Palmer, *Fourteen Years*, pp. 126-27. It is significant that Nettie noted, at so early a date, the exhaustion which was to prove Flora's downfall.

32. MB to NP, March 25, 1934.

33. MB to NP (fragment, probably from early 1940's).

34. MB to NP, February 13, 1935.

35. MB to NP, February 26, 1935. The pseudonym does not appear to have materialized.

36. MB to NP, June 9, 1936.

37. MB to NP, April 9, 1935.

38. MB to NP, September 4, 1931.

39. MB to NP, December 1, 1930.

40. MB to NP, December 14, 1936.

41. As late as 1933, with two novels published in four years, Marjorie wrote to Nettie concerning Leslie Rees, whom she had met and enjoyed in London, that "there is so little I can tell him of the world of letters here for I do not belong to it and never know what is happening unless you tell me" (October 9, 1933). The next year she wrote of the "rare pleasure," when Vance was in Sydney, of literary talk (July 8, 1934), for "we do not move in literary circles much" (December 23, 1934). To be confined by

jobs was the fate of most Australian authors, but for MBE there were the added restrictions of family and school living. Of a Christmas Eve party she attended in 1935, Marjorie wrote, no doubt typically, "The talk was good and getting better when I had to leave for the last boat"—the ferry home from Sydney to Longueville (MB to NP, December 29, 1935). It is comforting to find later evidence of the improvement that their new course of semifreedom brought about, as when, after attending some plays, Marjorie recorded: "We had a party at Flora's flat . . . oceans of talk and savories. We are trying to manage a weekly party, every Wednesday" (MB to NP, August 7, 1938). What the Eldershaws thought about Flora's literary ambitions I do not know, nor, from the Riverina, would it have much mattered; but the Barnard-Palmer correspondence is thick with references—some amusing, some painful—to the Barnards' lack of understanding of their brilliant daughter's career. The generation gap is no new thing.

Chapter Two

1. Both remain readily available, much read, and highly respected. *A House Is Built* ultimately appeared in American and Australian as well as English editions, and was translated at least once: into Swedish as *Vårt Hus I Sydney* (Stockholm, 1948).

2. "Australian Novel, Mr. Arnold Bennett's Praise," from the London *Evening Standard*, July 4, in the Melbourne *Argus*, July 5, 1929, p. 8; "Mr. Arnold Bennett Writes Appreciation of *A House Is Built*," Sydney *Morning Herald*, July 5, 1929, p. 14b.

3. It has even suffered the too great attention often accorded a classic: In 1945 MBE refused permission to an ambitious Australian editor who proposed an edition to include some fifty pages of his own annotations (MB to NP, May 3, 1945). But they had no defense against the separate publication as late as 1967 of a detailed study guide complete with commentary and discussion exercises calculated to rob the student of all the joy of personal discovery in his reading of this easily comprehended novel (A. K. Thomson, *Understanding the Novel*).

4. A Mr. James H. Watson of the Royal Australian Historical Society pointed out that a quartermaster in the Royal Navy was only a seaman in charge of stowing the stores and would have had no business experience, only an Army quartermaster being in charge of supplies ("Letter to the Editor," Sydney *Morning Herald*, January 10, 1930). Other history buffs found minor errors and anachronisms in details of the setting—errors that detract from the novel about as much as Keats's misnaming Balboa Cortez does from "On First Looking into Chapman's Homer."

5. *A House Is Built* (London, 1929), p. 239.

6. *Ibid.*, p. 141.

7. *Ibid.*, p. 59.

8. *Ibid.*, p. 150.

9. *Ibid.*, p. 43.

10. *Ibid.*, p. 20.

11. *Ibid.*, pp. 152-53.

12. *Ibid.*, p. 359.

13. *Ibid.*, p. 69.

14. *Ibid.*, p. 41.

15. *Ibid.*, pp. 53-54.

16. *Ibid.*, p. 301.

17. *Ibid.*, p. 34.

18. *Ibid.*, p. 83.

19. *Ibid.*, pp. 347-49.

20. MB to NP, November 16, 1930.

21. *Green Memory* (London, 1931), p. 45.

22. *Ibid.*, p. 279.

23. *Ibid.*, p. 288.

24. *Ibid.*, p. 279.

25. *Ibid.*, pp. 15-16.

26. MB to NP, December 1, 1930.

27. "The Novels of Seaforth Mackenzie," *Meanjin*, XIII (Summer, 1954), pp. 503-4. See also p. 162.

28. MB to NP, September 4, 1931.

Chapter Three

1. MB to NP, September 10, 1933.

2. MB to VP, January 22, 1935.

3. MB to NP, February 26, 1936.

4. *The Glasshouse* (London, 1936), p. 37.

5. *Ibid.*, p. 31.

6. *Ibid.*, p. 35.

7. *Ibid.*, p. 58.

8. *Ibid.*, p. 284.

9. *Ibid.*, p. 260.

10. *Ibid.*, p. 86.

11. *Ibid.*, pp. 35-36.

12. *Ibid.*, pp. 36-37.

13. *Ibid.*, p. 73.

14. *Ibid.*, p. 76.

15. *Ibid.*, p. 11.

16. MB to NP, February 26, 1936.

17. MB to VP, February 14, 1935.
18. MB to NP, April 28, 1935.
19. MB to NP, July 2, 1935.
20. *The Glasshouse,* p. 302.
21. *Ibid.,* p. 315.
22. *Ibid.,* p. 288.
23. MB to VP, March 10, 1936.
24. MB to NP, February 26, 1936.
25. MB to NP, October 8, 1935.
26. MB to NP, December 29, 1935.
27. MB to NP, June 9, 1936.
28. MB to NP, July 13, 1936.
29. *Plaque with Laurel* (London, 1937), p. 109.
30. *Ibid.,* p. 110.
31. *Ibid.,* p. 235.
32. *Ibid.,* pp. 161-62. This philosophy appears also in *The Glasshouse* in "Helen Weatherell's Story" (Chapter IX). Helen had been innocently and indirectly responsible, as a child, for her father's death. As an old woman she reflects, "There is no bitterer tragedy than to find you have destroyed what you love best, or even to know that you have been, however unwittingly, on the side of those impersonal forces that destroyed him" (p. 190).
33. *Ibid.,* p. 214.
34. *Ibid.,* pp. 127-28.
35. *Ibid.,* p. 287.
36. *Ibid.,* p. 117.
37. *Ibid.,* p. 231.
38. *Ibid.,* pp. 290-91.
39. *Ibid.,* p. 276.
40. *Ibid.,* p. 133. While *Plaque with Laurel* was being written, Marjorie wrote to Nettie, "We inevitably nose round the journalism question and achieve a savage epigram. 'Journalists,' one of the crassest of them remarks, 'are people who take in one another's washing and sell it.'" Answering Nettie's warning against going into journalism now that she had freed herself to write, she declared, "It has in truth no attractions for me. . . . So if I *have* to take to journalism for a living I'll certainly do something else" (May 5, 1936).
41. *Ibid.,* p. 32.
42. *Ibid.,* p. 21.
43. *Ibid.,* p. 9.
44. *Ibid.,* p. 288.
45. *Ibid.,* p. 21.
46. *Ibid.,* p. 288.

47. MB to VP, September 12, 1937.

48. MB to VP, December 12, 1937.

49. MB to NP, April 22, 1941.

50. MB to VP, May 8, 1941.

51. *Ibid.*

52. "How 'Tomorrow and Tomorrow' Came to be Written," *Meanjin*, XXIX (Spring, 1970), p. 329.

53. MB to VP, December 6, 1941.

54. MB to NP, Saturday (apparently mid-1942).

55. MB to NP, July 14, 1942.

56. FE to NP, July 17, 1942.

57. FE to VP, undated (apparently 1947).

58. MB to VP, May 8, 1941.

59. MB to NP, Saturday (apparently late 1941).

60. Fewer than half of these were completed. Lectures 1-16, 28 and 50, with outline of the complete series, are available in manuscript and typescript at the Mitchell Library in Sydney.

61. MB to NP, April 23 (apparently 1942).

62. MB to NP, June 15 and 16, 1942.

63. MB to NP, August 23, 1944.

64. MB to NP, December 15, 1944.

65. MB to NP, April 13 (apparently 1947). An account of the publisher's unnecessarily submitting the manuscript to the censor and the consequent deletion of all references to Russia, among other things, appears in MB's "How 'Tomorrow and Tomorrow' Came to be Written," pp. 329-30.

66. MB to VP, September 9, 1947.

67. *Tomorrow and Tomorrow* (Melbourne, 1947), p. 4.

68. *Ibid.*, p. 5.

69. *Ibid.*, p. 11.

70. *Ibid.*, p. 9.

71. *Ibid.*, p. 10.

72. *Ibid.*, p. 13.

73. *Ibid.*, p. 5.

74. *Ibid.*, p. 21.

75. *Ibid.*, p. 9.

76. *Ibid.*, p. 24.

77. *Ibid.*, p. 466.

78. *Ibid.*, p. 463.

79. "Australian Literature 1947," *Southerly*, 9:3 (1948), pp. 138-45.

80. "This Battered Caravanserai," *Southerly*, 9:4 (1948), pp. 222-23. His opinion of *Tomorrow and Tomorrow* appears in substantially the same words in book form two years later, save that there he modifies Harry's inheriting of the earth with "spiritually"—no more

applicable (Colin Roderick, *An Introduction to Australian Fiction*, Sydney, 1950, p. 119).

81. *An Introduction to Australian Fiction*, p. 120.

82. "Hail Tomorrow" in Notes and Comments, *Southerly*, 11:1 (1950), p. 58, presumably from the pen of the journal's editor, R. G. Howarth.

83. "How 'Tomorrow and Tomorrow' Came to be Written," p. 330.

84. *Ibid.*

85. Robert Burns, "Flux and Fixity: M. Barnard Eldershaw's 'Tomorrow and Tomorrow,'" *Meanjin*, XXIX (Spring, 1970), pp. 320-27. A year later Tom Inglis Moore's long-awaited *Social Patterns in Australian Literature*, in a section on the effects of the depression, paid tribute to this novel as "the most penetrating analysis in fiction" for that period (p. 262).

Chapter Four

1. MB to NP, November 26, 1931.

2. MB to NP, July 19, 1932.

3. *Home*, August 1, 1941.

4. Cecil Mann, ed., *Coast to Coast 1941* (Sydney, 1941), p. 93.

5. "The Plover" curiously reappeared in the 1960's in an anthology of wildlife rather than childlife stories—suggesting that it was selected by its title alone or that there was a shortage of wildlife (Bill Wannan, ed., *A Treasury of Wildlife Stories*, 1963, republished as *Australian Wildlife Stories*, 1970).

6. MB to VP, December 7, 1934.

7. MB to VP, January 22, 1935.

8. MB to NP, May 5, 1936.

9. Frank Dalby Davison, *The Road to Yesterday* (Sydney, 1964), Author's Note.

10. MB to NP, November 20, 1936.

11. Among them: the Sydney *Morning Herald*; the *Bulletin*; the *A.B.C. Weekly*; the *Australian Women's Digest*; *Home*; the *Home Annual*; and *Coast to Coast*.

12. *Australian Encyclopaedia*, vol. 7, p. 63.

13. MB to NP, Monday (apparently early January, 1946).

14. MB to NP, November 10, 1949. This remark was made in connection with the MB story, "Say Goodbye and Mean It," which Nettie had asked to use (and did) in the edition of *Coast to Coast 1949-50* she was editing.

15. MB to VP, February 2, 1937.

16. To one who, like Marjorie, had repeatedly spoken of the importance of format to a book's success, the appearance of *The Per-*

simmon Tree must have been a bitter disappointment. The deficiencies of paper and binding in this slim volume may be excusable as wartime necessities, but there is surely no excuse for the frequency of misprints.

17. This story first appeared in *Home*, September 1, 1937.

18. *The Persimmon Tree and Other Stories* (Sydney, 1943), pp. 53-54.

19. MB to NP, March 19, 1933.

20. *The Persimmon Tree*, p. 125.

21. With this volume the series shifted from annual to biennial frequency.

22. Ken Levis, in a review of *Coast to Coast 1949-1950*, in *Southerly*, 12:3 (1951), p. 167.

23. *Coast to Coast 1945*, p. 86.

24. Beatrice Davis, ed., *Short Stories of Australia: The Moderns* (Sydney, 1967). "The Persimmon Tree" was also chosen by Cecil Hadgraft, a discerning critic, for his anthology *A Century of Australian Short Stories* (1963).

25. "The Persimmon Tree" in *The Persimmon Tree*, pp. 21-25. Marjorie's letters to Nettie Palmer contain two interesting sidelights on this remarkable story, one concerned presumably with its genesis in her childhood (p. 16): "Long ago when we lived in Eastwood and had an orchard there was a row of persimmon trees down one side of the house. . . . In autumn the rooms were filled with red light. The persimmon trees dominated it. Such passionate trees" (MB to NP, April 21, 1948). The other points up the difficulties of publishing the elusive in Australia: Two weeks after the initial appearance of the story in *Home* (July 1, 1942), Marjorie wrote to Nettie from the hospital in which she was recovering from pneumonia that her doctor "had (unfortunately) read 'The Persimmon Tree' and demanded that I explain it. There it lay on the bed open to the regrettable picture of the naked woman. How could Gellert [then *Home*'s editor] bring down a steam hammer on what was meant to be a delicate point?" (July 14, 1942).

26. MB to NP, April 29, 1938. This Australian ability to see beauty in dessication emerges also in Marjorie's fine descriptive piece "O Country under Drought" (*Home*, August 1, 1942), an account of the landscape by day and by night under "normal" drought conditions.

27. A swagman (see "Waltzing Matilda") used to wander around the Australian outback with all his possessions in a bundle, or "swag." To "do a perish" is almost to die for want of water.

28. This story first appeared in the *Home Annual*, 1940; next, in *Coast to Coast 1941*. It is the closing story in *The Persimmon Tree*

(pp. 152-60). It also appeared in Australia's first major anthology, Walter Murdoch and H. Drake-Brockman, eds., *Australian Short Stories* (Oxford University Press, 1951).

29. Leslie Rees, ed., *Australian Radio Plays* (Sydney, 1946), pp. 139-51; *Eight One-Act Plays* (Melbourne: Nelson, 1961), No. 6; *Theatregoer*, vol. 2, no. 4 (February, 1962).

Chapter Five

1. MB to NP, November 8, 1936.
2. MB to VP, April 8, 1937.
3. MB to NP, July 31, 1937.
4. *Phillip of Australia: An Account of the Settlement of Sydney Cove 1788-92* (London, 1938), p. 117.
5. *Ibid.*, pp. 9-10.
6. *Ibid.*, pp. 9, 20.
7. *Ibid.*, pp. 26-27.
8. *Ibid.*, p. 33.
9. *Ibid.*, p. 98. If this second figure still seems high, take into account the extremes of age, the undernourishment, and the bad health of many of the convicts upon embarkation, as well as the conditions of the long voyage.
10. *Ibid.*, p. 108.
11. *Ibid.*, p. 110.
12. *Ibid.*, p. 112.
13. *Ibid.*, p. 244.
14. *Ibid.*, p. 245.
15. *Ibid.*, p. 53.
16. *Ibid.*, p. 135.
17. *Ibid.*, p. 140.
18. *Ibid.*, pp. 71-72.
19. *Ibid.*, p. 267. This text is immortalized on an ornate shaft in downtown Sydney, where Castlereagh Street joins Hunter and becomes Bligh, an area denoted "Richard Johnson Square." It was erected in 1925 "To the glory of God and in commemoration of the first Christian service held in Australia February 3rd 1788 [understandably delayed until the second Sunday after the Saturday landing on January 26], R^{ev} Richard Johnson B A the Chaplain being the preacher." This memorial further marks the site of the first church erected in Australia, opened August 25, 1793, burned down October 1, 1798—but no mention is made of the cause of the fire, the convicts' resentment over Governor Hunter's edict of compulsory attendance on R^{ev} Johnson's services. See *Phillip of Australia*, pp. 267-70, for the engrossing details.

20. *Ibid.*, p. 246.

21. *Ibid.*, p. 82.

22. MB to NP, June 28, 1938.

23. MB to VP, October 20, 1938.

24. MB to VP, February 13, 1940. The book has brought as much as $100 in recent sales.

25. *The Life and Times of Captain John Piper* (Sydney, 1939), p. xiii.

26. *Ibid.*, p. xii.

27. *Ibid.*, p. xiii.

28. *Ibid.*, pp. 6-7.

29. *Ibid.*, p. 7.

30. *Ibid.*, p. 10.

31. *Ibid.*, p. 12.

32. *Ibid.*, p. 16.

33. *Ibid.*, p. 34. The name is commonly spelled "Macarthur."

34. *Ibid.*, p. 96.

35. *Ibid.*, p. 97.

36. *Ibid.*, p. 123.

37. *Ibid.*, p. 147.

38. *Ibid.*, p. 153.

39. *Ibid.*, p. 191.

40. *Ibid.*, p. 13.

41. *Ibid.*, p. 20.

42. *Ibid.*, p. 15.

43. *Ibid.*, p. 8.

44. *Ibid.*, p. 195.

45. *Ibid.*, p. 10.

46. *Ibid.*, p. 100.

47. *Ibid.*, p. 158. The triangle was a frame to which a convict was secured while his bared back received from a cat o' nine tails the number of lashes officially prescribed for his offense.

48. *Ibid.*, p. 159.

49. *Ibid.*, pp. 175-76.

50. The paper that Flora read to the Royal Australian Historical Society in 1933 (p. 140) includes the statement: "I have proved, or hope that I have proved, that history is a creative art" ("History as the Raw Material of Literature," p. 4). The same thought appears through Marjorie's works, as separated in time as a letter to Nettie Palmer in 1931 (September 4) and "The Georgian Context: New South Wales," in Max DuPain, *Georgian Architecture in Australia* (Sydney, 1963), p. 13.

51. MB to VP, New Year's Eve, 1938.

52. MB to NP, January 28, 1939.

53. MB to NP, August 27, 1939.
54. *My Australia* (London, 1939), p. 23.
55. *Home*, March 1, 1938, p. 25 f.
56. *My Australia*, p. 11.
57. *Ibid.*, p. 16.
58. *Ibid.*, p. 56.
59. *Ibid.*, p. 21. In the revised edition of 1951, wood and wheat have been added to rum, wool, and gold as key commodities.
60. *Ibid.*, pp. 227, 246.
61. *Ibid.*, p. 309.
62. *Ibid.*, p. 130. This remark long preceded Robin Boyd's *The Australian Ugliness* (Melbourne, 1960), a title that has become a byword.
63. *Ibid.*, p. 47. There is some justice in H. M. Green's classifying *My Australia* as "descriptive writing" in his *A History of Australian Literature* (2 vols., 1961), as did E. Morris Miller in his bibliography *Australian Literature* (2 vols., 1940). But it is much more.
64. *Ibid.*, p. 153.
65. *Ibid.*, pp. 262-63.
66. *Ibid.*, p. 290.
67. *Ibid.*, p. 293.
68. *Ibid.*, p. 306.
69. MB to NP, November 10, 1939.
70. MB to NP, November 19, 1939.
71. MB to VP, December 2, 1939.

Chapter Six

1. MB to VP, August 16, 1940.
2. MB to VP, July 10, 1940.
3. MB to NP, October 18, 1940.
4. MB to VP, December 28, 1940.
5. MB to VP, January 5, 1941.
6. MB to NP, April 22, 1941.
7. MB to NP, Saturday (probably late 1942).
8. MB to NP, August 7, 1938.
9. *Macquarie's World* (Melbourne, 1946), p. 23.
10. *Ibid.*, p. 25.
11. *Ibid.*, p. 34.
12. *Ibid.*, p. 35.
13. *Ibid.*, pp. 59-60.
14. *Ibid.*, p. 161.
15. *Ibid.*, p. 145.
16. *Ibid.*, p. 147.

17. *Ibid.*, p. 160.
18. A "cornstalk" was so called because of the superior height to which his generation attained in Australia.
19. *Macquarie's World,* p. 150.
20. *Ibid.*, p. 16.
21. *Ibid.*, p. 19.
22. *Ibid.*, p. 214.
23. *Ibid.*, p. 220.
24. *Ibid.*, p. 225.
25. Sydney Tomholt, *Southerly,* 8:4 (1947), p. 239.
26. *Macquarie's World,* p. 182.
27. *Australian Outline* (Sydney, 1943), p. 26.
28. *The Sydney Book* (Sydney, 1947), p. 6.
29. *Ibid.*, p. 10.
30. *Ibid.*, p. 11.
31. *Ibid.*, p. 22.
32. *Macquarie's World,* p. 191.
33. *Lachlan Macquarie* (Melbourne, 1964), p. 18.
34. "The Georgian Context: New South Wales," in Max DuPain, *Georgian Architecture in Australia* (Sydney, 1963), p. 13.
35. *Ibid.*, p. 14.
36. *Ibid.*, p. 13.
37. "The First Australian," *Home,* January 3, 1938, p. 27.
38. "Prelude to History," *Home,* March 1, 1938, p. 35.
39. *Home,* April through December, 1938.
40. Mrs. Chisholm (1808-1877), the emigrant's friend, is named in the *Australian Encyclopaedia* as "possibly 'the greatest of women pioneers in the history of Australia'" (vol. 2, p. 354). A long tribute to her by novelist Eleanor Dark appears in the sesquicentennial *The Peaceful Army,* edited by Flora Eldershaw. Marjorie Barnard allows Chisholm a full-page portrait (op. p. 551) in *A History,* but refers only briefly to her work (pp. 255-56, 589).
41. "Historic Muster," *Home,* November 1, 1938, p. 76.
42. "Vice-Regal Guests," *Home,* April 1, 1938, p. 38 f.
43. *Australia Week-end Book* (Sydney, 1942), pp. 113-22. This was the first of five consecutive annual anthologies; MB is represented in 1942, 1943, and 1945.
44. *A History of Australia* (Sydney, 1962), p. 302.
45. *Ibid.*, p. 157.
46. *Ibid.*, p. 549.
47. *Ibid.*, p. 347.
48. *Ibid.*, p. 402.
49. *Ibid.*, p. 396.
50. *Ibid.*, p. 1. The same thought, in a few of the same words,

opens "The Landscape Writers" (p. 141), published years earlier under Flora's name.

51. *Ibid.*, p. 15.
52. *Ibid.*, p. 632.
53. *Ibid.*, p. 3.
54. *Ibid.*, p. 662.
55. *Ibid.*, p. 666.
56. *Ibid.*, p. 576.
57. *Ibid.*, p. 345.
58. *Ibid.*, p. 637.
59. *Ibid.*, p. 156.
60. *Ibid.*, p. 674. This personal note is charming but startling, on the concluding page of so monumental and objective a book.
61. *Ibid.*, p. 549.
62. *Ibid.*, p. 671.
63. *Ibid.*, p. 673.

Chapter Seven

1. "Eleanor Dark," *Essays in Australian Fiction,* pp. 182-83.
2. "The Period Novel, an Infinity of Problems," Sydney *Morning Herald,* 1929: I, November 23, p. 13b; II, November 30, p. 13g. "The Genetic Novel Has a Wide Field," I, December 21, p. 10f; II, December 28, p. 7f.
3. "The Period Novel," I, November 23, p. 13b.
4. *Ibid.*, II, November 30, p. 13g.
5. "The Genetic Novel," II, December 28, p. 7f.
6. "The Period Novel," I, November 23, p. 13b.
7. "The Genetic Novel," II, December 28, p. 7f.
8. "History as the Raw Material of Literature," Royal Australian Historical Society, *Journal and Proceedings,* vol. XX, part I (1934), pp. 1-17. Read before the Society, October 31, 1933.

On July 30, 1940, Flora read a second paper before this Society, "Captain John Piper," drawn in content and often in language from the MBE book of the previous year (vol. XXVI, part VI [1940], pp. 479-98).

9. *Ibid.*, p. 6.
10. *Ibid.*, p. 2.
11. *Ibid.*, p. 14.
12. *Ibid.*, p. 9.
13. *Meanjin,* XI (Spring, 1952), p. 218.
14. *Ibid.*, p. 215.
15. *Ibid.*, pp. 218-19.
16. *Ibid.*, p. 219.

17. *Ibid.*, p. 225.

18. *Ibid.*, p. 228. Editor T. Inglis Moore uses an acknowledged extract in *A Book of Australia* (London, 1961), pp. 288-90, but well over half of the essay in *Australia Writes: An Anthology* (Melbourne, 1953), pp. 22-30, without an indication that it is abridged.

19. "The Future of Australian Literature," *Australian Writers' Annual*, p. 13.

20. *Southerly*, 15:1 (1954), p. 39.

21. Frank Dalby Davison both edited and contributed to the 1943 collection, as did Vance Palmer with the 1944.

22. "Australian Literature Since 1929," *Books Abroad*, University of Oklahoma Press (October, 1960), p. 283.

23. *Essays in Australian Fiction* (Melbourne, 1938), p. 183.

24. Nettie Palmer, *Modern Australian Literature 1900-1923* (Melbourne, 1924), p. 24.

25. *Southerly*, 6:1 (1945), p. 32.

26. *Laughter, Not for a Cage* (Sydney, 1956), p. 215.

27. MB to VP, January 7, 1936.

28. *Essays in Australian Fiction*, p. 4.

29. *Ibid.*, pp. 13-14.

30. *Ibid.*, p. 20.

31. *Ibid.*, p. 24.

32. *Ibid.*, p. 33.

33. *Ibid.*, p. 26.

34. *Ibid.*, p. 129. An early and prominent American critic of Australian literature, Bruce Sutherland of Pennsylvania State University, is one who quotes this sentence, but with an "It has been called . . ." unfortunately instead of giving credit to MBE. *University of Toronto Quarterly* (October, 1946), p. 71. The MBE—and MB—style encourages quotation.

35. *Ibid.*, p. 129.

36. *Ibid.*, p. 131.

37. *Ibid.*, pp. 135-36.

38. Twenty years later Marjorie herself was still complaining of Australian criticism that "writers take in one another's washing, and impartiality flies out of the window" ("Australian Literature Since 1929," *Books Abroad*, p. 284). That she was personally conscious of the problem is seen in a postscript written to Nettie after first meeting the Palmers: "Am glad I completed the lecture on Vance Palmer before coming to Melbourne—it is not quite the same plunging one's critical fork into one's friends" (March 19, 1933). The following year Vance dedicated his third volume of short stories (*Sea and Spinifex*, 1934) "To Marjorie Barnard." MBE wanted Vance to write

a foreword to their *Essays,* an honor he understandably declined since he was one of the subjects.

39. *Essays in Australian Fiction,* p. 84.

40. *Ibid.,* p. 83.

41. *Ibid.,* pp. 84-85.

42. *Ibid.,* p. 98.

43. *Ibid.,* pp. 108-9.

44. In the discussion of Palmer's success in interpreting the world of common experience, following this, we get one of our few glimpses into the opinion of these two critics of the literary world outside of Australia—this one, of their conservative attitude toward the stream-of-consciousness school then relatively new but already critically acclaimed abroad: "If the author merely holds the mirror we get something like the *Ulysses* of James Joyce or the naturalistic ramblings of Gertrude Stein, which are exasperating and antipathetic to the average intelligence" (p. 113).

45. This book, for which even these critics can say little, leads them—authors of *A House Is Built,* remember—into a most revealing discussion of the disadvantages of writing a successful first novel!

46. *Essays in Australian Fiction,* p. 52.

47. *Ibid.,* p. 59. A notable example of Australian critical insensitivity is a contemporary review of *Man-Shy* by John Reed, who found the inevitable tinge of anthropomorphism in the book to be "false sentimentality," and concluded that its publication was "basically harmful and damaging to our cultural reputation" ("'Man-Shy,' a Criticism—Mainly Destructive," *Angry Penguins,* 1945, pp. 167-68).

48. *Ibid.,* p. 60.

49. *Ibid.,* p. 65.

50. *Ibid.,* p. 80. His short stories, uncollected, were omitted.

51. *Ibid.,* p. 140.

52. *Ibid.,* pp. 143-44.

53. *Ibid.,* pp. 146-47. Critics have inevitably made frequent comparisons between *The Montforts* and MBE's *A House Is Built,* Australian family chronicles published only a year apart.

54. *Ibid.,* p. 160.

55. *Ibid.,* p. 176.

56. *Ibid.,* p. 174.

57. *Ibid.,* p. 176.

58. *Ibid.,* pp. 178-79. Quoted from Stead's *The Beauties and the Furies,* p. 148.

59. *Ibid.,* p. 181.

60. All of the others discussed, save Stead, were older than Barnard and Eldershaw, although Davison and Mann were newer to publishing.

61. *Ibid.*, p. 184.

62. *Ibid.*, p. 190.

63. *Ibid.*, p. 194.

64. G. A. Wilkes, who holds the Chair in Australian Literature at the University of Sydney, provides an interesting item concerning an earlier influence: Mrs. Dark's interest in history, which flowered in her later great novels, stemmed from the research she had to do in order to write an essay on Caroline Chisholm for *The Peaceful Army* edited by Flora in 1938 (p. 94). "The Progress of Eleanor Dark," *Southerly*, 12:3 (1951), p. 145.

65. My own justification for having devoted more space to this book than to any one of the others is that despite its occasional flaws it was for its time a rare and remarkable achievement. As late as 1961 H. M. Green placed it "among the landmarks of Australian criticism" (*A History of Australian Literature*, p. 1201). As recently as 1971 T. Inglis Moore leaned on it as an authority for Vance Palmer's fatalism (*Social Patterns in Australian Literature*, p. 262). It therefore seems strange to find the *Essays* not so much as mentioned in the introduction to Clement Semmler's anthology *Twentieth Century Australian Literary Criticism* (1967)—perhaps because its existence conflicts with the editor's opening thesis that instead of a gradual development, "there was a flurry of critical writing at the turn of the century; an obvious gap in the 1920s and 1930s; and a building-up from the 1940s on" (p. ix).

66. MB to NP, June 28, 1938.

67. MB to NP, August 7, 1938.

68. MB to NP, November 6, 1938. An interesting reflection on one of the deficiencies in Australian criticism appears in this same letter: "There was quite a long review in *Desiderata* but the reviewer admitted he had never read the authors who were the subjects of the essays. That did not deter him from passing judgement on our judgement. Amazing isn't it?"

Chapter Eight

1. "The Harp in the Orchestra," review of Ruth Park, *The Harp in the South* (1948), *Southerly*, 9:3 (1948), pp. 182-84.

2. Review of R. M. Crawford, *Australia* (1952), *Meanjin*, XII (Summer, 1953), pp. 479-80.

3. Review of Thelma Astley, *A Descant for Gossips* (1960), "Fiction Chronicle," *Meanjin*, XIX (Summer, 1960), p. 435.

4. Review of Vance Palmer, *Golconda* (1948), *Meanjin*, VIII (Autumn, 1949), p. 58.

5. Review of Helen Heney, *Dark Moon* (1953), *Southerly*, 16:1 (1955), p. 45.

6. Review of Elyne Mitchell, *Flow River, Blow Wind* (1953), *Southerly*, 16:1 (1955), p. 42.

7. "The Harp in the Orchestra," p. 183.

8. Review of Nourma Handford, "Blood on the Leaves," *Southerly*, 16:4 (1955), p. 225.

9. "These Careful People," review of Helen Fowler and Bernard Harris, *The Careless People* (1954), *Southerly*, 17:1 (1956), p. 49.

10. Marjorie's disappointment in one book hailed as the "great Australian novel" led her to say, "One always has hopes when someone new comes into the field, I'm so anxious for the books to be a success that I nearly get out and push" (MB to NP, August 6, 1935).

11. "Fiction Chronicle," *Meanjin*, XVI (Winter, 1957), p. 208.

12. Review of Ken Levis, ed., *Coast to Coast 1951-52* (1952), *Southerly*, 51:1 (1954), p. 38.

13. *Ibid.*, p. 39. Whether the weakness of this volume indicates a trend in Australian writing or the taste of the editor, the reviewer doesn't purport to know.

14. Review of Russell Ward, *The Australian Legend* (1958), *Southerly*, 20:1 (1959), p. 46.

15. "Facts on Fiction," review of Colin Roderick, *An Introduction to Australian Fiction* (1950), *Southerly*, 11:4 (1950), p. 203.

16. *Ibid.*, p. 204.

17. "Fiction Chronicle," *Meanjin*, XVI (Winter, 1957), p. 205.

18. Reviews of Vance Palmer: *Golconda* (1948), *Meanjin*, VIII (Autumn, 1949), pp. 58-60; *Seedtime* (1957), *Meanjin*, XVII (Autumn, 1958), pp. 94-96.

19. "Miles Franklin," *Meanjin*, XIV (Summer, 1955), pp. 469-87.

20. "The Novels of Seaforth Mackenzie," *Meanjin*, XIII (Summer, 1954), pp. 503-11.

21. *Ibid.*, p. 503. See page 47 here for the possible connection of this remark with MBE's own *Green Memory*.

22. *Ibid.*, p. 511.

23. *Miles Franklin* (New York, 1967), p. 161.

24. "The Four Novels of Patrick White," *Meanjin*, XV (Winter, 1956), p. 156.

25. *Ibid.*, p. 157.

26. *Ibid.*, p. 158.

27. *Ibid.*, p. 157.

28. *Ibid.*, p. 161.

29. *Ibid.*, p. 160.

30. *Ibid.*, p. 165.

31. "Theodora Again," essay on Patrick White, *The Aunt's Story*, *Southerly*, 20:1 (1959), p. 51.

32. "The Four Novels of Patrick White," pp. 165-66.

33. *Ibid.*, pp. 167-68.

34. *Ibid.*, pp. 169-70.

35. *Ibid.*, p. 170.

36. "Theodora Again," p. 54.

37. Geoffrey Dutton, *Patrick White* (Australian Writers and Their Work, Melbourne, 1961), p. 40.

38. "Books," *Meanjin*, XVII (Autumn, 1958), p. 96.

39. *Ibid.*, p. 99.

40. *Ibid.*, p. 100.

41. "Scribbling on the Map," *Walkabout*, vol. 6 (August 1, 1940), pp. 36-38. The theme here has something in common with "The Landscape Writers," published years later under Flora's name, but is larger in concept.

42. "Our Literature," *Australian Writers Speak* (1942), pp. 97-105.

43. *Ibid.*, p. 102.

44. *Ibid.*, p. 97.

45. *Ibid.*, p. 98.

46. *Ibid.*, p. 101.

47. "A Survey of Australian Literature," *Chambers's Encyclopaedia* (London, new ed., 1950), I, pp. 817-22.

48. "Notes and Comments," *Southerly*, 11:4 (1950), p. 238.

49. "Australian Literature Since 1929," *Books Abroad* (October, 1960), p. 284.

50. *Ibid.*, p. 280.

51. *Ibid.*, p. 284.

52. MB to NP, November 25, 1935; August 4, 1936.

53. *Meanjin*, XIV (Summer, 1955), pp. 469-87.

54. *Miles Franklin*, p. 16.

55. *Ibid.*, Preface (unnumbered first page).

56. *Ibid.*, p. 66.

57. *Ibid.*, p. 14.

58. Miles Franklin, *Childhood at Brindabella, My First Ten Years* (Sydney, 1963).

59. *Miles Franklin*, p. 42.

60. *Ibid.*, p. 160.

61. *Ibid.*, p. 49.

62. *Ibid.*, p. 61.

63. *Ibid.*, p. 148.

64. MB to NP, September 25, 1931.

65. *Miles Franklin*, p. 100.

66. *Ibid.*, p. 118.

67. *Ibid.*, p. 111.

68. *Ibid.*, p. 132.

69. *Ibid.*, p. 140.

70. *Ibid.,* p. 146.

71. *Ibid.,* p. 165.

72. *Ibid.,* p. 167.

73. *Ibid.,* p. 150, quoted from Dymphna Cusack, *Miles Franklin: A Tribute* (Melbourne, 1955), p. 25, who in turn is quoting Miles's own words.

74. *Ibid.,* p. 154. Marjorie likens it in this respect to *My Career Goes Bung,* written in Miles's adolescence.

75. *Ibid.,* p. 151.

76. *Ibid.,* p. 157. Furphy (p. 13) is the "Tom Collins" who published Australia's remarkable *Such Is Life* in 1903 at age 60. He greatly admired Miles, met her once, corresponded with her, and encouraged her at length.

77. *Ibid.,* p. 158.

78. *Ibid.,* p. 161.

79. *Ibid.,* p. 163.

80. *Ibid.,* p. 145.

81. *Ibid.,* p. 18.

82. *Ibid.,* p. 19.

83. "How 'Tomorrow and Tomorrow' Came to be Written," *Meanjin,* XXIX (Summer, 1970), pp. 328-30.

Conclusion

1. MB to NP, February 13, 1933.

2. MB to NP, December 29, 1935.

3. MB to NP, Christmas Day, 1932.

4. For example, C. B. Christesen's *Australian Heritage* (1949), a collection of seventeen pieces of prose, uses four: one each from MBE's *My Australia, A House Is Built,* and *Tomorrow and Tomorrow;* another from MB's *Macquarie's World.*

Selected Bibliography

PRIMARY SOURCES

M. Barnard Eldershaw—Major Works

1. Novels

A House Is Built. London: Harrap, 1929. Sydney: Australasian Pub. Co., 1945.
Green Memory. London: Harrap, 1931.
The Glasshouse. London: Harrap, 1936. Sydney: Australian Pocket Library, 1945.
Plaque with Laurel. London: Harrap, 1937.
Tomorrow and Tomorrow. Melbourne: Georgian House, 1947. London: Phoenix House, 1948.

2 Histories

Phillip of Australia: An Account of the Settlement of Sydney Cove 1788-92. London: Harrap, 1938. Reissued in 1972.
The Life and Times of Captain John Piper. Sydney: B. Waite for the Australian Limited Editions Society, 1939.
My Australia. London: Jarrolds, 1939; cheap ed., 1943; rev. ed. 1951.

3. Criticism

Essays in Australian Fiction. Melbourne: Melbourne University Press, 1938. Freeport, N. Y.: Books for Libraries Press, 1970.

M. Barnard Eldershaw—Minor Works

1. Fiction

"The Mystery Grows" (Chapter 7). J. L. Ranken and J. C. Ross, eds., *Murder Pie*. Sydney: Angus and Robertson, 1936.
"The Plover" (short story). Cecil Mann, ed., *Coast to Coast 1941*. Sydney: Angus and Robertson, 1941, pp. 85-93.
"The Watch on the Headland" (radio drama). Leslie Rees, ed., *Australian Radio Plays*, 1946, pp. 137-51. Also in *Eight One-Act Plays*, Melbourne: Nelson, 1961, and *Theatregoer*, vol. 2, no. 4 (February, 1962).

2. History

"The Happy Pioneer: Elizabeth Macarthur." Flora Eldershaw, ed., *The Peaceful Army*. Sydney: Australia's 150th Anniversary Celebrations, Women's Executive Committee and Advisory Council, 1938, pp. 15-33.

3. Criticism

"The Period Novel, an Infinity of Problems." Sydney *Morning Herald*, 1929: I, November 23, p. 13b; II, November 30, p. 13g.
"The Genetic Novel Has a Wide Field." Sydney *Morning Herald*, 1929: I, December 21, p. 10f; II, December 28, p. 7f.

4. Editing

Coast to Coast 1946. Sydney: Angus and Robertson, 1947.

Marjorie Barnard—Major Works

1. Fiction

The Persimmon Tree and Other Stories. Sydney: Clarendon Publishing Co., 1943.

2. Histories

Macquarie's World. Sydney: B. Waite for the Australian Limited Editions Society, 1941. Melbourne: Melbourne University Press, 1946; 2nd ed., 1949; Melbourne Paperbacks, 1961. Sydney: Angus and Robertson, 1971.
A History of Australia. Sydney: Angus and Robertson, 1962; 2nd ed., rev., 1963. New York: Praeger, 1963.

3. Criticism

Miles Franklin. New York: Twayne Publishers, 1967. Melbourne: Hill of Content, rev., enlarged, illust., 1967.

Marjorie Barnard—Minor Works

1. Fiction

"A Mask of Australia." *Home*, March 1, 1938, p. 25f.
"Vice-Regal Guests." *Home*, April 1, 1938, p. 38f.

2. Histories

Australian Outline. Sydney: Ure Smith, 1943; new and rev. ed., 1949, Ure Smith Miniature Series, no. 1.
The Sydney Book. Sydney: Ure Smith, 1947.
Sydney: The Story of a City. Melbourne: Melbourne University Press, 1956.
Australia's First Architect: Francis Greenway. London: Longmans, 1961. Australian Landmarks Series.
Lachlan Macquarie. Melbourne: Oxford University Press, 1964. Great Australians Series.

3. Criticism

"Scribbling on the Map." *Walkabout,* vol. 6 (August 1, 1940), pp. 36-38.
"Our Literature." *Australian Writers Speak.* Sydney: Fellowship of Australian Writers, Angus and Robertson, 1942, pp. 97-105.
"A Survey of Australian Literature," *Chambers's Encyclopaedia,* London: new ed. 1950, vol. I, pp. 817-22.
"The Novels of Seaforth Mackenzie." *Meanjin,* XIII (Summer, 1954), pp. 503-11.
"Miles Franklin." *Meanjin,* XIV (Summer, 1955), pp. 469-87.
"The Four Novels of Patrick White." *Meanjin,* XV (Winter, 1956), pp. 156-70.
"Theodora Again." *Southerly,* 20:1 (1959), pp. 51-55.
"Australian Literature Since 1929." *Books Abroad,* University of Oklahoma Press, October 1960, pp. 280-84.

Flora Eldershaw—Minor Works

1. History

"Captain John Piper." Sydney: Royal Australian Historical Society, *Journal and Proceedings,* vol. XXVI, part VI (1940), pp. 479-98.

2. Criticism

"Contemporary Australian Women Writers." Sydney: Australian English Association, Offprint No. 4, 1931.
"History as the Raw Material of Literature." Sydney: Royal Australian Historical Society, *Journal and Proceedings,* vol. XX, part I (1934), pp. 1-17.
"Australian Literature Society Medallists." Sydney: Australian English Association, Offprint No. 20, 1935.
"The Landscape Writers." *Meanjin,* XI (Spring, 1952), pp. 215-28.

3. Editing

Australian Writers' Annual. Sydney: Fellowship of Australian Writers, 1936, vol. 1 (no more published).

The Peaceful Army: A Memorial to the Pioneer Women of Australia. Sydney: Australia's 150th Anniversary Celebrations Council, Women's Executive Committee and Advisory Council, 1938.

SECONDARY SOURCES

Articles about Flora Eldershaw

PALMER, NETTIE. "Flora Eldershaw," *Walkabout,* XVI (October 1, 1950), p. 8.

PRICHARD, KATHARINE SUSANNAH. "A Unique Collaboration, Tribute to Flora Eldershaw," *Westerly,* University of West Australia, no. 1 of 1957, pp. 35-36.

"Tributes to Flora Eldershaw," by Vance Palmer, Marjorie Barnard, T. Inglis Moore, Katharine Susannah Prichard, E. M. Miller, *Meanjin,* XV (Summer, 1956), pp. 390-94.

CRITICAL EVALUATIONS OF
M. BARNARD ELDERSHAW AND MARJORIE BARNARD

BLAKE, LESLIE. *Australian Writers.* Adelaide: Rigby, 1968. Praises the MBE and MB histories, especially *Phillip* and *Macquarie.* Discusses each of the five novels, preferring *A House Is Built* for its characters, *The Glasshouse* for its unusual technique, *Tomorrow and Tomorrow* for its portrayal of the social conditions of the depression and early war years. Concludes that "the techniques used by Barnard Eldershaw merit critical study."

BURNS, ROBERT. "Flux and Fixity: M. Barnard Eldershaw's 'Tomorrow and Tomorrow,'" *Meanjin,* XXIX (Spring, 1970), pp. 320-27. An examination in depth of this neglected final novel from the vantage of a quarter century.

ELLIOTT, BRIAN. *Singing to the Cattle* (collected essays). Melbourne: Georgian House, 1947. "The Historical Novel in Australia" (pp. 86-109) contains a comparison of *A House Is Built* with *The Montforts,* finding it good but lacking in the objectivity of Mills's novel.

Encyclopaedia of Australia. A. T. A. and A. M. Learmonth, comps. London: Frederick Warner & Co., 1968. Brief biographies of MB and FE, and mention of the five novels, naming *A House Is Built* and *Tomorrow and Tomorrow* as most important.

EWERS, JOHN K. *Creative Writing in Australia, a Selective Survey.* Melbourne: Georgian House, 1945. High praise for *A House Is Built* and for the evenness of the MBE collaboration throughout, but Ewers feels that a decline in creativity in the later novels may be responsible for the turn to history and criticism. Detailed appreciation of the MB short stories. The latest edition (1966) shows an understanding of *Tomorrow and Tomorrow.*

GRATTAN, C. HARTLEY. *Introducing Australia.* New York: John Day, 1942; Sydney: Angus and Robertson, 1944, 2nd ed., 1949. In a chapter on "Cultural Life," this early American student of Australia finds MBE "prolific," mentioning *A House Is Built* as staid and competent, *Plaque with Laurel* as witty but light— and places above them not only Richardson and Prichard but "Brent," the still "impenetrable pseudonym" for Miles Franklin.

GREEN, H. M. *An Outline of Australian Literature.* Sydney: Whitcombe and Tombs, 1930. Brief biographies of MB and FE, and a detailed discussion of *A House Is Built,* highly praised and favorably compared as a historical, realistic, and satiric novel with *The Monforts.*

————. "Literature," ch. XX of C. Hartley Grattan's anthology *Australia.* Berkeley: University of California Press, 1947. The United Nations Series. Feels Richardson and Prichard to be Australia's best, but credits MBE with their sensitive observations, their ironic and sometimes gently malicious humor. Green finds their first novel simple and objective, the later ones modernistic in method.

————. *Australian Literature 1900-1950.* Melbourne: Melbourne University Press, 1951. This slender survey lists *Essays in Australian Fiction* and *Phillip of Australia* in its Select Bibliography, but MBE are discussed only as novelists, their historical material and psychological approach being stressed. Contains a rare good statement of the theme of *Tomorrow and Tomorrow.*

————. *A History of Australian Literature, Pure and Applied.* A critical review of all forms of literature produced in Australia from the first books published after the arrival of the First Fleet until 1950, with short accounts of later publications up to 1960. Sydney: Angus and Robertson, 1961. 2 vols. This fullest treatment of the MBE and MB works is generally understanding and favorable. *Tomorrow and Tomorrow* is recognized as their finest novel, the *Essays* as overrating Palmer and Davison but valuable on Richardson and perceptive on the early Mann and Dark. The histories are praised for their imagination and human interest. The generally discerning discussion of MB's *The Persimmon Tree* is remarkable for its omission of the title story.

HADGRAFT, CECIL. *Australian Literature, a Critical Account to 1955.* London: Heinemann, 1960. A remarkably perceptive evaluation of MBE's *A House Is Built* and its irony, and MB's "The Persimmon Tree" and its sensitivity. *Essays in Australian Fiction* is briefly recognized; nothing else is more than mentioned.

HESELTINE, HARRY. "Australian Fiction Since 1920," in *The Literature of Australia,* Geoffrey Dutton, ed. Penguin Books, 1964 (pp. 181-224). *A House Is Built* is criticized for the narrative compression necessary in relating the Hyde family to the nation's history and for the intended irony, largely unrealized. Heseltine is kinder to MB's "The Persimmon Tree," finding it "a finely judged portrayal of feminine sensibility."

INGAMELLS, REX. *Handbook of Australian Literature.* Melbourne: Jindyworobak, 1949. Lists MBE among "names generally recognized as important" in the first thirty years of the century, and finds *A House Is Built,* like *The Montforts,* an important addition to historical fiction in Australia. Points out the book's indebtedness to Galsworthy for technique but credits it for the "artistic unobtrusiveness" with which the accurate historical research has been incorporated into the story. *Green Memory* and *Tomorrow and Tomorrow* are included, with comment, among suggestions for reading.

MACARTNEY, FREDERICK T. *A Historical Outline of Australian Literature.* Sydney: Angus and Robertson, 1957. MBE is listed chronologically among 64 novelists who first published between 1901 and 1951; only *A House Is Built,* for which they are "best known," is mentioned. Their *Essays in Australian Fiction* appears under "Criticism" among 23 entries, 1856 to 1950. MB is listed among 28 short story writers from 1915 to 1955, classed with those who "incline towards traditional merit" rather than those showing "freer diversions."

MILLER, E. MORRIS. *Australian Literature from Its Beginning to 1935.* A descriptive and bibliographical survey of books by Australian authors in poetry, drama, fiction, criticism and anthology with subsidiary entries to 1938. Melbourne: Melbourne Universty Press, 1940. 2 vols. Curiously divided by decades into "Novelists" and "Women Novelists," but it does rather florid justice to MBE, discussing their first two novels, listing the next two, their three histories, and their *Essays.* Thorough to the point of including their share in *Murder Pie,* and MB's youthful *The Ivory Gate.*

MILLER, E. MORRIS AND FREDERICK T. MACARTNEY. *Australian Literature, A Bibliography to 1938* by E. Morris Miller, extended to 1950 by Frederick T. Macartney. Sydney: Angus and Robertson,

1956. The prefatory "Historical Outline" here is almost identical with Macartney's *A Historical Outline of Australian Literature,* above, which is an abstract from it. The Bibliography itself has the fullest treatment of MB and MBE's lives and works to be found outside of H. M. Green's monumental *A History of Australian Literature* (also above). The *Essays* and the three MBE histories are only listed here, but the five novels are described and summarized in some detail, though not evaluated. MB's historical works to date (*Macquarie's World, Australian Outline,* and *The Sydney Book*) are mentioned, as is even the early minor *The Ivory Gate.* Several selections (including of course the title story) from *The Persimmon Tree* are examined.

MOORE, T. INGLIS. *Social Patterns in Australian Literature.* Sydney: Angus and Robertson, 1971. Includes numerous quotations from MB and MBE, and the latter's place among Australian novelists is frequently indicated. High praise for their *Tomorrow and Tomorrow* as a study of the depression, and reliance on their treatment of Vance Palmer in the *Essays.*

RODERICK, COLIN, ed. *The Australian Novel.* Sydney: Angus and Robertson, 1945. An anthology containing excerpts from nineteen novels including *A House Is Built,* which Roderick generally admires in both style and content. *Green Memory* he finds less appealing, *The Glasshouse* rich in dramatic characterization and subtle creation of atmosphere, *Plaque with Laurel* below the level of the rest. MBE's and MB's historical works are listed, as are the subjects of the *Essays'* "thoughtful studies." Welcome biographical material is provided on each author.

————. *An Introduction to Australian Fiction.* Sydney: Angus and Robertson, 1950. Biographies of MB and FE and discussions of *A House Is Built, Green Memory* (the first and best of the three intermediate "minor novels of fair average quality"), and *Tomorrow and Tomorrow.* The *House,* as a chronicle, lacks the sophistication and range of *The Montforts* (Boyd) and the exuberance of *All That Swagger* (Franklin); *Tomorrow* is superior as social criticism to *The Roaring Nineties* (Prichard). However, Roderick's earlier detailed and generally unfavorable review of *Tomorrow* (*Southerly,* 9:4 [1948], pp. 222-23) is reprinted here almost verbatim, with no indication of a change of heart or mind.

WILKES, G. A. *Australian Literature: A Conspectus.* Sydney: Angus and Robertson, 1969. Wilkes sees in *A House Is Built* the naturalistic tradition extended into the historical field, and feels that the book helped to set the vogue for the historical novel in the 1930's.

Index

(Multiple listings of works by MBE, MB, and FE appear under Criticism, Editing, Historical Sketches, Histories, Novels, and Short Stories. The more important items are also alphabetized separately.)